Front cover: © "The Maze", William Kurelek, 1953, reproduced by kind permission
of Bethlem Royal Hospital Archives and Museum.

First published in the United Kingdom by South London and Maudsley NHS Foundation Trust
(Formerly known as Bethlem and Maudsley NHS Trust) in 1987 by:

South London and Maudsley NHS Foundation Trust
Bethlem Royal Hospital
Monks Orchard Road
Beckenham
Kent
BR3 3BX

Tel: 020 3228 6000

www.slam.nhs.uk8

First Edition 1987

Fifth Edition revised 2019

A catalogue record for this book is available from the British Library. ISBN 978-0-9564425-4-3

Printed and bound by CPI Group (UK) Ltd, Croydon, CR0 4YY

Disclaimer

This Guide is intended to be informative and clear it should not be regarded as a substitute for the Mental Health Act or for usage of the MHA Code of Practice and the Reference Guide. Every care has been taken to ensure that these guidelines are up-to-date and accurate. It must be considered that this book is the end product of the author's interpretation on the Mental Health Act 1983. It should not be relied upon as a source of legal advice. Readers, individual practitioners and organisations will need to seek their own legal advice in particular cases. No liability is accepted for any injury, loss or damage howsoever caused. All information was correct at the time of printing.

The Maze - Fifth Edition 2019

A Practical Guide to the Mental Health Act 1983 (Amended 2007)

Incorporates the very significant changes in the Mental Health Act to police powers contained in the 2017 Policing and Crime Act

Written by: South London and Maudsley NHS Foundation Trust

Foreword

The Maze provides a practical guide to the Mental Health Act. It is aimed to assist Mental Health Practitioners, Mental Health Act Administrators, Associate Hospital Managers and staff working in general acute hospital settings, with their understanding of the Act. It will also be of interest to anyone with a general interest or who is studying mental health law.

The first version of The Maze was published by The Bethlem and Maudsley NHS Trust in 1987 with revisions in 1994, 1997 and 1999. As there were plans to revise the Mental Health Act, no further revisions were made until a new version was published by South London and Maudsley NHS Foundation Trust in 2010 after the Mental Health Act 2007 amendments. Further versions have been published which included the impact of key legal cases (especially the landmark Supreme Court ruling during 2014 known as the Cheshire West judgment). The updates reflect the growing complexity of mental health law particularly in terms of the interface between the Mental Health Act and the Mental Capacity Act – including Deprivation of Liberty Safeguards. Positive feedback had been received from readers about the use of flowcharts and these have been increasingly used in each edition.

This fifth edition includes the important changes to the Mental Health Act contained in the 2017 Policing and Crime Act which are dealt with in a substantially rewritten Chapter 7 of this Guide.

This current revision has been developed with contributions from a wide range of experts working in the field of mental health. I am grateful to them for their commitment to making this revised version a detailed text giving guidance on this interesting and complex area of law.

Dr Matthew Patrick
Chief Executive

March 2019

Preface

This 5th Edition contains important changes to the Mental Health Act contained within the 2017 Policing and Crime Act which are included within the Chapter on Police Powers. As with previous editions the Guide presents core information in a practical way including flow charts and a number of specialist chapters dealing with forensic patients, patients under the age of 18 and the role of those working in Mental Health Act administration.

Note the MHA applies to both England and Wales but not to other parts of the UK which have their own laws. The 'Welsh' MHA is identical to that in England though it has it's own Code and different statutory forms. Though this guide does not deal comprehensively with the MHA schedules and regulations it is important that people are familiar with them. An example of their importance is that they dictate the content and number of the statutory forms.

This Guide uses terminology such as patient and mental disorder. It does so because both the Mental Health Act and its Code of Practice use such terms. It is acknowledged that many readers of this Guide are more comfortable with terms such as 'client' or 'service user' rather than 'patient' and prefer terms such as 'mental health problem' or 'mental health distress' rather than the term 'mental disorder'. Note also that when quotes are made from the Act or it's Code the male pronoun is used.

Within this Guide quotes from the Mental Health Act (MHA) or the Mental Capacity Act (MCA) are in italics. Quotes from the MHA or MCA Codes or the Department of Health Reference Guide are also in italics as are direct quotes from legal judgements, official circulars or other acts of parliament.

The word 'organisation' is used in this Guide to describe the body of people with final responsibility for managing a particular service. Examples would be those managing within a Trust, Foundation Trust, independent hospital or local authority.

The word 'hospital' is used in the Guide to describe the place where patients are detained. This includes care homes managed by local authorities The word 'ward' is used to describe the part of a hospital where a patient is detained.

The phrases 'MHA Office' and 'MHA Officers' are used to describe staff employed by any organisation whose main functions are to administer the MHA.

This Guide does not attempt to compete with more academic publications but seeks to present information about what is often a confusing and complex subject in a way which is both user-friendly and accessible to its readers.

Though this Guide is intended to be both informative and clear it should be stressed that it should not be regarded as a substitute for the Act itself or the MHA Code of Practice and the Reference Guide. Nor should it be relied upon as a source of legal advice - individual practitioners and organisations will need to seek their own legal advice in particular cases.

Bob Lepper
South London and Maudsley NHS Foundation Trust (SLaM)
MHA Adviser and Policy Lead
March 2019

With thanks to the following people for their assistance with producing this Guide:

Ms Layo Afulape, former head of Social Care (MHOA) and AMHP SLaM

Mr Jason Andrews, MHA Management Team PA,

Ms Caroline Beamish, Associate Hospital Manager, SLaM

Ms Sarah Burleigh, Assistant Director of Nursing, SLaM

Ms Bernice Burns, Practice Development Nurse, SLaM

Ms Leena Kerosevic, Mental Health Law Team Leader, SLaM

Ms Kay Burton,Assistant Director of Mental Health Law, SLaM

Ms Sarah Cannell, Practice Manager and AHMP (CAMHS), SLaM

Dr Tony Davies, Consultant Psychiatrist, SLaM

Mr Peter Hasler, former Deputy Director of Nursing, SLaM

Ms Jackie Hone, former MHA Team Leader, SLaM

Dr Theresa Joyce, former MCA Clinical Lead, SLaM

Ms Yvette Leacock, former Development and Innovations Manager, SLaM

Mr Stuart Marchant, former Partner Bates Wells & Braithwaite Solicitors SLaM

Ms Babayami Oluwabukola acting MHA Mgt Team PA SLaM

Dr Alice Roberts,Consultant Psychiatrist ,SlaM and Trust MCA Clinical Lead

Mr Richard Sammut, former MHA Team Leader, SLaM

Dr Jane Sayer, former Programme Manager of Nursing Excellence & Magnet Recognition, SLaM

Dr Marisa Silverman, former Consultant Psychiatrist (MHOA) and Trust DOLS Lead, SLaM

Ms Susan Thompson Partner DAC Beachcroft

Mr Kevin Towers, Head of Mental Law and Clinical Records, West London Mental Health Trust

Ms Laura Wilkinson, former MHA Team Leader, SLaM

Ms Bernadette Pickerell, Mental Health Law Team Leader, SLaM

Glossary of Terms

A glossary of some of the most common terms used within the Mental Health Act and this Guide

ACRONYM	TERM	MEANING	MAIN CHAPTER(S) IN GUIDE
AC	**Approved Clinician**	Description of the suitably qualified professional who is authorised to perform particular functions within the Act.	**See Chapter 5**
AMHP	**Approved Mental Health Professional**	The role within the Act the most important of which is to make applications to detain patients under Part 2 of the Act.	**See Chapter 4**
Attorney	**Attorney**	Someone appointed under the MCA with a LPA who is authorised to make decisions on behalf of someone lacking capacity. The word 'donee' is also used to describe this person.	**See Chapter 23**
AWOL	**Absence Without Leave**	Description of a patient detained under the MHA or subject to a Community Treatment Order or Guardianship who is not where they are meant to be.	**See Chapter 11**
BNF	**British National Formulary**	The main guide used by those who prescribe, dispense and administer medication. Common terms used within psychiatry are 'BNF categories' and 'NF Limits'.	**See Chapter 10**
CCG	**Clinical Commissioning Group**	These are NHS organisations set up under the 2012 Health and Social Care Act to organise the delivery of NHS services in England.	**Referred to in several chapters**
CPA	**Care Programme Approach**	The term used to describe the care and support offered by secondary mental health services to patients with what is termed 'complex characteristics'.	**See Chapter 20**

ACRONYM	TERM	MEANING	MAIN CHAPTER(S) IN GUIDE
Code	**MHA Code of Practice**	The Code required within the MHA which defines good practice for those exercising powers and functions under the Act. Note also there are Codes of Practice for the MCA and for DOLS.	**See Chapter 15**
Court of Protection	**Court of Protection**	The court set up under the MCA which specialises in dealing with issues which relate to someone who lacks capacity to make decisions for themselves.	**See Chapter 23**
CTO	**Community Treatment Order**	The legal power which enables particular patients to leave hospital under CTO.	**See Chapter 21**
Consultee	**Consultee**	A term used within the MHA to describe a person who is consulted with by a SOAD when they are considering the approval of a patient's treatment plan.	**See Chapter 10**
Deputy	**Deputy**	Someone appointed under the MCA by the Court of Protection with ongoing legal responsibility to make decisions on behalf of someone who lacks capacity.	**See Chapter 23**
DOLS	**Deprivation of Liberty Safeguards**	A set of procedural safeguards introduced in April 2009 to provide protection for someone who lacks capacity and is being 'deprived of their liberty' within care homes or hospitals.	**See Chapter 24**
DVCVA	**Domestic Violence (Crime and Victims) Act 2004**	Gives the right of victims of particular crimes to make representation concerning the discharge and aftercare of the offender concerned. The 2007 MHA extends the rights of these victims in a number of ways.	**See Chapter 26**
ECT	**Electro Convulsive Therapy**	A particular treatment often used in psychiatry for which particular safeguards are contained within the MHA.	**See Chapter 10**

ACRONYM	TERM	MEANING	MAIN CHAPTER(S) IN GUIDE
ECHR	**European Convention on Human Rights**	The Convention introduced in 1950 which established the European Court of Human Rights and provided the framework in which the HRA was introduced into UK law.	**See Chapter 17**
FACS	**Fair Access to Care Services**	The term used for guidance given to social services councils to give them a framework for determining eligibility criteria for adult social services.	**See Chapter 20**
HRA	**Human Rights Act 1998**	The Act of Parliament which incorporated into UK legislation the 1950 European Convention on Human Rights.	**See Chapter 17**
IMCA	**Independent Mental Capacity Advocate**	A safeguard contained within the MCA giving access to an advocacy if major decisions are being made on behalf of someone who lacks capacity and who has no family member or friend to 'advocate' on their behalf.	**See Chapter 23**
IMHA	**Independent Mental Health Advocate**	A role introduced in April 2009 which makes available for 'qualifying patients' someone to assist them to understand and work with information they have been given under the MHA.	**See Chapter 18**
LPA	**Lasting Power of Attorney**	A term used within the MCA to describe someone who has been appointed to make particular decisions on behalf of someone who lacks capacity.	**See Chapter 23**
LSSA	**Local Social Services Authority**	A local authority which has responsibilities for adult social services. One function of a LSSA is to appoint people to perform the AMHP function.	**See Chapter 4**
MCA	**2005 Mental Capacity Act**	The legislation which provides a legal framework for those making decisions in relation to a person who lacks capacity.	**See mainly Chapter 23**

ACRONYM	TERM	MEANING	MAIN CHAPTER(S) IN GUIDE
MHA of 'the Act'	**1983 Mental Health Act**	The term used within this Guide to describe the legislation (including the 2007 amendments) which deals with the care and treatment of people who are 'mentally disordered'.	**All chapters**
MHCS	**Mental Health Casework Section**	Formerly the Mental Health Unit the part of the Ministry of Justice which manages aspects of the care and treatment of certain categories of forensic patients.	**See Chapter 26**
MHT	**Mental Health Tribunal**	An independent court of law which provides the safeguard within the MHA of hearing appeals and considering referrals for detained patients.	**See Chapter 13**
MHU	**Mental Health Unit**	The body within the Ministry of Justice which manages aspects of the care and treatment of certain categories of forensic patients.	**See Chapter 26**
MOJ	**Ministry of Justice**	The Government Department with particular responsibilities for patients detained under Part 3 of the MHA.	**See Chapter 26**
Nearest Relative	**Nearest Relative**	A term unique to the MHA describing someone identified by s26 who has various rights - the person may not be the same person as the patient's next of kin.	**See Chapter 6**
PACE	**The 1984 Police and Criminal Evidence Act**	This legislation and its accompanying Code provide the core framework for police powers and safeguards in areas such as arrest,detention and interviewing.	**See Chapter 7**
RC	**Responsible Clinician**	The AC (see above) who is in charge of the care and treatment of a particular patient.	**See Chapter 5**
RPA	**Representation of the People Act**	This term describes a number of Acts of Parliament which deal with all aspects of the electoral processes within the UK.	**See Chapter 19**

ACRONYM	TERM	MEANING	MAIN CHAPTER(S) IN GUIDE
Reference Guide	**Department of Health Reference Guide**	First published in 2008 and revised in 2015 this Guide in intended to assist people to understand the provisions of the Act.	**Referred to in several chapters**
S or s	**Section**	The relevant paragraph/clause of the MHA leading to phrases such as 'patient X is detained under s2'.	**See all chapters**
SOAD	**Second opinion appointed doctor**	A doctor appointed by the Care Quality Commission who provides an independent second opinion concerning particular aspects of Part 4 and Part 4A treatments.	**See Chapter 10**
S12 Doctor	**Section 12 Approved Doctor**	This describes a doctor who has been approved to act as an s12 doctor. The term is significant as the majority of sections require at least one of the two doctors submitting medical recommendations to be 's12 approved'.	**See many chapters - especially Chapters 3 and 25 which describe the permutation of doctors needed to make a particular section lawful**

Contents

Part One Overview of MHA - Main Roles and Civil Sections

Chapter 1 Introduction and MHA Overview

The 1983 Mental Health Act (MHA or the Act) provides the legal framework for the detention in hospital of people who are deemed to be suffering from mental disorder. The powers within the Act are used mainly to assess and treat these disorders. The Act contains a number of safeguards for anyone who is detained including the role of the Mental Health Tribunal, the Care Quality Commission and the Hospital Managers. The changes within the 2007 MHA - most of which were introduced in November 2008 - do not constitute a new Act; they are amendments to the 1983 MHA most of which has remained the same.

The MHA Code of Practice (the Code) is an important document as it provides guidance on how the MHA should be used by those with powers and responsibilities under the Act. The Code is also of value for patients, their carers and family as it defines best practice in the way the Act is used. Chapter 15 of this guide deals with the Code.

The main powers within the Act can be used to detain people in hospital. This is often referred to as when a person is 'sectioned'. The main powers are used either to bring a person into hospital or to detain someone who is already in hospital as a voluntary or informal patient. Other powers within the Act provide a framework for patients to receive treatment in the community for their mental disorder.

The main powers within the Act are exercised by Approved Mental Health Professionals and Approved/Responsible Clinicians. Doctors also have other important roles such as to make medical recommendations. Lesser powers are available to police officers and nurses within the legislation. As a result of a number of legal cases clinicians increasingly talk about admitting some patients 'under the Mental Capacity Act'. Where a patient is assessed as lacking capacity to consent to admission to hospital and/or lacks capacity to consent to medical treatment then the MCA provides an alternative legal framework for admission and treatment.

It is suggested that there are four types of admission.

With capacity and consenting - no formal procedures - **voluntary patient**

Without capacity and refusing - MHA used to admit the patient

With capacity and refusing - **MHA** used to admit the patient

Without capacity and **not resisting** – **MCA** or **MHA** used to admit the patient
(note some clinicians would prefer to use the MCA on the grounds that no powers are needed if the patient is 'compliant'. It does raise the question that - if the ward environment and the care plan *for that particular patient* amount to a **deprivation of liberty** - then a DOLs authorisation is necessary.

Chapter 2 MHA - Structure, Definitions and Exclusions

MHA - Structure

The MHA is split into ten parts which are summarized in the table below. Appendix A of this Guide summarises all the sections within the Act.

Each part of the MHA is further split into numbered paragraphs or groups of paragraphs. These paragraphs are often known as 'sections' and terms such as 'sectioning' and 'sectionable' are commonly used. Note that Part 7 which dealt with the management of property and affairs of patients was repealed in 2005 following the implementation of the Mental Capacity Act.

PART	SECTION (S)	DEALS WITH
1	**1** Application of the Acts	Definition of mental disorder and exclusions
2	**2-34** Compulsory Admission to Hospital and Guardianship	■ All civil admissions ■ Community Treatment Orders ■ Guardianship ■ Applications and Medical Recommendations ■ Nearest Relatives
3	**35-55** Patients concerned in criminal proceedings or under sentences	Covers patients concerned in criminal proceedings or under sentence
4 and 4A	**57-64** Consent	Consent to Treatment including Part 4A dealing with treatment of community patients not recalled to hospital
5	**65-79** Mental Health Tribunals	Mental Health Tribunals including applications and referrals and powers of Tribunal
6	**80-92** Removal and return of patients within the United Kingdom	Removal and return of patients within the United Kingdom including arrangements for Scotland, Northern Ireland, England and Wales and Channel Islands or Isle of Man
8	**114-123** Miscellaneous Functions of Local Authorities and the Secretary of State	■ Role of Mental Health Act Commission ■ Role of Code of Practice ■ Aftercare
9	**126-30** Offences	Ill treatment of patients Forgery and false statements
10	**130A-149** Miscellaneous and Supplemental	Includes ■ Independent Mental Health Advocates ■ Informal Admission ■ Duty of hospital managers to give information to detained and community patients ■ Patient correspondence ■ Police powers

The following chart summarises how the main sections operate

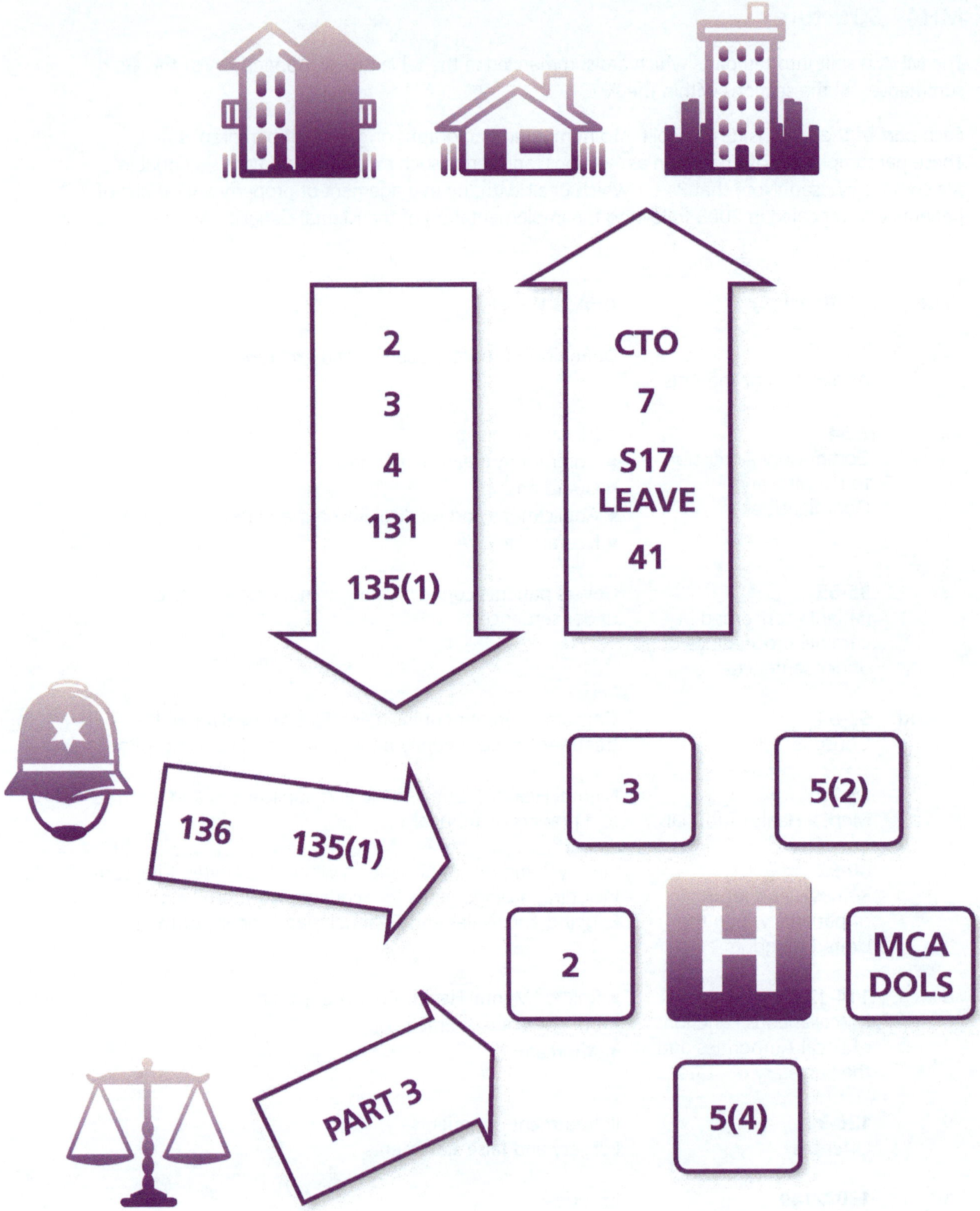

S1 - Definitions of Mental Disorder

Part 1, s1 (2), provides a definition of mental disorder which is *'any disorder or disability of the mind.'* This is a generic definition replacing the four categories of mental disorder contained within the 1983 MHA. The Act does not attempt to further define what is or is not mental disorder; the Code at 2.4 states; *'relevant professionals should determine whether a patient has a disorder or disability of mind in accordance with good clinical practice and accepted standards of what constitutes such a disorder or disability.'*

Whilst the MHA uses the term mental disorder it is also important to be familiar with the term 'unsound mind' which is used within the Human Rights Act - see Chapter 17.

Definitions of mental disorder of people with learning disabilities

The only remaining reference to the now abolished four categories of mental disorder concerns any patient with learning disabilities being detained for treatment. If such a patient is detained it is a requirement in s1 (2A) that the disability is 'associated with abnormally aggressive or seriously irresponsible conduct ' for them to be brought under compulsion within the Act. Note that the definition of learning disabilities is 'a state of arrested or incomplete development of the mind which includes significant impairment of intelligence and social functioning'. Also note that if the assessment and/or treatment of someone with learning disabilities are for a concurrent mental health problem this requirement does not apply. Further guidance about people with learning disabilities is contained within Chapter 20 of the Code.

Note that this narrower definition for someone with learning disabilities does not apply for s2, or for any section lasting less than 72 hours nor for detention under s7 guardianship.

Clinical Understanding of Mental Disorder

The absence within the MHA of any more detailed definition of what might or might not be a mental disorder is intended to allow clinicians the freedom to make their own professional judgements.

2.2 of the Code give examples of what clinically recognized conditions might fall within the s1 definition. Though the list is described as not exhaustive it mentions:

- affective disorders such as depression and bipolar disorder
- schizophrenia and delusional disorders
- neurotic, stress-related and somatoform disorders (such as anxiety, phobic disorders, obsessive compulsive disorders, post-traumatic stress disorders and hypochrondrical disorders)
- organic mental disorders such as dementia or delirium (however caused)
- personality and behavioural changes caused by brain injury or damage (however acquired)
- personality disorder
- mental and behavioural disorders caused by psychoactive substance misuse, eating disorders, non-organic sleep disorders and non-organic sexual disorders learning disabilities
- autistic spectrum disorders(including Asperger's syndrome)
- behavioural and emotional disorders of children and adolescents

The inclusion of personality disorder in this list is of significance - reiterated in 2.3 and 2.19 of the Code as it makes clear that the judgement as to whether someone with personality disorder is or is not detainable should be made in the same way as for any other type of disorder or illness. Chapter 21 of the Code gives further guidance on personality disorder in decision-making.

Clinical guidelines entitled 'Anti-Social Personality Disorder - Treatment Management and Prevention' and 'Borderline Personality Disorder- Treatment and Management' were published by the National Institute for Clinical Excellence (NICE) in January 2009.

MHA Definitions - Exclusions

Part 1, s1 (3) specifies that *'dependence on alcohol or drugs'* are not, in themselves, disorders or disabilities of mind. 2.9 – 2.13 of the Code gives guidance on the circumstances in which a person who is dependent on drugs or alcohol could lawfully be detained due to the concurrent existence of a mental disorder. Solvents and similar substances (which a psychoactive effect) are included in the definition of drug dependency.

These circumstances could include situations where the mental disorder concerned resulted from the person's alcohol or drug dependence or where the disorder (either organic or functional) was associated with prolonged abuse of drugs or alcohol including the effects of withdrawal.

The exclusions from detention on the grounds of *'promiscuity or other immoral conduct or sexual deviancy'* which were contained within the 1983 MHA were repealed in the amended MHA. 2.6 to 2.8 of the Code address the danger of confusing diagnosis with 'difference'. It reminds clinicians of the danger of labelling someone as mentally disordered simply because their behavior reflects beliefs and /or actions rooted in their culture or religion.

Chapter 3 MHA Civil Sections - s2, s3, s4, s5 (2) and s5 (4)

Part 2 of the MHA deals with civil sections commencing with s2. This chapter deals with s2, s3, s4, s5(2) and s5(4). Page 43 below summarises in table form key information about these sections.

Note the distinctive role of the Approved Mental Health Professional (AMHP) in making MHA applications for s2, s3 or s4 is dealt with in Chapter 4 of this Guide.

Section 2

Purpose of s2

The purpose of s2 is to allow compulsory admission and detention for assessment of someone with a mental disorder. This assessment may lead to treatment which can occur while under s2. S2 can either be used to admit someone from the community into hospital or to detain someone who is already an in-patient but who is not detained under the Act (such a patient is often referred to as a voluntary or informal patient).

Legal Criteria for s2

For this section the legal criteria are:

- *person is suffering from mental disorder of a nature or degree which warrants the detention of the person in a hospital for assessment (or for assessment followed by medical treatment for at least a limited period',* and
- *'detention is in the interests of the person's own health or safety or with a view to the protection of other persons'.*

Length of s2

The duration of s2 is for up to 28 days. S2 cannot be renewed nor is it considered good practice for one s2 to be followed by another s2 within a short period of time. Case law makes clear that the use of 'back to back' s2's (or use of one s2 followed after a brief gap by a second s2) to avoid securing the nearest relative's 'agreement' to s3 would not be lawful. Note that if s4 is converted to s2 the s2 begins from the date that the s4 began.

The only circumstances in which s2 could be extended are:

- if, during the 28 days, the process had begun of seeking to displace the patient's nearest relative to facilitate an application for detention under s3
- if a patient detained under s2 returns from being absent without leave during the final week of the 28 day period, s21 permits the s2 to be extended for a period of one week from the date of the patient's return. Note: s21 does not provide any authority to detain or 'retake' a patient who is absent without leave at the point at which the s2 runs out.

Displacement procedures and absence without leave are dealt with in Chapters 6 and 11 of this Guide.

Treatment under s2

S63 permits treatment of the patient's disorder, with or without consent, for the first three months of detention. This includes the period in which a patient is detained under s2. No MHA statutory form needs to be completed for s63 treatment. This covers the administration of medication for treatment of mental disorder; note that more stringent safeguards apply where the proposed intervention is Electro-convulsive Therapy (ECT) (dealt with in MHA Part 4A) or interventions covered by s57 of the MHA.

The legal criteria make clear that treatment with compulsion is lawful under s2. The statute places no restriction on the circumstances in which such treatment might occur. Statements implying that treatment on s2 could only be given with compulsion in 'emergency' or 'life and limb' circumstances have no legal basis.

In law the calculation of this period begins from when medication for the treatment of mental disorder is first administered, but 'custom and practice' is often to make the calculation from when the period of detention began.

Appeal Rights against s2

Any patient detained under s2 has the right of appeal to both the Mental Health Tribunal (MHT) and the Hospital Managers. If the patient makes an appeal (known in law as an application) to the MHT he or she must do so within the first 14 days of the section. If a patient on s2 is placed on s3 any MHT application they had made while on s2 would still be heard by the MHT (who would base their decision on the s3 criteria).

More information about the role of the MHT and the Hospital Managers are contained in Chapters 13 and 16 of this Guide.

Leave of Absence under s2

Patients detained under s2 can be granted leave of absence under s17 of the Act. Details about s17 leave of absence are dealt with in Chapter 11 of this Guide.

Absence without Leave under s2

See Chapter 11 of this Guide.

Ending of s2

S2 can be ended at any time during the 28 days in any one of the following ways:

- by the patient's RC
- by the Hospital Managers following a 'Hearing '
- by the patient's nearest relative's request for discharge which is not barred by the patient's RC
- by the MHT.

In the ways described in the first three bullet points the power to discharge is to be found in s23 of the MHA. The power of discharge in the final bullet point is to be found within MHA s72.

Though there is no statutory form for the ending of s2 by the RC it is suggested that organizations devise such a form. This is so that it is clear exactly when the section ends. There also needs to be a clear mechanism to inform detained patients that they are no longer detained.

The application of the 'least restrictive option and maximizing independence' principle within the Code does suggest that merely allowing detention under s2 to 'lapse' is not best practice unless detention for the full period of 28 days has a clinical rationale.

Note that during the 28 days duration of s2 it is possible for an application to be made for detention under s3 - see the following section.

s2 or s3?

14.27 of the Code give the following suggestions as to when s2 (as opposed to s3) should be used.

MHA s2 should only be used if:

- *'the full extent of the nature or degree of a patient's condition is unclear;'*
- *'there is a need to carry out an initial in-patient assessment in order to formulate a treatment plan or to reach a judgement about whether the patient will accept treatment on a voluntary basis following admission;'* **or**
- *'there is a need to carry out a new in-patient assessment in order to reformulate a treatment plan, or to reach a judgement about whether the patient will accept treatment on a voluntary basis'.*

Paperwork and rights leaflet for s2

The following forms must be completed in all cases when s2 is used

1 Form A3	or	2 Forms A4	(Medical)
1 Form A2	or		(AMHP Application)
1 Form A1			(Nearest Relative Application)
1 Form H3			(Record of Detention)

The rights leaflet for s2 is S2

S2 Medical Recommendations

Legal/best practice requirements

On the statutory form(s) doctors completing medical recommendations for s2 need to address the following issues:

- the s2 legal criteria (see above)
- what the issues are concerning the patient's health or safety or with a view to the protection of other persons which makes detention necessary
- the reason alternatives to s2 detention are not possible. This explanation should focus on the patient's symptoms/behavior and on the way this is connected to the reason why other forms of care (i.e. as informal patient or in the community) are not appropriate.

Detention under s2 requires the completion of medical recommendations by two doctors. The doctors can either make a joint medical recommendation on a single statutory form **A3** or separate medical recommendations on two separate statutory forms **A4**. If form A3 is used the two doctors must assess the patient and complete the form at the same time. Good practice suggests that at least one of the doctors should assess with the AMHP.

It is suggested that doctors who decide to complete recommendations – where applicable – should refer to why the Mental Capacity Act (MCA) could not have been used to admit the patient.

The following material applies to both s2 and s3

Status of two doctors and meaning of 'previous acquaintance'

One of the two doctors must be s12 approved (see Glossary for explanation of the term). If the doctor who is s12 approved does not have 'previous acquaintance with the patient', the second recommendation - if practicable - should be made by a doctor who does have such previous acquaintance. It is also preferable if a doctor does not have previous acquaintance that they are s12 approved. If neither doctor has previous acquaintance the AMHP making an application for s2 or s3 needs to explain on the form why they could not obtain a recommendation from a doctor who did have previous acquaintance with the patient.

Conflicts of interests

Chapter 39 of the Code identifies possible conflicts of interest (financial, business, personal or professional) which might put restrictions on medical recommendations provided by doctors. Key points are:

- good practice is that at least one of the two recommendations is provided by a doctor not on the staff of the admitting hospital. Note that the material in the Code is based on the MHA regulations-there are plans to amend the regulations to make this a statutory requirement – not just best practice. Note that for someone being admitted to an independent hospital it is already a **statutory requirement** that one of the two doctors must not work at that hospital.
- the Code provides guidance relating to where there is a professional relationship between the two doctors providing medical recommendations. The relationships which would indicate a conflict of interests are (a) one of the doctors is line managed or employed by the other doctor

  (b) both doctors are members of the same team, (c) the AMHP making the Application either employs or manages one of the doctors. 39.11 of the Code defines a team as *'a group of professionals who work together for clinical purposes on a routine basis. That might include a community mental health team, a crisis resolution or home treatment team, or staff on an in-patient unit (but not necessarily the staff of an entire hospital)' only in case of genuine emergency should the two doctors and AMHP belong to the same team'.*

Time Limits for Medical Recommendations

- If separate medical recommendations are completed there cannot be more than five clear days between the examinations completed by the two doctors. This means that (for example) if the first examination is completed on the 1st May and the second completed on the 7th May then the requirements of the law have been met.

  Note the gap is between the examinations and not the signing of the recommendation.

- Where separate medical recommendations are provided the date of signing of both recommendations cannot be later than the date of the application made by an AMHP. The patient's admission to hospital (or if the patient is already in hospital, the receipt of the documents by a person authorized to receive them) must take place within 14 days starting from the date of the later of the two medical examinations.

Applications by AMHP - legal and best practice requirements

Recommendations lawfully completed by two doctors do not mean that the patient is detained. The process of someone being 'sectioned' is only completed when an AMHP has decided to complete an application which is founded on the completion of the appropriate recommendations.

Time limits for applications

- The applicant (nearest relative or AMHP) must have personally seen the patient within 14 days ending with the date of signing the application
- On the form they must give the date on which they last saw the patient
- On their form their signature confirms that 'I have interviewed the patient and am satisfied that detention in hospital is in all the circumstances of the case the most appropriate way of providing the care and medical treatment of which the patient stands in need'.

Note that a fuller description of the Role of the Nearest Relative can be found in Chapter 6 of this Guide.

End of material common to both s2 and s3.

S2 - Nearest Relative Issues

Informing the nearest relative

The AMHP considering making a s2 application is required to attempt to define the patient's nearest relative according to the 'list' within s26 of the Act. See Chapter 6 of this guide. For s2 the requirement according to the Code is for the AMHP to *'take such steps as are practicable to inform the nearest relative and, if different, carer, that the application is to be (or has been) made and of the nearest relative's power to discharge the patient'*.

The meaning of 'practicable' is to take into account the practical difficulties in identifying and informing the nearest relative. Examples of those difficulties could be:

- the nearest relative's own health or mental incapacity
- difficulty establishing the identity of or location of the nearest relative
- even if the identity or location of the nearest relative were possible to establish doing so would entail an excessive amount of investigation or involve unreasonable delay (due to the pressing need to make an application).

Right of nearest relative to make application

In law the nearest relative does have the right to make the s2 application instead of that application being made by an AMHP. This right can be exercised either because the nearest relative wishes to do so or because the AMHP has decided not to make an application. Note that the Code guidance is that a doctor or doctors approached by a nearest relative wishing to make an application should advise them that an AMHP is the preferred applicant.

14.30 of the Code make clear the preference for the AMHP. *'An AMHP is usually a more appropriate applicant than a patient's nearest relative, given an AMHPs professional training and knowledge of the legislation and local resources. This also removes the risk that an application from a nearest relative might have an adverse effect on their relationship with the patient.*

If the nearest relative makes the application they need to complete statutory form A1. Note also the subsequent requirement in s14 for the Local Social Services Authority (LSSA) from which the patient came to interview the patient and then provide the hospital with a report on the social circumstances of the patient.

Scrutiny of s2 papers

Any scrutiny - either medical or administrative - of s2 detention papers should check:

- consistency in the spelling of the patient's name and address
- that all doctors and applicants have given their own full name and address
- medical recommendations must be signed on or before the date of the application
- for doctors completing medical recommendations that they clearly indicate whether they are (a) s12 approved or not (b) whether they have had 'previous acquaintance or not with the patient'
- all applications and medical recommendations are signed and dated. Note that an unsigned application or medical recommendation cannot be amended and would render the detention invalid.
- there can be no more than five clear days between separate examinations by the two doctors.
- if neither doctor did have previous acquaintance with the patient the applicant on form A2 must give reasons why they could not obtain a recommendation from a doctor who did know the patient
- the applicant has signed their application within 14 days of seeing the patient
- the patient has been admitted to hospital within 14 days of the last examination by a doctor completing a medical recommendation
- the hospital to which the patient is admitted is the hospital named on the AMHP or Nearest Relative Application.

More thorough guidance on the procedures contained within s15 for rectifying errors (and those which cannot be rectified) is contained in Chapter 8 of this Guide.

Section 3

Note that at the end of the material on s3 it's processes are summarized in a flow chart

Purpose of s3

The purpose of s3 is to allow compulsory admission and detention for treatment of someone with a mental disorder. S3 can either be used to admit someone from the community into hospital or to detain someone who is already an in-patient. Prior to being placed under s3 an in-patient may have been an informal/voluntary patient or may have been detained under s2, s4, s5 (2) or s5 (4). Note that detention under s3 may follow revocation of a patient's Community Treatment Order (CTO) - see Chapter 21 of this guide.

Legal Criteria for s3

For this section the legal criteria are:

'person is suffering from mental disorder of a nature or degree which makes it appropriate for them to receive medical treatment in a hospital', and

'it is necessary for the health or safety of the person or for the protection of other persons that they should receive such treatment', and

'such treatment cannot be provided unless they are detained under this section', and 'appropriate medical treatment is available to them'.

Note that the 'appropriate treatment test' was introduced into the MHA in November 2008. Chapter 23 of the Code gives guidance on how this test should be applied in decisions about the use of the Act.

Length of s3

The initial duration of s3 is for up to six months. S3 can be renewed if the above legal criteria are still met with the additional requirement that the treatment for the patient cannot be provided unless they continue to be detained. If s3 is renewed, the first renewal is for up to six months and subsequent renewals for a year at a time. The circumstances in which a detained patient is referred for a Tribunal are dealt with in Chapter 13 and the arrangements by which Hospital Managers review detention are dealt with in Chapter 16.

Treatment under s3

S63 permits treatment of the patient's disorder, with or without consent, **for the first three months of detention**. If a s2 is 'converted' to s3 without a break the calculation of the 'three month rule' is from when the s2 began. No MHA statutory form needs to be completed for s63 treatment. This covers the administration of medication for treatment of mental disorder; note that more stringent safeguards apply where the proposed intervention is Electro-convulsive Therapy (ECT) or interventions covered by s57 of the MHA. These safeguards are covered in Chapter 10 of this guide.

In law the calculation of this period begins from when medication for the treatment of mental disorder is first administered but 'custom and practice' is often to make the calculation from when the period of detention began. If the detention under s3 follows - without a gap - detention under s2, the calculation of the three month period can be from when the s2 began.

Treatment is not confined to the administration of medication. S145 says that medical treatment for mental disorder includes *'nursing, psychological intervention and specialist mental health habilitation, rehabilitation and care'*. The significance of the term 'psychological intervention' is to clarify that for some patients with personality disorder or borderline personality disorder this will be the main (or only) form of treatment offered to them.

Rehabilitation means that the detained patient is receiving treatment to enable him or her to return to the community and be able to function within it. Habilitation is a much less commonly used word but is correctly used if the patient prior to treatment had never lived in the community nor functioned within it.

Appeal Rights against s3

Any patient detained under s3 has the right of appeal to both the Mental Health Tribunal (MHT) and the Hospital Managers.

More information about the role of the MHT and the Hospital Managers is contained in Chapters 13 and 16 of this Guide.

Leave of Absence under s3

Patients detained under s3 can be granted leave of absence under s17 of the Act. Material about s17 leave of absence is dealt with in Chapter 11 of this Guide.

Absence without Leave under s3

See Chapter 11 of this Guide.

Ending of s3

S3 can be ended at any time during the detention period in any one of the following ways:

- by the patient's RC
- by the Hospital Managers following a 'Hearing '
- by the patient's nearest relative's request for discharge which is not barred by the patient's RC
- by the MHT.

In the ways described in the first three bullet points the power to discharge is to be found in s23 of the MHA. The power of discharge in the final bullet point is to be found within MHA s72. Though there is no statutory form for the ending of s2 by the RC it is suggested that organizations devise such a form.

This is so that it is clear exactly when the section ends. There also needs to be a clear mechanism to inform detained patients that they are no longer detained.

S3 or S2?

14.28 of the Code gives the following suggestions as to when s3 (as opposed to s2) should be used:

- *'the patient is already detained under s2 (detention under section 2 cannot be renewed by a new s2 application)' or*
- *'the nature and current degree of the patient's mental disorder,the essential elements of the treatment plan to be followed and the likelihood of the patent accepting treatment as an informal patient are already sufficiently established to make it unnecessary to undertake a new assessment under section 2'.*

The application of the 'least restrictive option and maximizing independence' principle within the Code does suggest that merely allowing detention under s3 to 'lapse' is not best practice unless detention for the full period has a clinical rationale.

The process of s3 being 'superseded' by CTO is dealt with in Chapter 21 of this Guide. Note also that patients who have been detained under s3 are entitled to s117 aftercare - see Chapter 20 of this Guide.

Paperwork and rights leaflet for s3

The following forms must be completed in all cases when s3 is used.

1 Form A7	or 2 Forms A8	(Medical Recommendations)
1 Form A6	or	(AMHP Application)
1 Form A5		(Nearest Relative Application)
1 Form H3		(Record of Detention)

The rights leaflet for s3 is S3

S3 Medical Recommendations

Legal / best practice requirements

The doctors completing medical recommendations for s3 need on the statutory forms to address the following issues:

- whether the patient is suffering from a mental disorder of a nature or degree which makes it appropriate for the patient to receive medical treatment in a hospital
- the nature and current degree of the patient's mental disorder, the essential elements of the treatment plan to be followed and the likelihood of the patient accepting treatment as an informal patient are already sufficiently established to make it unnecessary to undertake an new assessment under section 2
- the reason alternatives to s3 detention for treatment are not possible. This explanation should focus on the patient's symptoms/behavior and on the way this is connected to the reason why other forms of care (i.e. as an informal patient or in the community) are not appropriate
- that they are satisfied that appropriate treatment will be available for the patient concerned. This requires the name of the hospital (or hospitals) at which such treatment will be available to be written onto the form(s). If the appropriate treatment is only available in a particular part of a hospital this should also be stated. It is suggested that doctors who decide to complete recommendations –where applicable – should refer to why the Mental Capacity Act (MCA) could not have been used to admit the patient.

If the patient is actually admitted to a hospital which is not named as providing appropriate treatment on either the separate or joint medical recommendations this would invalidate the section.

Detention under s3 requires the completion of medical recommendations by two doctors. The doctors can either make a joint medical recommendation on a single statutory form A7 or separate medical recommendations on two separate statutory forms **A8**. If Form **A7** is used, the two doctors must assess the patient and complete the form at the same time.

All other legal and best practice requirements which are the same for s2 and s3 are dealt with above.

S3 - Nearest Relative Issues

Note that a fuller description of the Role of the Nearest Relative can be found in Part One Chapter Six of this Guide.

Consultation

Consultation

The AMHP considering making an s3 application is required to attempt to define the patient's nearest relative according to the 'list' to be found within s26, see page 51 of this guide. For s3 the requirement, according to the Code at 4.58 is *'Before making an application for detention under section 3, the AMHP must consult the nearest relative, unless it is not reasonably practicable or would involve unreasonable delay.'*

The meaning of 'practicable' is to take into account the practical difficulties in identifying and informing the nearest relative.

Examples of those difficulties could be:

- the nearest relative's own health or mental incapacity
- difficulty establishing the identity of or location of the nearest relative
- even if the identity or location of the nearest relative were possible to establish doing so would entail an excessive amount of investigation or involve unreasonable delay (due to the pressing need to make an application).

The difference within the legislation between 'informing' (s2) and 'consulting' (s3) relates to the fact that the nearest relative has the right to object to a s3 application being made. This is summarized in 14.65 of the Code which states *'If the nearest relative objects to an application being made for admission for treatment under section 3, the application cannot be made. If it is thought necessary to proceed with the application to ensure the patient's safety and the nearest relative cannot be persuaded to agree, the AMHP will need to consider applying to the county court for the nearest relative's displacement under section 29 of the Act.'*

Chapter 6 of this Guide gives more information about these processes.

Right of nearest relative to make application

In law the nearest relative has the right to make the s3 application instead of that application being made by an AMHP. This right can be exercised either because the nearest relative wishes to do so or because the AMHP has decided not to make an application. Note that the Code guidance is that a doctor or doctors approached by a nearest relative wishing to make an application should advise them that an AMHP is the preferred applicant.

14.30 of the Code says this preference is because *'An AMHP is usually a more appropriate applicant than a patient's nearest relative, given an AMHP's professional training and knowledge of the legislation and local resources, together with the potentially adverse effect that an application by the nearest relative might have on their relationship with the patient'.*

If the nearest relative makes the application they need to complete statutory form A5. Note also the subsequent requirement in s14 for the Local Social Services Authority (LSSA) from which the patient came to interview the patient and then provide the hospital with a report on the social circumstances of the patient.

Scrutiny of s3 papers

Any scrutiny - either medical or administrative - of s3 detention papers should check:

- consistency in the spelling of the patient's name and address
- that all doctors and applicants have given their own full name and address
- medical recommendations must be signed on or before the date of the application
- for doctors completing medical recommendations that they clearly indicate whether they are (a) s12 approved or not (b) whether they have had 'previous acquaintance or not with the patient'
- All applications and medical recommendations are signed and dated. Note that an unsigned application or medical recommendation cannot be amended and would render the detention invalid
- there can be no more than five clear days between separate examinations by the two doctors See page 25 of this guide
- if neither doctor did have previous acquaintance with the patient the applicant on form A6 must give reasons why they could not obtain a recommendation from a doctor who did know the patient
- the applicant has signed their application within 14 days of seeing the patient
- the patient has been admitted to hospital within 14 days of the last examination by a doctor completing a medical recommendation
- the hospital to which the patient is admitted is the hospital (or one of the hospitals) named as providing appropriate treatment on the separate recommendations or join recommendation
- the hospital to which the patient is admitted is the hospital named on the AMHP or Nearest Relative Application.

If the patient is actually admitted to a hospital which is not named as providing appropriate treatment on either the separate or joint medical recommendations this would invalidate the section. The view of some experts is that s15 could be used to replace a single medical recommendation which failed to name the 'right' hospital with one which did.

More thorough guidance on the procedures contained within s15 for rectifying errors (and those which cannot be rectified) is contained in Chapter 8 of this Guide.

THE PATIENT'S JOURNEY – ADMISSION FOR TREATMENT

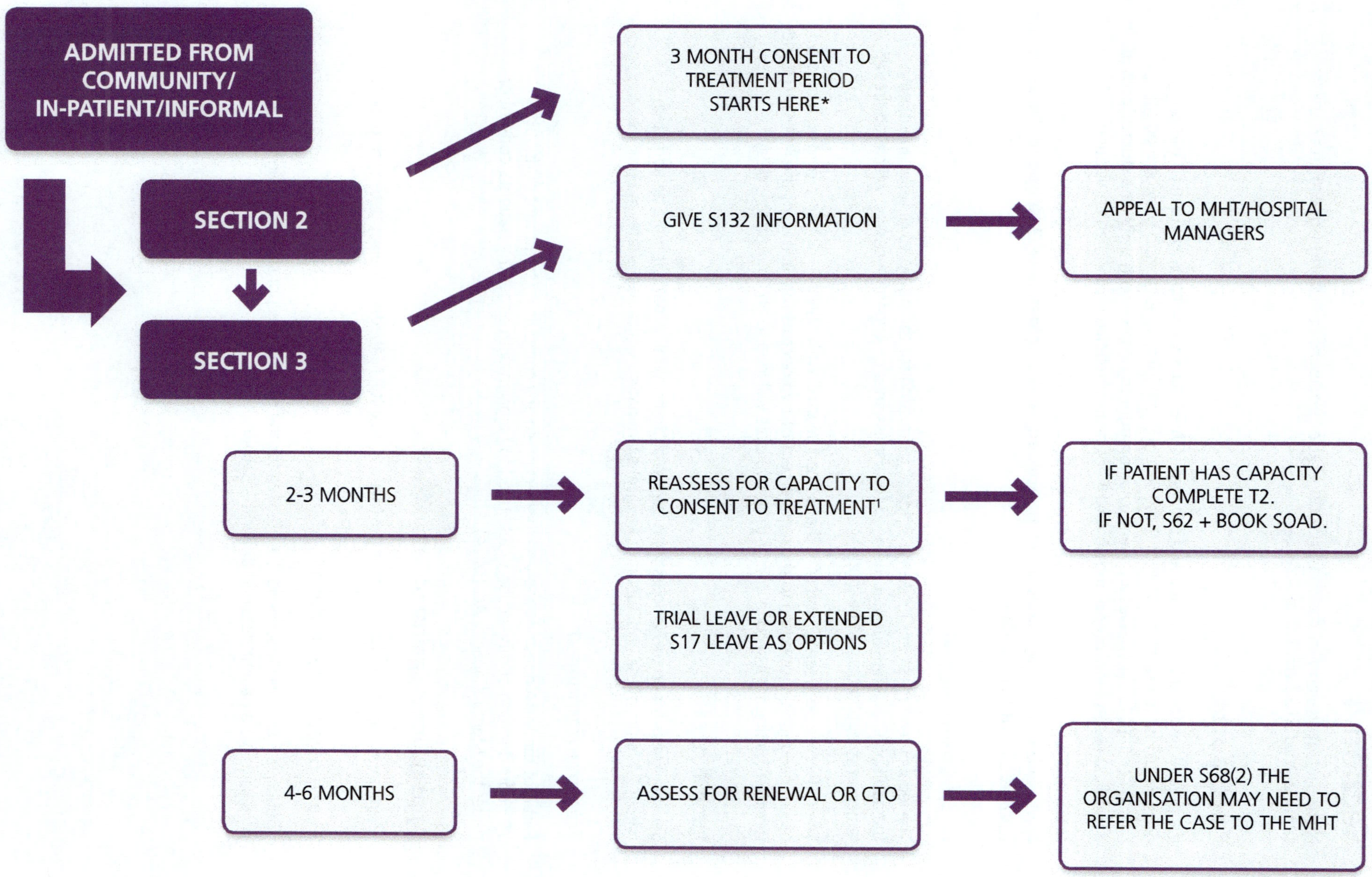

* This chart assumes a continuous period of detention [1] And capacity is assessed at point of admission and at regular intervals.

Section 4

Note that at the end of the material on s4 the processes for changing a s4 to s2 are summarized in a flow chart.

Purpose of s4

If a patient needs to be detained and brought to hospital the normal way in which this is done would be to use s2 or s3. Both these sections require two doctors to provide medical recommendations. S4 enables a patient to be brought to hospital with **only one doctor providing a medical recommendation** and an AMHP (or nearest relative) making an application.

Note that s4 cannot be used to detain someone already a hospital in-patient but can lawfully be used - for example - in an Accident and Emergency or Outpatient's Department if the legal criteria are met.

Legal Criteria for s4

The legal criteria for s4 are the same as for s2 (admission for the purposes of assessment) with the additional requirement that the need for admission is of *'urgent necessity'* which requires an 'emergency application' to be made.

The difference between s2 and s4 is that s4 can be used with only one doctor providing a medical recommendation as opposed to the requirement of two doctors for s2. It is for the AMHP to decide whether waiting for a second doctor to be available will lead to an *'undesirable delay'.*

Length of s4

Section 4 lasts for up to 72 hours from admission to hospital. A patient must be admitted within 24 hours of the application or medical examination whichever is later in time.

Treatment under s4

Part 4 of the MHA does not apply to this section so any compulsory treatment during the 72 hours duration of this section would need to be given with either the patient's consent or under the Mental Capacity Act (MCA).

Appeal Rights against s4

There are no appeal rights to either the MHT or Hospital Managers against detention under s4.

Leave of absence under s4

Though it is an unlikely scenario it is possible for the patient's Responsible Clinician to grant leave of absence to a patient detained under this section.

THE PATIENT'S JOURNEY INTO DETENTION USING S4 – S2

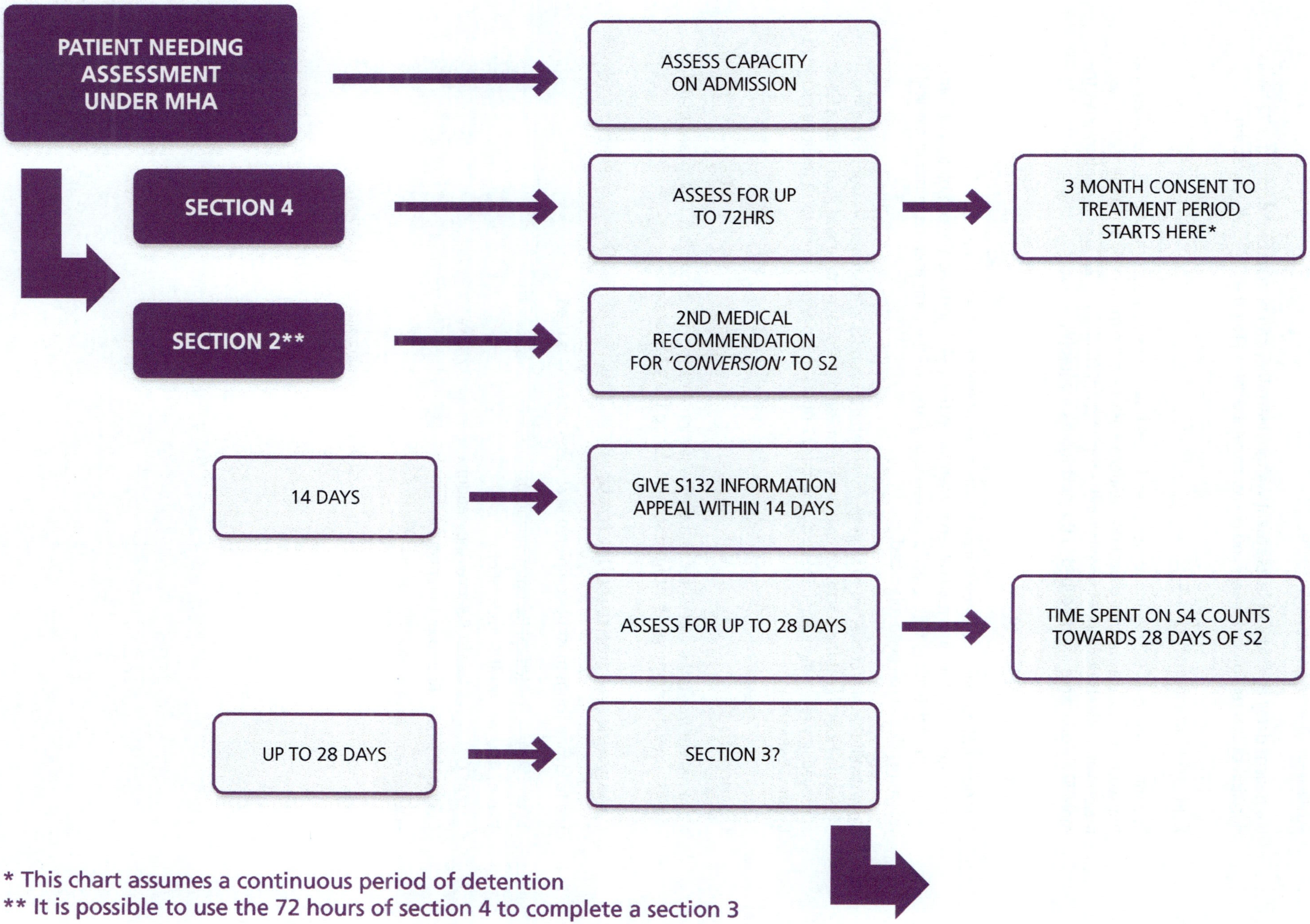

* This chart assumes a continuous period of detention

** It is possible to use the 72 hours of section 4 to complete a section 3

Absence Without Leave under s4

If a patient detained under s4 goes absent without leave they can be 'retaken' during the 72 hours duration of this section but there is no power to retake them after the 72 hours has lapsed.

Ending/Conversion of s4

Though the patient's RC has the power to end the s4 during its 72 hours duration it is unlikely that this would be done as further detention - under s2 or s3 - is the most likely outcome for the vast majority of patients brought to hospital under this section. During the 72 hours duration of s4 the more likely outcomes are described in the next three paragraphs.

Conversion to s2

This does not require a new application by either an AMHP or nearest relative but does require the completion of the 'missing' medical recommendation (form **A4**) and also the completion of form **H3** (record of detention) with specific reference on **Part 2** of the form that the 'missing' medical recommendation has been submitted.

Note that if the s4 is converted to s2 in this way detention under s2 commences from when the s4 began. Note that if the doctor completing the 'missing' medical recommendation is not s12 approved any recommendation made during the 72 hours to 'convert' the s4 to s2 must be provided by an s12 doctor.

Change to s3

If the patient meets the criteria for s3 then the section 4 cannot be converted. This means that if s3 is to be used the processes 'start from scratch' during the 72 hour period.

Paperwork and rights leaflet for s4

The following forms must be completed in all cases when s4 is used.

1 Form A11	(Medical Recommendation)
1 Form A10 or	(AMHP Application)
1 Form A9	(Nearest Relative Application)
1 Form H3	(Record of Detention)

The rights leaflet for s4 is S4

Legal/best practice requirements for s4 medical recommendation and application.

For doctor

The doctor completing the medical recommendation must have seen the patient within the last 24 hours.

The doctor completing form A11 needs on the statutory form to address the following issues:

- whether the patient is suffering from a mental disorder of a nature or degree which warrants their detention in hospital for assessment (or assessment followed by medical treatment) for at least a limited period
- what the issues are concerning the patient's health or safety or with a view to the protection of other persons which make detention necessary
- Why it is of urgent necessity that the person needs to be detained and admitted and why the 'normal' route of admission under s2 would involve a delay which would be both undesirable and present risk issues. The doctor needs to specify how long the delay would be before a second medical recommendation could be obtained. He or she also needs to describe what the risks - to the patient or other people - would be if such a delay occurred.
- Why alternatives to s4 detention are not possible. This explanation should focus on the patient's symptoms/behavior and the way this is connected to the reason why other forms of care (i.e. as informal patient or in the community) are not appropriate.

For applicant

On form A9 or A10 the applicant must state that the legal criteria for s2 have been met and that to comply with the 'normal' requirements i.e. obtaining a second medical recommendation would involve 'undesirable delay'. The application must be made within 24 hours of the examination by the doctor.

When should s4 be used?

Chapter 15 of the Code gives guidance as to when s4 should or should not be used. 15.8 of the code defines an emergency as when there is evidence of:

- *an immediate and significant risk of mental or physical harm to the patient or others*
- *danger of serious harm to property* **or**
- *a need for the use of restrictive interventions.*

Scrutiny of s4 papers

Any scrutiny - either medical or administrative - of s4 detention papers should check:

- consistency in the spelling of the patient's name and address
- that the doctor and applicant have given their own full name and addresses
- that both application and medical recommendation are signed and dated
- Note: an unsigned application or medical recommendation cannot be amended and would render the detention invalid
- the applicant has signed their application within 24 hours of seeing the patient
- that the doctor completing their medical recommendation must have seen the patient within the last 24 hours
- the hospital to which the patient is admitted is the hospital named on the AMHP or Nearest Relative Application.

Note that s15 cannot be used to rectify s4 papers.

Section 5(2)

Note that at the end of this section of the chapter the processes for changing s5 (2) to s2 or s3 are summarised in flow chart form.

Purpose of s5(2)

If an informal in-patient decides they no longer want to be assessed and/or treated or wishes to leave hospital they may need to be assessed to be detained under s2 or s3 in the ways described above.

These processes take time to begin and complete which is why s5 works as a 'holding power'. S5(2) allows one person - either a doctor or an Approved Clinician who is not a doctor - to 'hold' the patient for up to 72 hours to enable the s2 or s3 assessments to take place.

It needs to be stressed that it is not automatic that s5 (2) is superseded by s2 or s3. This is because those assessing the patient may decide the patient does not meet the criteria for those sections.

It is important to stress that on all occasions if s5 (2) has been used the assessments for s2 or s3 must be prioritised. Organisations may wish to set targets/standards regarding the way these assessments are carried out. It is extremely bad practice not to undertake these assessments within the 72 hour period and/or simply to allow detention under s5 (2) to lapse.

Legal Criteria for s5 (2)

The view of the doctor (or Approved Clinician who is not a doctor) is *'that an application ought to be made under this Part of this Act for the admission of the patient to hospital'.*

The meaning of the word 'application' refers to the use of s2 or s3. It should be stressed that the patient must be an in-patient. This section could not - for example - be used in an A&E Department. The Code at 18.7 defines the term hospital in-patient as meaning *'any person receiving in-patient treatment in a hospital'.*

In cases where a recently admitted informal patient wanted to discharge themselves the term 'treatment' can lawfully be interpreted to including such interventions as 'nursing' and 'care' (see s145).

Note that a CTO patient who has been admitted informally (i.e. not recalled) cannot be prevented from leaving hospital by the use of s5 (2). The only power to keep that person in hospital would be to recall them. Recall procedures are dealt with in Chapter 21 of this Guide.

Length of s5 (2)

Section 5(2) lasts for up to 72 hours.

Treatment under s5(2)

Part 4 of the MHA does not apply to this section so any compulsory treatment during the 72 hours duration of this section would need to be given with either the patient's consent or under the Mental Capacity Act (MCA).

Appeal Rights against s5(2)

There are no appeal rights to either the MHT or Hospital Managers against detention under s5 (2).

Leave of Absence

It is not possible to grant leave of absence to a patient detained under s5 (2).

Absence Without Leave

Though a s5(2) ends automatically when the patient leaves the hospital and it's grounds, if the patient becomes AWOL from hospital the law does allow the patient to be 'retaken' during the 72 hour period.

Ending / Conversion of s5(2)

The following are the options for the outcome of detention under s5 (2):

- conversion to s2 or s3 (see information above on these two sections)
- the consultant for the patient may decide to 'end' the detention though technically this does not involve using the discharge power contained within s23 - see next bullet point
- if either of the two doctors asked to submit medical recommendations for s2/s3 or the AMHP asked to consider making a s2/s3 application conclude that the person is not 'sectionable' detention under s5(2) ends. It is suggested that organisations use a form to record this and to have in place mechanisms for ensuring the patient is aware of their reversion to informal status.

Paperwork and rights leaflet for s5(2)

The following form must be completed in all cases when s5 (2) is used. **1 Form H1** Report by doctor/approved clinician

The statutory form is divided into two parts. The first part of the form must be completed by the registered medical practitioner or approved clinician who is in charge of the patient's care or their 'nominee'.

The 2007 MHA amendments mean that someone who is not a doctor may be authorised to use s5 (2). As more non-doctors take up the Approved Clinician role, organisations will need to decide upon the circumstances in which someone who is not a doctor (either an Approved Clinician or their deputy) should be placing someone on a s5(2).

Chapter 18 of the Code gives helpful guidance on a number of aspects of the use of s5 (2) and it is recommended that organisations consider devising their own protocols using the Code as the framework for such protocols.

Unlike s2, s3 or s4 no record of detention (Form H3) needs to be completed for S5 (2). However **Part 1** of **Form HI** does require the person applying this section to indicate how they are submitting the form to the relevant 'MHA Officer', and **Part 2** of the form requires the relevant 'MHA Officer' to confirm that the form has been submitted. Organisations need to decide who should complete Part 2 of the form (options are a ward-based nurse or someone working in an MHA Office) and whether it is appropriate for internal mail systems to be used to deliver the completed form to an MHA office.

The rights leaflet for s5 (2) is **S5 (2)**.

THE PATIENT'S JOURNEY – USING S5(2) – S2/S3

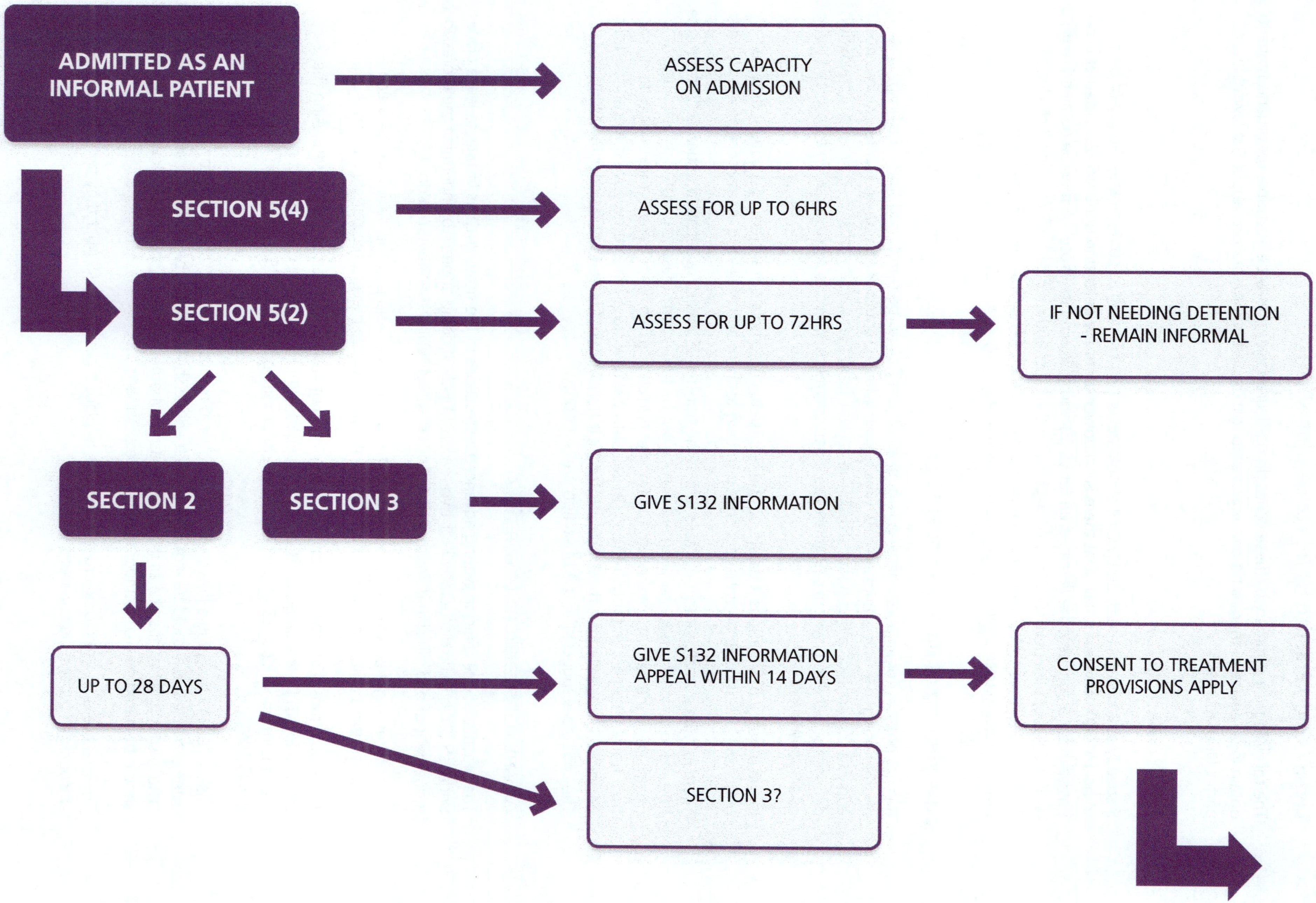

Legal / Good Practice Issues concerning s5(2)

The following is a summary of these issues. In particular cases it may be advisable for organisations to obtain legal advice as there is no consensus amongst 'expert commentators' about the lawfulness of particular practices.

Back to Back s5 (2)

If speedy assessments are undertaken it should never be necessary to contemplate the use of back to back s5 (2). It is clear in law that there is no power to renew detention under s5 (2). Whether it is unlawful for a patient to be detained under s5 (2) and following its 'lapse' to then be detained (with or without a gap) on a new s5 (2) would depend on the facts and may be subject to legal challenge. 18.38 of the Code states *'Detention under section 5(2) or 5(4) cannot be renewed but that does not prevent it being used again on a future occasion if necessary.'*

Transferring of patients under s5 (2)

It is not possible for a patient detained under s5 (2) or s5 (4) to be transferred from one hospital to another using s19. This is because s19, which deals with the transfer of detained patients, does not apply to someone detained under s5 (2). This is clear from the wording of s19 (1) (a) and (2) (a) which defines the patient to whom s19 applies as a person who is *'liable to be detained in a hospital by virtue of an application.'*

In the majority of situations it would not be helpful to contemplate transferring a patient detained under s5 (2) as it could be unhelpful and unsettling to them and make the assessment process harder.

There may be a small number of cases where the transfer of someone detained under s5 (2) from one hospital to another is necessary. An example might be for security reasons or for reasons of urgent treatment. If the patient consents to the transfer (which requires them to have the capacity to do so) then transfer can occur, though the s5 (2) will automatically lapse when they leave the hospital. If the person lacks capacity then the legal basis for their transfer would need to be under the MCA. The code does suggest the use of section 4 as an option.

Advance Instructions to use s5 (2)

The practice of one clinician writing advanced instructions in the notes such as 'if tries to leave place under s5 (2)' is to be discouraged for two reasons. Firstly, it could appear to undermine the professional judgement of one clinician if another clinician is in effect telling them what to do.

Secondly, it might be seen to amount to 'de facto detention' and blur the distinction between an informal and a detained patient if the clinician's intent was to prevent the patient leaving.

This would most probably amount to a 'deprivation of liberty' that can only be lawful using the Deprivation of Liberty Safeguards(DOLS) contained within the Mental Capacity Act or by sectioning the patient under s2 or s3 of the MHA. More information about DOLS is contained in Chapter 24 of this Guide.

It is lawful and acceptable however for the notes to record that s5 (2) should be considered if a patient attempts to leave. It could be argued that such advice should in fact be applied to any informal patient who wishes to leave hospital as the decision as to whether someone should be allowed to leave hospital should be based on a contemporaneous risk assessment.

The practice of any doctor instructing a nurse to place a patient on s5 (4) if they try to leave is discouraged for the same reasons.

Section 5(4)

Purpose of s5(4)

This allows a nurse of the 'prescribed class' to detain an in-patient who is already receiving treatment for mental disorder.

The definition of 'prescribed class' is any nurse registered in sub-parts 1 or 2 of the register maintained by the Nursing and Midwifery Council (NMC) whose entry on the register indicates that their field of practice is either mental health or learning disability.

Legal Criteria for s5 (4)

A hospital in-patient who is already receiving treatment for mental disorder who the nurse believes:

- *'appears to be suffering from a mental disorder to such a degree that it is necessary for the patient's health or safety or for the protection of others that they need to be immediately restrained from leaving hospital'* ***and***
- *'it is not practicable to secure the immediate attendance of a clinician for the purposes of furnishing a report under subsection (2) above'.*

Length of s5 (4)

S5 (4) lasts for up to six hours or until the doctor (or Approved Clinician who is not a doctor) attends. Note that it is the arrival of this person which ends the s5 (4) rather than the commencement of their assessment for s5 (2). Note also that if that person arrives and applies s5 (2) the 72 hour period of the s5 (2) runs from when the s5 (4) was first applied.

Treatment under s5 (4)

Part 4 of the MHA does not apply to this section so any compulsory treatment during the 6 hours duration of this section would need to be given with either the patient's consent or under the Mental Capacity Act (MCA).

Appeal Rights

There are no appeal rights to either the MHT or Hospital Managers against detention under s5 (4).

Leave of Absence

It is not possible to grant leave of absence to a patient detained under this section.

Absence Without Leave

If a patient detained under s5 (4) goes absent without leave they can be 'retaken' during the 6 hours duration of this section if they are located on the hospital premises. There is no power to retake them after the 6 hours has lapsed.

Ending of s5 (4)

As stated above the arrival of the person who is to assess for s5 (2) automatically ends s5 (4). If such a person has not attended within the six hours the s5 (4) ends at that point and cannot be renewed. 18.38 of the Code states *'Detention under section 5(2) or 5(4) cannot be renewed but that does not prevent it being used again on a future occasion if necessary.'*

Paperwork and rights leaflet for s5(4)

The nurse applying this section needs to complete Form H2 which requires them to address the relevant legal criteria (see above) and describe the category of their registration (see above).

There is no longer a form to record the ending of s5 (4) but the Code advises at 18.37 that *'the time at which a patient ceases to be detained under section 5(2) or s5 (4) should be recorded, preferably using a standardised system established by the hospital managers for this purpose.'*

The rights leaflet for s5 (4) is **S5** (4).

Other Notes about the use of s5(4)

- The criteria for its use (see above) are more rigorous than for s5 (2) which is an indication of the intention within the legislation that s5 (2) should always be the preferred option. There will be cases when it is appropriate for a nurse to detain someone using this power but it is important that organisations have in place robust systems for ensuring that doctors (or Approved Clinicians) promptly and swiftly respond to situations in which patients wish to leave hospital and need to be assessed.
- It is not unknown for patients wishing to leave hospital to be prevented from doing so by being told by nursing staff 'you cannot leave until you have seen a doctor' or - on a ward where the doors are locked - for staff not to open the door. This may amount to a deprivation of liberty at the point at which the patient states a desire to leave. Section 5(4) should be used to provide the patient with a formal and transparent procedure and to avoid the suggestion of unlawful detention. Note also that s139 offers any nurse who has used s5 (4) protection from any proceedings brought against them providing they can demonstrate that their intervention was *'not done in bad faith or without reasonable care'*.

Note that a CTO patient who has been admitted informally (i.e. not recalled) cannot be prevented from leaving hospital by the use of s5 (4). The only power to keep that person in hospital would be to recall them. Recall procedures are dealt with in Chapter 21 of this Guide.

Additional guidance on both s5 (4) and s5 (2) can be found in Chapter 18 of the Code.

Though a s5(4) ends automatically when the patient leaves the hospital and it's grounds this does not apply if the patient had become AWOL where the law does allow the patient to be 'retaken' during the 6 hour period.

MHA 1983 - Summary of Civil Sections (MHA Part 2)

Section	Length	Part 4 applies	Appeal Rights	Professional Requirements to use	Forms
2	Up to 28 days	Yes	To MHT and Hospital Managers	Two doctors (one s12 approved) providing medical recommendations + AMHP or Nearest Relative application	■ **1 Form A3 or 2 Forms A4** ■ **1 Form A2 or Form A1** ■ **1 Form H3 (Part 2 only)**
3	Up to six months *(renewable)*	Yes	To MHT and Hospital Managers	Two doctors (one s12 approved) providing medical recommendations + AMHP or Nearest Relative application	■ **1 Form A7 or 2 Forms A8** ■ **1 Form A6 or Form A5** ■ **1 Form H3 (Part 2 only)**
4	Up to 72 hours	No	None	One doctor + AMHP or Nearest Relative application	■ **1 Form A11** ■ **1 Form A10 or Form A9** ■ **1 Form H3 (Part 2 only)**
5(4)	Up to six hours	No	None	One nurse	■ **1 Form H2**
5(2)	Up to 72 hours	No	None	One doctor or approved clinician (or nominated deputy) Usually done by a doctor	■ **1 Form H1**

Chapter 4 Role of the Approved Mental Health Professional

Introduction

As from November 2008 the role of Approved Social Worker (ASW) was replaced by the role of Approved Mental Health Professional (AMHP). This change enables suitably trained and accredited people who are not social workers by background to become AMHPs. The role is not open to doctors but can be undertaken by social workers, psychologists, occupational therapists and nurses.

The Regulations for the accreditation of an AMHP are contained in the AMHP Regulations for England (Statutory Instruments No 1206 2008). Note there are separate regulations for Wales.

Local Social Services Authorities

Responsibility for ensuring a robust and adequate supply of AMHPs lies with Local Social Service Authorities (LSSAs). It will be possible for an AMHP to be employed by an organisation other than the LSSA, but the LSSA will remain responsible for the quality and availability of the services offered by AMHPs in that area and clear governance arrangements will need to be in place. This will enable the AMHP to be clear about their training needs, access to legal advice and legal indemnity cover.

The Distinctive Role of the AMHP

The role of the AMHP can be seen as providing a counterbalance to the role of the doctor who operates to some extent within the 'medical model'. In order for decisions about compulsion to be both objective and appropriate the AMHP brings to the role what can be summarised as being a 'social perspective.'

The perspective brought by the AMHP is to focus on the overall circumstances of the patient's case including issues (e.g. social and educational factors) which may affect the patient and thus put into context the needs of that patient for assessment or treatment. Aspects of the role include:

- Looking at the issues of concern in a way which attempts to engage the patient themselves
- Ensuring that any interventions are the 'least restrictive' possible and are also in strict compliance with all aspects of the law. This includes the MHA as well as other legislation such as the Human Rights Act 1998 and the Children Act 2004
- Taking into account the wishes of relatives and all other relevant circumstances of the case.

It is helpful to see aspects of the AMHP role in the context of the Guiding Principles contained within Chapter One of the Code - see Chapter 15 of this Guide.

Summary of AMHP role

- To consider making applications for s2, s3, s4 and s7
- To be involved in the making, extension and revocation of Community Treatment Orders
- To be involved - if patient is known to them - as 'second professional' when consideration is being made by an RC to renewing detention under s3 or s37
- To enter and inspect premises (other than NHS hospitals) in which a mentally disordered person is living and where there is reasonable cause to believe the person is not under proper care. This function is to be found in s115
- To apply for a warrant to enter specified premises and - if appropriate - remove the patient using the powers in s135 (1). An alternative outcome of the use of this power is that the assessment of the patient takes place in the premises concerned leading to the patient being detained under s4, s2 or s3 or agreeing to informal admission
- To interview a person who has been removed to a place of safety under s135 or s136 (see Chapter 7 of this Guide).

Role in MHA assessments

Within the context of an MHA assessment the role of the AMHP includes:

- having overall responsibility for co-ordinating the process
- making their own professional judgements as to whether the statutory criteria are met
- interviewing the patient in a suitable manner
- considering whether the use of compulsion is necessary and appropriate and how this should be reflected in any proposed care and treatment.

Chapter 5 The role of the Approved Clinician and Responsible Clinician

Introduction

The roles of Approved Clinician (AC) and Responsible Clinician (RC) were introduced in November 2008 as part of the amended MHA. The RC replaced the role of the Responsible Medical Officer (RMO) whereas the AC role was a completely new one. The change means that suitably qualified ACs who are not doctors by background can move into the role of RC i.e. the person who is in overall charge of the care and treatment of a detained patient. Note that ACs who are not RCs can be responsible for authorising treatment under Part 4 or Part 4A of the Act.

Before a person can be an RC, they must first be an AC. The role of AC can usefully be described as being a qualification. Approval is delegated from the Department of Health to local approval bodies.

Approval to act as An Approved Clinician

The following is a summary of the approval requirements to be found within s.12ZA-C and the Instructions with respect to the Exercise of Approval Functions 2014. Additional information about the role of the AC can be found in 'Mental Heath Act 2007 New Roles - Guidance for approving authorities and employers of Approved Mental Health Professionals and Approved Clinicians' published by the National Institute for Mental Health in England (NIMHE) in October 2008.

Summary of the approval requirements

The relevant approval body can approve someone to be an Approved Clinician from the following range of registered and professionally qualified groups:

- registered medical practitioners (i.e. doctors)
- chartered psychologists
- first level nurses (whose field of practice is either mental health or learning disabilities)
- registered occupational therapists
- registered social workers.

Approval is not automatic for anyone from the groups described above: the person needs to demonstrate specific competencies before they can be approved. These competencies are to be found in Schedule 2 of the AC directions. In addition the person needs to have completed in the last two years a course for the initial training of an Approved Clinician, and been approved or been treated as approved to act as an Approved Clinician in England or Wales in the last five years.

This table on the next page is reproduced from the NIMHE guidance referred to above and focuses on the competencies required for approval.

Summary of competency required	Description of what this means
Comprehensive understanding of the role of the AC and RC	Includes understanding of legal responsibilities and key functions of the role
Legal and policy framework	■ Applied knowledge of the 1983 MHA; related Codes of Practice and national and local policy and guidelines ■ Applied knowledge of other relevant legislation and its Codes - in particular 1998 Human Rights Act, 2005 Mental Capacity Act and Children Acts ■ Applied knowledge of relevant NICE guidance.
Assessment of mental disorder	■ Ability to identify the presence of mental disorder and to identify its severity and to determine whether the disorder is of a nature or degree to warrant compulsory confinement ■ Ability to undertake mental health assessments (which incorporate biological, psychological, cultural and social perspectives).
Assessment of risk	■ Ability to assess all levels of clinical risk including risk to the safety of the patient and others. To do so using evidence-based frameworks for risk assessment and management.
Treatment of mental disorder	■ Understanding of mental health related treatments (i.e. physical, social and psychological interventions) ■ Ability to formulate, review appropriately and lead on treatment (where the clinician is appropriately qualified) within the context of a multi-disciplinary team.
Assessment of capacity	High level of skill in determining whether a patient has the capacity to consent to treatment.
Care Planning	Ability to manage and develop care plans which combine health, social services and other resources (ideally but not essentially within the context of the Care Programme Approach).
Leadership and Multi-Disciplinary Team Working	■ Ability to effectively lead a multi-disciplinary team including the ability to assimilate the (potentially diverse) views and opinions of other professionals, patients and carers whilst maintaining an 'independent' view. ■ Ability to manage and take responsibility for making decisions in complex cases without the need to refer to supervision in each case. ■ Understanding of and recognition of limits to own skills and recognition of need to seek other professional views to inform decisions.

Summary of competency required	Description of what this means
Equality and Cultural Diversity	■ Up to date knowledge and understanding of equality issues (including those concerning race, gender, disability and sexual orientation) ■ Ability to identify, challenge and - where possible - redress discrimination and inequality in all its forms in relation to approved clinical practice ■ Understanding of the need to sensitively and actively promote equality and diversity, and understanding of how cultural factors and personal values impact on professional judgment and the ways in which mental health legislation and policy are applied.
Communication	■ Ability to communicate effectively with professionals, patients, carers (in particular in relation to decisions taken and the underlying reasons for these). ■ Ability to keep appropriate records including an awareness of the legal requirements to do with record-keeping. ■ Understanding of, and ability to manage competing requirements of confidentiality and effective information-sharing to the benefit of patients and other stakeholders. ■ Ability to compile and complete statutory documentation and to provide written reports. ■ Ability to present evidence to courts and tribunals.

Summary of the functions of the AC and RC

Functions of the AC

The main function of the AC is: To decide upon treatment without consent using the powers within MHA Part 4 and Part 4A. This includes being in charge of medication given to a patient where the authorisation has been provided by a Second Opinion Appointed Doctor (SOAD). Note that in terms of Part 4 and Part 4A the approval clinician who authorises the treatment does not need to be the patient's RC though in most cases it will be the same person.

Note also that if the RC for a patient is not medically qualified to prescribe medication (for example) another professional who is qualified to prescribe will need to be involved and will be in charge of that aspect of the patient's treatment.

Functions of the RC

All patients detained s2 or s3 or Part 3 (forensic sections) must have a RC. The exception is patients detained under s35. Note that someone detained under s5 (2), s5 (4), s135 (1) or s136 does not have an RC. The functions of the RC can be summarised as:

- having overall responsibility for the patient's care and treatment within the context of the care being provided by a multi-disciplinary team. This role includes responsibility for regularly reviewing whether the patient still meets the criteria for detention;
- having powers to grant leave of absence:
- having powers to end the patient's section;
- having powers to bar discharge by the patient' nearest relative;
- having powers to renew a patient's section (subject to the need for the agreement of another professional who has been involved in the patient's care and treatment);
- having the power for certain categories of patients to make a Community Treatment Order (CTO).

Allocation of the RC

The RC is the person who has overall responsibility for the care and treatment of a patient.

Each patient can only have one RC at any point in time and the decision as to who that should be is determined by the needs of the patient. An example might be in a team which contained both a doctor and a psychologist who were ACs. Initially the doctor might be the RC if the main treatment at that stage was anti-psychotic medication. Later on, as psychological interventions became central to the patient's treatment, the psychologists might replace the doctor as the RC.

Chapter 36 of the Code is entitled 'Allocating or changing a responsible clinician'. It emphasises the need for local protocols within organisations which seek to ensure that the person allocated to be the RC should be the individual AC with the most expertise to meet the assessment and treatment needs of the patient. At any point in time it is important that the identity of the RC is clear and that there are appropriate cover arrangements for when the regular RC is not available.

Change of RC

The Code suggests that - because the needs of a patient may change over time - there needs to be a review mechanism in place which enables consideration to be given to changing the RC. The change should always be made with the intention of enabling the patient's needs to be met more effectively. It is suggested that the Guiding Principles within Chapter One of the Code are a useful tool for reviewing which professional within an organisation is best equipped to be the patient's RC.

Chapter 6 The role of the nearest relative

Introduction

The role of the nearest relative is very important within the MHA and can be regarded as a valuable 'check and balance' to the very significant powers granted within the legislation to professionals.

The term nearest relative is unique to the MHA and should not be confused with terms such as 'next of kin' or 'carer'. The essential difference is that the 'nearest relative' is defined within s26 of the MHA with the patient having only very limited choice as to whom that person is. In making an application under s2, s3 or s4 the Approved Mental Health Professional (AMHP) needs to decide who the patient's nearest relative is. Note that restricted patients and patients detained under s35, s36 or s38 do not have a nearest relative for the purposes of the MHA.

Note that specific issues involving identification of the nearest relative for children and young people are dealt with in Chapter 26 of this Guide.

S26 - Identification of Nearest Relative

S26 (1) contains a hierarchical list of who can be the Nearest Relative within the meaning of the Mental Health Act. This is:

- husband or wife or civil partner
- son or daughter
- father or mother
- brother or sister
- grandparent
- grandchild
- uncle or aunt
- nephew or niece.

The AHMP needs to work their way down the list until they are able to identify someone who is the nearest relative of the patient in question.

General points

Anyone on the list can move to the top of the list if they 'ordinarily reside with' or 'care' for the patient.

Husband/Wife/Civil Partner

If a man and woman have been living together in a relationship for more than six months or more, they can be counted as being each other's nearest relative irrespective of whether they are married.

If a same-sex couple have been living together in a relationship for six months or more they can be counted as being each other's nearest relative irrespective of whether they are in a civil partnership or not.

Where the couple are not currently living together it is only where there is a permanent separation by agreement between the two people that they cease to be each other's nearest relative.

In the case of one of the two partners having deserted the other that person ceases to be the nearest relative.

Age

In cases where there is more than one person in each category of the list it is always the older who is the nearest relative. For example if the patient has both a son and daughter it is the older of the two who is the nearest relative. Anyone under the age of 18 cannot be the nearest relative of a patient (unless they are the patient's spouse or parent).

Residency

Anyone on the list who does not ordinarily reside in the UK, Channel Islands or the Isle of Man cannot be the patient's nearest relative. The exception would be if the patient themselves did not ordinarily reside in the UK in which case this exclusion does not apply. Note that the term 'ordinarily resides' is contained within s26 (4) and there will be cases when an AMHP will need to interpret whether a person does ordinarily reside in the UK or not.

Half-blood/whole blood relationships

Where there is more than one person in any category a relationship of the whole blood ranks higher than a relationship of the half-blood.

Illegitimacy

If the patient is 'illegitimate' the patient's mother should always be regarded as the nearest relative unless the patient's father has established parental responsibility under Section 3 of the 1989 Children Act.

Five Year Rule

If there is no one on the list it is possible for someone with whom the patient lives but is not in a 'relationship' with them to become the nearest relative.

Changes to identity of nearest relatives

There are four main ways in which the identity of the nearest relative can change or for a nearest relative to be appointed, which are described in the next section of this Chapter.

County Court appointment of nearest relative

The first way is when a county court appoints someone to the role of nearest relative in circumstances which s29(3)(a) describes as *'where the patient has no nearest relative within the meaning of the Act, or that it is not reasonably practicable to ascertain whether he has such a relative, or who that relative is.'*

A significant number of patients do not have a nearest relative and it may be valuable if someone in a befriending or advocacy role takes on the responsibility. Local authorities may proactively seek to take on the role but it is recognised that they have only limited available resources to do so.

Displacement procedures

The second way is when a county court displaces the current nearest relative following the initiation of displacement procedures. These procedures can be initiated either by an AMHP or another relative of the patient or someone with whom the patient lives or lived prior to admission to hospital. Under the 2007 amendments **the patient themselves** can initiate the process. This amendment to the MHA was triggered by the 'JT case' where the patient was found in court to have had her Article 8 Human Rights (Right to Family and Social Life) breached as the 1983 MHA had made no provision for the patient themselves to initiate displacement procedures.

There are in law a number of different reasons as to why displacement procedures are initiated. These are described in table form on the next page of this Guide.

Summary of Grounds for displacement	MHA Reference	Notes on these grounds
Incapacity of existing nearest relative	S29(3)(b) where *'the nearest relative of the patient is incapable of acting as such by reason of mental disorder or other illness'*	■ This could be either a physical or mental disorder. It would be for the court to decide whether to displace. Simply because a nearest relative has or had a serious mental health problem(possibly including periods of MHA detention) does not automatically bar them from the role. ■ A more appropriate response might be for the nearest relative to delegate the responsibility to someone else on the s26 list (see below).
Unreasonable objection to sectioning	S29(3)(c) where *'the nearest relative of the patient unreasonably objects to the making of an application for admission for treatment or a guardianship application'.*	■ When a nearest relative opposes an AMHP making a s3 application this is a fairly common trigger for displacement procedures to begin. ■ Note that the nearest relative has no legal right to oppose s2 being instigated but case law has made clear it is unlawful to use s2 solely to avoid the barrier to s3 detention presented by the nearest relative.
Inappropriate use by nearest relative of power of discharge	S29(3)(d) where the power to discharge has been used by the nearest relative *'without due regard to the welfare of the patient or the interests of the public or is likely to do so'*	Though the MHA allows the nearest relative to request discharge from s2 or s3 the law recognises that in certain situations attempts to exercise this power are not appropriate and can be grounds for instigating displacement procedures.
Unsuitability	s29(3)(d) where *'the nearest relative is otherwise not a suitable person to act as such'.*	This clause was inserted into the MHA in November 2008; at the time of this Guide's publication there is no case law interpreting what 'suitable' may or may not mean.

Summary of displacement procedures

S29 enables the existing nearest relative to be displaced by a county court and the role handed over to someone else. This person could be another relative of the patient but the role is more commonly given to a named local authority. The order of displacement will be time-limited if the grounds for displacement are due to unsuitability or incapacity (see table above). Case law has established that it is lawful for an interim displacement to be made pending the final court decision.

Delegation by nearest relative

The third way in which the identity of the nearest relative can change is where the current nearest relative authorises someone else to take on the role. This person does not need to be someone on the s26 list. There is no statutory form for this change to be recorded but a number of local authorities will have devised forms for enabling it to be made. It is essential that both the current nearest relative and the person they are authorising to become the nearest relative sign any form or document. If such a change occurs it is essential that MHA Officers are made aware of the change.

If delegation occurs it is not limited to the time duration of the current period of detention and continues beyond that.

Change of circumstances

The fourth way in which the identity of the nearest relative changes is where circumstances change. One example is where the patient's son or daughter reaches the age of 18 and - assuming there is no husband or wife or civil partner - they therefore become the Nearest Relative. Another example would be where the patient's son - assuming there is no husband or wife or civil partner - has been living abroad and returns to ordinarily reside in the United Kingdom.

If such a change occurs (which may first come to the attention of local authority or ward based staff) it is essential that MHA Officers are made aware of the change so that the necessary procedures can be followed.

Wrong identification of the nearest relative

This is a particularly complex area and it is advised that organisations should seek legal advice in situations in which issues of whether a section is 'valid' or not are being discussed.
Key terms are within s6; especially s6 (2) which refers to an AMHP application which is 'duly completed' and s6 (3) which refers to an application which 'appears to be duly made and founded on the necessary medical recommendations'.

Section 11(4) states that the AMHP cannot make an application for admission under s3 or guardianship, if the AMHP has not consulted the person (if any) 'appearing to be' the nearest relative (unless the requirement to consult that person does not apply if it appears to the professional that in the circumstances such consultation is not reasonably practicable or would involve unreasonable delay).

If the wrong nearest relative has been identified by an AMHP the organisation will need to satisfy itself whether the AMHP reasonably believed that the person identified was the nearest relative, in other words whether the person 'appeared to be' the nearest relative. If so, the application is valid. If not, the application will be invalid. Organisations should seek information from the AMHP service to help them decide whether the AMHP acted reasonably and take advice if necessary.

If an application is invalid, the hospital will nevertheless have a defence under s6 (3) if the application appeared to be duly made. Accordingly the organisation shall have authority to detain at least until it becomes aware of the error. This is supported by recent case law including TTM v London

Borough of Hackney, (2011). Once the detaining organisation becomes aware of the error it can no longer rely on the application as providing adequate authority for continued detention. In the case of a s3 application it may be necessary to invalidate the section as there has been a failure to the part of the statutory process which concerns consultation with the nearest relative. For a s2 application the duty is only to inform the nearest relative – the failure to have done so probably does not require invalidation to occur but – as soon as the nearest relative has been correctly identified – it would be important for the detaining organisation to inform that person of their legal rights (subject to the patient's agreement).

Note the Code's advice is that s23 powers should be used to end the section.

The AHMP Role in consulting the nearest relative (s3)

The MHA starts from the assumption that normally before a s3 application is made the nearest relative should be identified and consulted. 14.59 of the Code says it is only if there would be 'unreasonable delay' or it would not be 'reasonably practicable' that consultation should not happen.

Examples of this are given in 14.60 of the Code.

- 'it is not practicable for the AMHP to obtain sufficient information to establish the identity or location of the nearest relative or where to do so would require an excessive amount of investigation including unreasonable delay'.
- 'consultation is not possible because of the nearest relative's own health or mental incapacity'.

The issue of what the word practicable means has been explored by the courts in a number of cases. In several cases the judge ruled that the AMHP could have done more to identify and consult. Another potentially difficult area is where the patient knows who their nearest relative is and tells the AMHP they do not wish that person to be consulted. This issue was first explored in the 'Bristol Case' and revisited in the TW v Enfield case. 14.62-14.65 of the Code gives guidance for AMHP in this area. In all cases the AMHP will need to balance the patient's Article 8 rights (respect for their privacy and family life) with the patient's Article 5 rights (the right to liberty).

Rights and Responsibilities of the nearest relative

These can be summarised as the following:

- the right to make applications for detention under s2, s3 or s4
- right to be consulted by AMHP (s3 and s7) and right to object
- notification of admission under s2 and s4
- right to be invited to a MHT
- notification of sectioning by hospital and of impending discharge by hospital (if patient agrees) (s132 and s133)
- the right to order the discharge of a patient detained under s2 or s3 or CTO and rights of appeal to MHT if discharge barred (unless s2).

The next section of this Chapter deals with the nearest relative's power of discharge.

Nearest relative powers of discharge

This power is contained in s23 but note that s25(1) means that the patient's RC has up to 72 hours to consider this request and to block the discharge if they believe the patient would *'if discharged likely to act in a manner dangerous to other persons or to himself'*. Note this power to request discharge does not apply to Part 3 patients.

Organisations need to have in place protocols enabling requests from nearest relatives to be clearly identified and promptly dealt with. This is to safeguard the rights of the nearest relative and also to ensure the RC or a covering AC is able to consider the request before the 72 hours has passed.

There is no statutory form for the nearest relative to use but page 356 of the Code gives a sample letter that could be used. Note the nearest relative does not need to use that letter. If another format is used and is in anyway ambiguous about whether or not it constitutes a discharge request the nearest relative should be contacted as a matter of urgency so they can clarify their intention. An example of possible ambiguity is where the letter contains a number of negative comments about the hospital ward and its staff which could be interpreted to be more appropriately treated as a complaint.

There are four possible outcomes to the request:

- the nearest relative withdraws the request; they have the right to do so but can only do so before the 72 hours have ended
- the RC considers the request and decides to end the section themselves.
- the RC considers the request and allows the 72 hours to pass in which case the patient is no longer detained.
- the RC considers the request and issues a barring certificate during the 72 hours. If they do so they must certify this on statutory form **M2**.

If the RC bars discharge the patient and the nearest relative need to be informed. If the barring of discharge was on an s3 the nearest relative needs to be told that they have a subsequent right to apply for an MHT but that they must exercise that right within 28 days of being informed that the discharge has been barred. Both for s2 and s3 the Hospital Managers must also consider whether to review detention at this point - their role is dealt with in Chapter 16 of this Guide.

Other points concerning discharges by nearest relatives

Meaning of 'dangerousness'

The RC cannot bar discharge simply because they believe the patient continues to meet the statutory criteria for detention. Dangerousness constitutes a much higher threshold than the references in the statutory criteria to *'health or safety of the patient or the protection of others'*. 32.23 explains this difference by stating that the question the RC needs to focus on is *'the probability of dangerous acts, such as causing serious physical injury or lasting psychological harm not merely on the patient's general health or safety and others' general need for protection'*.

It is suggested that best practice would always be for the RC to make a risk assessment before deciding whether to bar discharge or not.

Discharge from hospital or section?

In most cases the intention in discharge is to allow the patient who is under s2 or s3 to leave hospital. It is however possible for the patient to remain as an informal patient if discharge is not blocked. Discharges by nearest relatives do not remove the duty of the hospital and local authority to provide aftercare; including s117 for s3 patients.

Consequences of barring discharge

If discharge is barred the nearest relative cannot seek discharge again before the end of the current period of detention (either 28 days on s2 or six months or one year on s3). Note also the possibility of seeking displacement if it is believed the power has been exercised inappropriately (see table above).

Chapter 7 The role of the police (including s135, s136 and conveying)

This chapter has been updated to include changes to MHA s135,136 and s138 which were included in the Policing and Crime Act of 2017. Note that the Department of Health have updated the s135 and s136 rights leaflets to reflect these changes. Note also this chapter uses the term police officer throughout unless it is a direct quote from the Act which uses the term constable.

Section 135

Purpose of s135 (1)

This section permits a justice of the peace to issue a warrant enabling any 'constable' to enter premises named on the warrant and to remove the person involved to a place of safety. The warrant is issued only after an AMHP has submitted evidence the person meets the following criteria.

Purpose of s135(2)

Section 135(2) deals with obtaining a warrant to enable a police officer to enter premises to 'retake' someone who is AWOL under the MHA. This includes patients AWOL under guardianship or community treatment orders. This warrant can be obtained by an AMHP or anyone authorised by the detaining authority to do so. In contrast to the execution of a s135 (1) warrant, the police officer does not have to be accompanied by the person who has obtained the warrant.

Length of Warrants

For both s135 (1) and s135 (2) entry to the premises must be within three months of the date of issue.

Legal criteria for s135(1)

S135 (1) (a) and (b) requires the justice of the peace to have:

- *'reasonable cause to suspect that a person believed to be suffering from mental disorder - has been, or is being, ill treated, neglected or kept otherwise than under proper control, in any place within the jurisdiction of the justice'* ***or***
- *'being unable to care for himself, is living alone in any such place'.*

Legal criteria for s135(2)

S135 (2) (a) and (b) requires the justice of the peace to have:

- *'reasonable cause to believe that the patient is to be found on premises within the jurisdiction of the justice;* ***and***
- *that admission to the premises has been refused or that a refusal of such admission is apprehended'.*

Removal of person

Section 135(3) enables the 'constable' (i.e. police officer) or an AMHP to remove the person to a 'place of safety'. Note that the constable must always be accompanied by an AMHP and a doctor. The Code says it is helpful if the doctor concerned is also s12 approved.

The constable may use reasonable force in executing the warrant. In circumstances when police believe that a breach of the peace is occurring (or is imminently likely to occur) they have powers under the 1984 Police and Criminal Evidence Act to enter private premises without needing a warrant.

If the premises where the person lives has a co-owner or co-occupier, that person's permission is sufficient for entry to take place without the need for a s135 (1) warrant.

Meaning of 'place of safety'

Section 135(6) defines a place of safety as:

- *'residential accommodation provided by a local social services authority under Part 111 of the National Assistance Act 1948'*
- *'a hospital as defined by this Act' (i.e. MHA)*
- *a police station'*
- (an independent hospital or care home) *'for mentally disordered persons'* **or**
- *'any other suitable place'.*

Note that this is the definition of a place of safety as applicable to s136 - see below. The Code's view in 16.5 is *'Where it is reasonably practicable, the intended place of safety should be identified, and the necessary arrangements made, before a warrant is applied for under section 135(1). Proper planning should ensure that it is not necessary to use a police station as a place of safety for people removed under section 135(1), other than in the exceptional circumstances described in paragraph 16.38'.* which states *'if the person's behaviour would pose an unmanageably high risk to other patients, staff or other users if the person were to be detained in a healthcare setting'*. This guidance applies to both s135 and s136.

If the plan had been to use the s135(1) only to enter premises and then remove the person under s2, s3 or s4 then the 'place of safety' would probably be the hospital ward to which the admission was planned.

Length of s135 (1)

The person can be detained in the place of safety for up to 24 hours. Transfers between one place of safety and another are lawful but never extend the length of detention. The period can be extended by another 12 hours as authorised by a registered medical practitioner but only if it has not been possible to complete the assessment of the patient within the 24 hours. It is suggested that organisations should have protocols identifying the seniority of the doctor making that decision.

How s135(1) is used

The most common use of s135 (1) is not actually to remove the person from somewhere under this power but to use the s135 (1) to enter premises and then to assess for s2, s3 or s4 leading to hospital admission under section (or possibly informal admission if the patient agrees to this).

Appeal Rights against s135 (1)

There are no appeal rights against s135 (1). The patient should be given information about their detention in the same way as would happen for other sections. The rights leaflet is **S135.**

Treatment under s135(1)

Part 4 of the MHA does not apply to this section so any compulsory treatment duration of this section would need to be given with either the patient's consent or under the Mental Capacity Act (MCA).

Outcome of s135(1)

If used only to secure entry to premises, leading to the person leaving the premises under s2, s3 or s4, the s135 (1) is superseded by that section.

A patient taken to hospital under s135(1) can only be kept for 24 hours (plus 12 more hours if applicable) while assessments take place. This assessment should be conducted by a doctor and an AMHP. Best practice is considered to be that the doctor is s12 approved.

If early indications are that sectioning under Part 2 is required, the role of the doctor and AMHP may be not only to assess under s135 (1) but also to begin the process of sectioning under s2, s3 or s4.

Detention under s2, s3 or s4 (or the decision to not make an application by an AMHP) ends detention under s135 (1). S135 (1) also ends when other arrangements for care and treatment are made or at the end of 24 hours (plus 12 more hours if applicable).

If no assessments have been made/completed during the maximum length of the s135(1) the person is free to leave the place of safety. If it was a hospital setting s5 (4) or s5 (2) could not be used to detain them as they would not be a hospital in-patient.

Conveying patients to hospital

This part of the Chapter focuses on the processes by which a patient is conveyed from the community to the hospital where they are to be detained. It does **not** deal with other forms of conveying which include the following:

- transferring patients between hospitals
- returning patients to hospital who are absent without leave(AWOL)
- taking CTO or conditionally discharged patients to hospital who have been recalled
- taking and returning to the place of residence guardianship patients
- taking patients to and between places of safety (s135 and s136)
- taking patients to and from court.

Organisations need to have local protocols (including police, ambulance and patient transport services input) to deal with all aspects of conveying.

Section 6 of the Act authorises the conveying of patients to hospital.

The power to convey a person to hospital requires a completed application by an AHMP or the patient's nearest relative. The Act allows such force as necessary to convey the person to hospital and the applicant (nearest relative or AMHP) has all the powers that a police officer has when taking a person into custody. From the place of origin to hospital the person is in legal custody and if they escape they can be retaken under s138.

Where an application for s2 or s3 has been completed and the patient escapes whilst being conveyed to hospital, he/she may be retaken within 14 days beginning with the date of the examination by the last doctor who provided a medical recommendation as part of the sectioning process.

Where an application for s4 has been completed and the patient escapes whilst being conveyed to hospital, he/she may be retaken within 24 hours from the time of the medical examination or the time when the application was made, whichever is the earlier.

Note that if the patient who has escaped from custody and has returned to their flat or house of other private premises a warrant under s135 would be needed to secure entry.

Section 136

Purpose of s136

This sentence authorises a police officer to detain somebody appearing to be mentally disordered and take them to a place of safety.

Legal Criteria for s136

Section 136(1) & (2) states:

'If the person appears to a constable to be suffering from mental disorder and to be in immediate need of care and control, the constable may, if he thinks necessary to do so in the interests of that person or for the protection of other persons-remove that person to a place of safety within the meaning of section 135 above.' and

'A person removed to a place of safety under this section may be so detained there for a period not exceeding term permitted period of detention for the purpose of enabling him to be examined by a registered medical practitioners and to be interviewed by an approved mental health professional and of making any necessary arrangements for his treatment of care.'*

To enable s136 to be lawfully and appropriately used it is advised that organisations develop local protocols in conjunction with local authorities, ambulance and police services.

The following notes deal with aspects of the legal criteria described above.

**normally 24 hours unless 12 hour extension needed*

Meaning of 'appears to'

This wording recognises that a police officer is not considered, in law, competent to make a diagnosis that someone is or is not mentally disordered. It is recommended that organisations providing mental health care offer training to local police forces in how best to identify and respond to individuals who may or may not have mental health problems.

Meaning of 'public place'

Note the term 'place to which the public have access' (commonly referred to as a 'public place') has been removed from the Act. This means the s136 power can be used in any place with the exception of the following:

- any house, flat or room where that person, or any other person is living or
- any yard, garden, garage or outhouse that is used in connection with the house, flat or room, other than one that is also used in connection with one or more other houses, flats or rooms

Meaning and choice of 'place of safety'

The definition within s136 of a place of safety is taken from s135 (6) (see above under s135 (1). Local policies should identify 'designated' places of safety within a healthcare setting. For a whole range of reasons the use of polices stations as places of safety should be avoided as much as possible. 16.38 of the Code states *'A police station should not be used as a place of safety except in exceptional circumstances, for example it may be necessary to do so because the patient's behavior would pose an unmanageably high risk to other patients, staff or other uses if the person were to be detained in a healthcare setting'.*

Length of s136

Section 136 lasts for up to 24 hours (see above for grounds for 12 hour extension). Transfers between one place of safety and another are lawful but never extend the length of detention.

Appeal Rights against s136

There are no appeal rights against s136. The patient should be given information about their detention in the same way as would happen for other sections.

The rights leaflet is **S136**.

Treatment under s136

Part 4 of the MHA does not apply to this section so any compulsory treatment while the s136 is in place either the patient's consent or under the Mental Capacity Act (MCA).

Outcomes of s136

Whilst s136 is in place the following are the possible outcomes:

- the person is assessed under the MHA and agrees to informal admission
- the person is assessed as having medical problems and is admitted to a medical ward. This might be when assessment concludes there is no mental disorder or that the medical problem is more pressing than any mental health problem
- assessment leads to the conclusion that the person does not have a mental health problem at all.*

*Though s136(2) requires the patient to be seen by an AMHP the meaning of the statute is that if a doctor sees the patient first and concludes they have no mental disorder the patient can no longer be detained and must immediately be released.

Other changes to s136

These are;

- before using s136 the police officer if it is practicable to do so must consult with either a registered medical practitioner, registered nurse or AMHP;
- the power is added to allow the police officer(s) to undertake protective searches and the circumstances in which they can do this;
- clarification of the circumstances in which the person placed on s136 can be taken to a police station rather than a place of safety. These changes are supplemented within the Regulations which include specific guidance as to how the person should be looked after. Note these changes make it unlawful to take a child to a police station (a child is defined as somebody under 18).

Chapter 8 The Role of MHA Administration

Many organisations will employ staff to work in MHA Administration. The Code refers to such staff as 'MHA Officers' which is the terminology used in this Chapter of the Guide. These staff have a key role to play in ensuring their organisation secures compliance with both the MHA and its Code.

This Chapter focuses on their role in receiving, scrutinising and rectifying section papers. These staff may also have a role in giving MHA advice and arranging Tribunals and Managers' Hearings.

Receiving Papers

TThe meaning of receipt is described in 35.6 of the Code as a process that *'involves physically receiving documents and checking that they amount to an application that has been duly made (since that is sufficient to give the managers the power to detain the patient)'*.

When a patient is to be detained under s2, s3 or s4 statutory form H3 needs to be completed (in addition to the medical recommendations and the AMHP application).

If the patient has been detained under s5 (2) form H3 should not be completed. Instead form H1 needs to be completed. Note this form is divided into two parts. The first part is completed by the clinician who has used s5 (2). The second part is completed by a person authorised to receive section papers.

Organisations need to have protocols as to who can receive section papers. If papers are received during 'office hours' by MHA Officers arrangements will need to be in place to ensure that papers are received out of hours. Often this task will be undertaken by nursing staff working on wards where patients are detained and organisations will need to decide whether those staff receive papers on all occasions or only out of office hours.

Staff undertaking the role of receiving papers need to be competent to do so and organisations may decide that the role is only undertaken by staff at a particular level of seniority or with a particular level of expertise.

There is no legal barrier to photocopies of the original blank forms being used or to the use of computer-generated versions. More than one firm has published versions of the new statutory forms which were introduced in November 2008. There is no legal problem with using different versions of the form providing that the wording corresponds to the wording set out in the Regulations - Schedule 1 of the Mental Health (Hospital, Guardianship and Treatment) Regulations 2008.

It is advised that if a patient is being formally transferred from one hospital that the receiving hospital has sight of faxed copies of the section papers before transfer occurs.

The Code stresses the importance of the person receiving the papers also scrutinising them. It then describes the more detailed and thorough scrutiny process.

Scrutinising Papers

Administrative Scrutiny

The most effective way of receiving and checking accuracy of papers is to use some form of checklist. The checklist should include the following points.

- Do the forms relate to the same section?
- Does the Application give the name of the hospital and the detaining organisation - the patient must be admitted to the hospital named on the Application?
- Are all forms dated and signed?
- Are names and addresses spelt correctly?
- If neither doctor knew the patient (s2 and s3) has the AMHP stated why on the Application?
- Is at least one of the doctors s12 approved (s2 and s3)?
- S4 only - has the doctor signed within 24 hours of seeing the patient?
- Where there are two medical recommendations, were the two examinations carried out no more than five clear days apart (s2 and s3)?
- Has the patient been admitted to hospital within 14 days of the last medical examination?
- Is the nearest relative resident in the UK (s2 and s3)?.

The final part of this Chapter explains s15 of the MHA and how it can be used to rectify errors which have been made by those completing section papers. Some errors are not rectifiable and these can be seen in the table below.

Note that a joint medical recommendation can not be rectified if the error is that neither doctor was s12 approved or there were more than five clear days between the medical recommendations. Only errors such as wrong spelling of names could be rectified using s15.

Medical Scrutiny

In addition to the role of administrative scrutiny the medical recommendations should be scrutinised by someone with appropriate clinical expertise. This person would normally be a doctor probably working at consultant level.

Rectifying errors

The next section of this Chapter is based on practical experience. It is recommended that organisations develop their own protocols as on a number of issues there is no legal precedent for those who need to make day to day judgements about rectifying errors.

To distinguish between rectifiable and non-rectifiable errors this section uses the words 'invalid' or 'invalidated' to describe more serious non-rectifiable errors. These terms are used for convenience and do not attempt to make a distinction in law between sections which 'began' and then were 'ended' or between sections which could be argued had never 'begun' at all.

Note that issues concerning the identification of the 'wrong'nearest relative are dealt with in Chapter 6 of this Guide.

S15 Summary

There will be occasions when a doctor or AMHP puts the wrong date down - e.g. at the beginning of a new year accidentally puts down the date of the year which has just ended. Such an error is rectifiable. The following part of the chapter presents in table form issues dealing with the main sections of the MHA as relating to s15 rectification.

The procedures available within s15 for the rectification of errors do not apply to the following sections:

- part 3 (forensic) sections where any necessary amendments would need to be made - where applicable - by the courts
- CTO applications - note for this that it is suggested that the papers are scrutinised by a MHA Officer before the RC completes the final part of the Form.
- s7 guardianship applications
- s19 transfers.
- s5
- s4 emergency applications once they have expired unless converted to s2.
- s20 or s20A (CTO) renewals.

Note that these papers do still need to be scrutinised. If 'minor' errors are found a file note should be made and kept with the patients records. If more serious errors are found (e.g. the CTO1 form was completed after the s3 had expired) the CTO is clearly not valid.

Those working in MHA offices should be aware of the Bostridge v Oxleas NHS Foundation Trust case in 2014. This case concerned a patient placed on a CTO after their s3 had expired. Only nominal damages were paid to the patient as the error was felt to be a technical one. This judgement does not undermine the importance of scrutiny as the reputation of a particular organisation – and the NHS in general – is damaged by such cases.

PART 1 - ALL SECTIONS

DESCRIPTION OF ERROR	S15 APPLIES?	SUMMARY OF RECTIFICATION PROCESS	OTHER NOTES
Misspelling of name/address of patient	YES	For s2 and s3 complete within 14 days and good practice to amend for other sections	In some cultures there is no definitive spelling of a person's name but a consensus will need to be reached.
Inconsistencies in spelling of name/address	YES	For s2 and s3 complete within 14 days and good practice to amend for other sections	Judgement may be needed as to correct details as records may differ.
Incomplete addresses (e.g. post codes)	YES	For s2 and s3 complete within 14 days and good practice to amend for other sections	Post codes are needed.
No name or address for patient	YES	For s2 and s3 complete process within 14 days but if not possible to establish patient's true identity by 14th day section would remain valid	■ Homeless person should be recorded as NFA ■ If patient long stay on a ward may be OK to put ward as residence but will need to be consistent on all forms ■ If patient does not give name (e.g. mute) or gives false name(s) note should be made with papers. A brief description of the patient should be given (e.g. white female aged approximately 50)
Nearest Relative - no details given or just telephone number	YES	May not be possible to complete process within 14 days or at all	Find out if more information has been obtained from AMHP. It is a matter for the AMHP's professional judgment as to whether it was practicable to have identified and consulted with nearest relative before making application.
Doctors or AMHP don't give full name or address (initials are not acceptable)	YES	Complete within 14 days and good practice to amend for other sections	If not possible to get this done within 14 days (e.g. because doctor or AMHP is on holiday) judgement needs to be made as to whether error is sufficiently serious to require invalidation but unlikely to be considered so.

DESCRIPTION OF ERROR	S15 APPLIES?	SUMMARY OF RECTIFICATION PROCESS	OTHER NOTES
No hospital or wrong hospital named in application	NO	Section invalid as 'not duly completed ' (see s6 and s11)	The Application must name the actual hospital to which the patient has been admitted.
Both doctors have not stated the hospital where the patient is admitted as having the appropriate treatment available.	NO	Section invalid as 'not duly completed' (see s6 and s11)	The requirements within the 'appropriate treatment' test mean the hospital to which the patient is actually admitted to be named by the doctors on both medical recommendation(s) or the joint medical recommendation (s3). This has not been tested in court but the view of some experts is that s15 can be used to replace a single medical recommendation naming the 'wrong' hospital with one which does.
More than 5 complete days between medical recommendations	YES	Complete within 14 days - notice must be given in writing to the applicant and a fresh medical recommendation must be furnished to the hospital managers within 14 days	■ 'Custom and practice' is often for those working in MHA Administration to manage this process but the applicant should be made aware of the problem ■ The oldest of the medical recommendations needs to be replaced with a new one ■ s12 uses the phrase 'not more than 5 days must have elapsed between the days on which the separate examinations took place' i.e. if first examination happened on (e.g.) 1st March and second examination on 7th March that would be lawful.
Neither doctor s12 approved	YES	■ Obtain medical recommendation by a s12 doctor and furnish to the hospital managers within 14 days - as above, notice must be given in writing to the applicant ■ 'Custom and practice' is often for those working in MHA Administration to mange this process but the applicant should be made aware of the problem	A joint medical recommendation is not rectifiable under s15 in this situation.

DESCRIPTION OF ERROR	S15 APPLIES?	SUMMARY OF RECTIFICATION PROCESS	OTHER NOTES
Neither doctor knew patient and AMHP has not given reason	YES	Ask AHMP to add reasons to their form	If AMHP (e.g. due to leave) will not be able to complete within 14 days another option would be to obtain a fresh recommendation from a doctor who did know the patient but such a doctor may not exist if (e.g.) the patient is newly living in the United Kingdom or is not registered with a GP.
Medical recommendation(s) or application not signed	NO	Invalidation needed	This applies also to s5.
Application made more than 14 days after AMHP last saw patient or application made more than 14 days from date of last medical examination or patient conveyed and admitted to hospital more than 14 days from date of last medical recommendation	NO	Invalidation needed	
Doctors have different views as to whether 'health' 'safety' 'protection of others' apply on their forms	NA		There is no legal requirement for the 2 doctors to agree on each or any of these criteria but the medical scrutineer may comment if there is inconsistency between what the doctor's clinical description says and which legal criteria that doctor believes to apply.
Inadequacy of one or both medical recommendation or of a joint medical recommendation	YES (if single medical recommendation) Or NO (if joint medical recommendation)	Complete within 14 days. If one medical recommendation is inadequate that doctor may be asked to make additions or the recommendation could be replaced by a more adequate one using s15. It is not possible to amend joint medical recommendations in this set of circumstances.	■ The views of the medical scrutineer will give guidance as to how inadequate a recommendation is. An example of inadequacy might be a description of the patient's 'history' but no narrative as to the patient's current condition. ■ An example where the section would be invalid would be where the medical recommendation(s) suggest the admission's purpose was only for the treatment/assessment of a physical disorder.

PART 2 - SECTION 5(2) ONLY

DESCRIPTION OF ERROR	S15 APPLIES?	SUMMARY OF RECTIFICATION PROCESS	OTHER NOTES
Doctor does not indicate whether they are the RC or nominated deputy or has wrongly identified themselves.	NO	s15 does not apply to the furnishing of a report under s5 (2).	

PART 3 - SECTION 4 ONLY

DESCRIPTION OF ERROR	S15 APPLIES?	SUMMARY OF RECTIFICATION PROCESS	OTHER NOTES
AMHP has made the application more than 24 hours after last seeing patient	NO	Invalidation needed	
Doctor not S12 approved	NA		If 'converting' s4 to s2 the new medical recommendation would need to be made by an s12 approved doctor.
Doctor did not know patient and AMHP has not given reasons	YES (but only if applied prior to expiration of the emergency application or prior to the 'conversion' to s2).		
Doctor not S12 approved nor knowing the patient	NA		There are differing legal views here but - if a genuine emergency and such a doctor were not available - the section remains valid. The AMHP would need to give reasons on form A10.

PART 4 - SECTION 20 & 20A (CTO) RENEWALS ONLY

DESCRIPTION OF ERROR	S15 APPLIES?	SUMMARY OF RECTIFICATION PROCESS	OTHER NOTES
Form H5 or CTO7 not completed either by the patient's RC or in that RC's absence (due to sickness or leave) by the covering RC.	NO	Invalidation needed	
Form H5 or CTO7 not completed until after the s3/37/CTO has expired or completed more than 2 months before renewal permitted.	NO	Invalidation needed	

Part Two The Use of the MHA on Hospital Wards/Units

Chapter 9 Giving Information to Patients

Section 132 of the MHA deals with the giving of information to detained patients. Section 132A deals with the giving of information to patients subject to Community Treatment Orders (CTO).

Section 132(4) and s133 deal with the giving of information about the patient's detention to their nearest relative. Section 132A (3) deals with the giving of information to the nearest relative of a CTO patient.

What information should be given?

Patients detained under any section need to be informed:

- what section they are detained under
- how long that section lasts
- the implication for them of being detained under that section
- what appeals rights - if any - they have against their detention
- the role of the Care Quality Commission and the Code of Practice
- the circumstances in which correspondence sent by the patient might not be delivered
- (NB: particular procedures only apply to patients detained in high security psychiatric settings)
- the consent to treatment provisions applicable to the section
- the rights of discharge if applicable by the patient's Responsible Clinician or their nearest relative
- the role of the Independent Mental Health Advocate (IMHA).

This constitutes a large amount of information, some of which involves quite technical language and is being given often at a stage when the patient is still quite unwell. The repeating of information is **crucial** – see below.

How should the information be given?

Information should be given both orally and in writing. It is not a mandatory requirement to use the rights leaflets referred to in the text of this Guide but it is suggested these leaflets should form the core information organisations give to detained patients (possibly supplemented by locally produced information). To record that this information has both been given and understood it is suggested that organisations develop and use what is often described as a 's132 form'.

Who should give the information?

Neither the MHA nor the Code are prescriptive as to who should give the information to detained patients. In many organisations it will be nursing staff that have this role. Those with ultimate responsibility for the MHA within organisations will need to have governance arrangements so they are satisfied that information has been appropriately given to patients and that those patients understand the information given to them. Even where the core responsibility for giving information is delegated within organisations to nursing staff it will often be appropriate for other members of the multi-disciplinary team to share the role.

When should the information be given?

The MHA says the information should be given 'as soon as practicable' after the period of detention has begun. This recognises that there may be barriers to understanding, particularly during the early stages of detention.

Examples of such barriers are:

- linguistic barriers
- hearing or visual impairments
- difficulties in reading and writing
- cultural barriers
- patient's own mental state or their refusal to listen
- patient's lack of capacity - either short or long-term
- effects of medication.

How often should information be given?

The Code stresses the importance of regular checks to ensure that detained patient's continue to understand the information which has been given to them. This will involve repeating information. Organisations should have policies which determine as a minimum when information should be repeated (e.g. at least once a month for all patients). For some patients more frequent repeating may be necessary – this should form part of their care plan. Note when CQC visits take place towards this may be an area they focus on.

Examples of when repeating information must or should be considered are:

- when a new section is implemented or when a section is renewed
- when the patient has appealed against their section or is considering making an appeal either to the MHT or the Hospital Managers
- when a significant change in treatment is being considered
- when there are changes in the applicability of Part 4 or Part 4A to the patient (e.g. at the three month point of detention)
- when a patient is transferred from one ward to another or from one hospital to another.

Giving information to nearest relative

If the patient has a nearest relative, that person has a statutory right to receive information. Information about the patient's detention is dealt with in s132 (4) and information about discharge from hospital of the detained patient is dealt with in s133.

The MHA states that a *'copy of any information'* given to the patient about detention should be given to the nearest relative (if there is one) at the same time as when the patient is given the information or soon afterwards. The precise wording in the MHA s132 (4) is *'those steps shall be taken when the information is given to the patient or within a reasonable time thereafter.'*

This information should be routinely given to the nearest relative *'except where the patient otherwise requests'*.

Note that in some situations - despite the patient having a 'veto' on the nearest relative being given information - that person may still be aware of the patient's detention through the AMHP role in the sectioning process. Also note that the patient cannot prevent the nearest relative being invited to a MHT which is their statutory right.

Where the patient's objection to their nearest relative receiving information is in the context of their mental disorder it may be helpful to check that the patient still has the same view when repeating information (see above). An example would be when a nurse was giving information very soon after a patient had been admitted and that patient had a delusional belief about their nearest relative (e.g. that the person had been trying to poison them). As the patient became less unwell it would be appropriate to discuss that issue with them as they might now wish their nearest relative to be given information about the section. If the patient lacks capacity a decision should be taken whether the objection is valid.

Giving information to nearest relative about patient discharge from hospital

S133 (1) gives the nearest relative the right (unless the patient requests otherwise) to be given information about the patient's discharge from hospital. Where practicable this information should be given at least seven days before the patient's discharge.

Note also that the nearest relative themselves can request that they not be given this information.

Chapter 10 Consent to Treatment (Part 4 of the MHA)

Note that Part 4A of the Act which deals with Community Treatment Order (CTO) patients is dealt with in Chapter 21 of this Guide.

Note also that this Chapter makes frequent references to the Care Quality Commission (CQC) which now has responsibility for statutory functions which previously were undertaken by the Mental Health Act Commission (MHAC). The role of the CQC is dealt with in Chapter 14 of this Guide.

Overview of Part 4

The consent to treatment provisions within Parts 4 and 4A of the MHA cover situations in which patients are given *'medical treatment for mental disorder'*. The provisions are meant to provide a balance between giving clinical staff the autonomy to provide treatment for detained patients and providing safeguards for those patients. Though the MHA does permit treatment in the absence of consent in particular circumstances, attempts should always be made to obtain the patient's informed and valid consent for any intervention as would happen with any other form of treatment offered to any patient.

Part 4 of the Act deals with the treatment of people who have been detained in hospital, including those on section 17 leave, those who are absent without leave (AWOL) and Community Treatment Order (CTO) patients who have been recalled to hospital. This Chapter concludes with a flow chart summary of the main aspects of Part 4.

Definitions and Scope of Part 4

Definitions

In addition to the use of medication, s145 of the Act states that medical treatment includes *'nursing, and also includes psychological intervention and specialist mental health habilitation, rehabilitation and care.'*

This treatment is defined in s145 (4) as 'for the purpose of alleviating or preventing a worsening of the disorder or one or more of its symptoms or manifestations.'

The treatment of physical health problems is only part of treatment under the Act to the extent that such treatment is part of, or ancillary to, treatment for mental disorder. Otherwise the Act does not regulate medical treatment for physical health problems. Clinicians should refer to the Mental Capacity Act for guidance in this regard. Information about ancillary treatment is given later in this Chapter.

Section 64(3) sets out the appropriate treatment test. This states; *'For the purposes of this Act, it is appropriate for treatment to be given to a patient if the treatment is appropriate in his case, taking into account the nature and degree of the mental disorder from which he is suffering and all other circumstances of his case'.*

Scope

Some patients detained in hospital under the Act are not covered by the rules contained in Part 4. Section 56(3) defines these patients as including patients detained under s4, s5 (2), s5 (4), s35, s135, s136, s37, s45A and conditionally discharged patients.

These patients are in the same position as those who are not subject to the Act and have exactly the same right to consent to or refuse treatment.

Summary of sections 57, 58 and 58A

Part 4 provides three different 'regimes' for treating mental disorder which are sections 57, 58 and 58A of the Act. Each of these regimes sets out types of medical treatment for mental disorder to which special rules and procedures apply, including in many cases the need for a certificate from a second opinion appointed doctor (SOAD) approving treatment.

- Section 57 covers neurosurgery for mental disorder and the surgical implantation of hormones to reduce male sex drive
- Section 58 covers medication (after an initial 3 month period) except Electro-convulsive therapy (ECT)
- Section 58A covers ECT and medication administered as part of ECT.

Summary of section 63

Unless sections 57, 58 or 58A apply, s63 of the Act means that detained patients may be given medical treatment for mental disorder if they:-

- consent to it; **or**
- have not consented to it but the treatment is given by or under the direction of the approved clinician in charge of the treatment in question.

A prerequisite of consent is the patient's capacity and someone lacking capacity cannot consent or not consent to proposed treatment.

If sections 57, 58 or 58A apply, detained patients may be given treatment only if the rules in those sections are followed. (see below).

Key Principles

Giving of Information

Detention does not itself preclude the professional obligation to give information about proposed treatments.

Meaning of Consent

The following definition from the Code 24.34 makes clear that, for consent to be meaningful, it has to be both informed and valid.

'Consent is the voluntary and continuing permission of a patient to be given a particular treatment, based on a sufficient knowledge of the purpose, nature, likely effects and risks of that treatment including the likelihood of its success and any alternatives to it. Permission given under any undue or unfair pressure is not consent'.

The Code at 24.36 stresses the importance of giving information in a helpful way. It says *'It is the duty of everyone seeking consent to use reasonable care and skill, not only in giving information prior to seeking consent,but also in meeting the continuing obligation to provide the patient with sufficient information about the proposed treatment and alternatives to it.'*

The Code at 24.37 states that *'The information which should be given should be related to the particular patient, the particular treatment and relevant clinical knowledge and practice. In every case, sufficient information must be given to the patient to ensure that they understand in broad terms the nature, likely effects and all significant possible adverse outcomes of that treatment, including the likelihood of its success and any alternatives to it. A record should be kept of information provided.'*

A professional who chooses not to disclose information must be prepared to justify that decision.

Patients should be told that they can withdraw consent to treatment at any time. Where they withdraw consent they should be given a clear explanation of the consequences of not receiving treatment and the circumstances in which treatment may be given without their consent.

By definition a person who lacks capacity to consent to treatment does not consent even if they co-operate with the treatment or actively seek it.

Establishment and meaning of capacity

A prerequisite of the process for giving information and obtaining (or not obtaining) the patient's consent is that the patient has the capacity (competence) to make a decision. For people aged 16 years or over capacity to consent is defined by the Mental Capacity Act (MCA). Under the MCA:

- people must be assumed to have capacity unless it is established they lack capacity in relation to a particular matter
- people are not to be treated as unable to make a decision unless all practicable steps to help them do so have been taken without success
- people are not to be treated as unable to make a decision merely because they make an unwise decision.

According to the MCA *'a person lacks capacity in relation to a matter if at the material time he is unable to make a decision for himself in relation to the matter because of an impairment of, or disturbance in the functioning of, the mind or brain'* if

- he is unable to understand the information about the decision to be made; or
- he is unable to retain that information; or
- he is unable to use or weigh that information in the balance as part of the decision-making process; or
- he is unable to communicate that decision (by talking, using sign language or any other means). When making decisions about patients under the MHA it should be remembered that:
- mental disorder does not necessarily mean that a patient lacks capacity to give or refuse consent
- any assessment of an individual's capacity is decision specific and has to be made in relation to the proposed treatment.

A person may have the capacity to consent to one form of treatment but not another

- capacity in an individual with mental disorder can vary over time and should be assessed at the time the decision needs to be made
- explanations should be appropriate to the patient's assessed ability to understand
- all assessments of capacity should be fully recorded.

Key Procedures

First three months of detention

During the first three months of detention the approved clinician has the lawful authority to give medication for the treatment of mental disorder. Note that this includes any time a patient is detained under s2 before that detention is changed - without a break - to s3.

Note Chapter 24.41 of the Code which states: *'During this time the patient's consent should still be sought before any medication is administered ,wherever practicable .The patient's consent, refusal to consent, or a lack of capacity should be recorded in the case notes. If a person has capacity to consent, but such consent is not forthcoming or is withdrawn during this period, the clinician in charge of the care and treatment must consider carefully whether to proceed in the absence of consent, to give alternative treatment or stop treatment'.*

It has been argued that, because the MCA starts with the presumption of capacity – it is wrong to test capacity for a detained patient. The rationale for the Code's requirement is that it enables evidence for the authority to treat to be established.

At and after three months of detention

Section 58 applies to the administration of medication to detained patients for the treatment of mental disorder once three months have passed with the exception of medication administered as part of ECT which is covered by section 58A.

Patients cannot be given medication to which s58 applies unless:

- the approved clinician in charge of treatment or a Second Opinion Appointed Doctor (SOAD) certifies that the patient has the capacity to consent and has done so (by completing form **T2**); **or**
- a SOAD certifies that the treatment is appropriate and either that: the patient does not have the capacity to consent; or the patient has the capacity to consent but has refused to do so (by completing form **T3**).

Where an approved clinician certifies that a patient consents, a record of the discussion with the patient and a confirmation of capacity to consent should be made in the patient's notes.

Certificates under this section must clearly set out the specific forms of treatment to which they apply. All the relevant drugs should be listed including medication given PRN (as required) either by name or by the classes described in the British National Formulary (BNF). If drugs are specified by class, the certificate should state clearly the number of drugs authorised in each class and whether any drugs within the class are excluded. The maximum dosage and route of administration should be clearly indicated for each drug and category of drugs proposed. The Code says 'particular care' should be exercised if BNF limits are exceeded.

Treatment for ECT

Section 58A applies to ECT and to medication administered as part of ECT to detained patients and to all patients aged under 18 years (whether detained or not).

Key differences for section 58A:

- patients who have the capacity to consent may not be given ECT unless they consent to it
- no patient under 18 years can be given ECT unless a SOAD has certified that the treatment is appropriate
- a certificate is required for ECT at any time even in the first three months which should include medication administered as part of the ECT.

A patient who lacks the capacity to consent may not be given ECT under section 58A unless a SOAD certifies that the patient lacks capacity to consent and that:

- the treatment is appropriate
- no valid and applicable advance decision has been made by the patient under the Mental Capacity Act refusing the treatment
- no suitably authorised attorney or deputy objects to the treatment on the patient's behalf and
- the treatment would not conflict with a decision of the Court of Protection which prevents the treatment being given.

If the SOAD decides to authorise treatment with ECT for an adult **without capacity** they will do so on form **T6**. If ECT is to be given to an adult patient **with capacity** the Approved Clinician should complete form **T4**. In all cases SOADs should indicate on the certificate the maximum number of administrations of ECT approved.

ECT and under 18's

For any child or young person under 18 there are specific procedures about ECT within the Act. These procedures apply to all persons under 18 whether consenting or not and whether detained or not. In all cases - except in an emergency - a SOAD needs to approve the ECT. If the young person is detained under the Act authorisation of ECT by the SOAD is sufficient authority for ECT then to be given.

If however the young person is not detained under the Act the SOAD certificate needs to be accompanied by an additional legal authority which would consist of:

- the young person's own consent (which presumes capacity) or
- possibly, the authorisation of the person with parental responsibility for the young person

19.84 - 19.85 of the Code advises that relying on the authority of someone with parental responsibility to give ECT would not be prudent. If the young person is under 16 the Code suggests court authorisation - except in an emergency - should be sought and that this should occur before a SOAD visit is arranged. Whether or not s58A applies, all patients to be treated with ECT should be given written information beforehand about its nature, purpose and likely effects.

One of the information leaflets published at the same time as the reissue of the Rights Leaflets is about ECT and might be of value to be given to and discussed with patients. The leaflet focuses on ECT in the context of the MHA and would not be helpful to use with patients who were not detained under the MHA. The leaflet is ECT and can be downloaded in the same way as other Rights Leaflets referred to in various parts of this Guide.

Treatments requiring consent and a second opinion under section 57

Section 57 applies to neurosurgery for mental disorder and to surgical implantation of hormones to reduce male sex drive. It applies to all patients whether or not they are otherwise subject to the Act. Where s57 applies these treatments can be given only if all three of the following requirements are met:

- the patient consents to treatment;
- three independent people appointed by the CQC - one of whom must be a doctor - must agree the patient has capacity, understands the proposed treatment and has consented to it
- The doctor's role is also to certify that it is appropriate to give the treatment. Before issuing a certificate this doctor must also consult with the patient's RC and two other 'consultees'.

The role of 'consultees' is explained below.

SOAD Procedures

The Care Quality Commission (CQC) has issued a number of guidance notes for the benefit of clinical staff, consultees and their own SOADs, details of which can be found on their website.

The treatment proposal for the patient, together with notes of any relevant multidisciplinary discussion, must be given to the SOAD before or at the time of the visit. Organisations will need to have protocols to ensure that the people whom the SOAD needs to meet (including the clinician in charge of the treatment and the statutory consultees) are available, at least by telephone, at the time of the visit together with all relevant documentation.

SOADs have the right to access records without the patient's consent, if necessary, but only those records relating to the treatment in the hospital. The SOAD's attention should be drawn to any recent review of the patient's medication. Organisations will also need to have protocols in place to ensure the SOAD is able during the visit to access the records for the patient or patients being visited. This should include arrangements to view electronic records where these are used.

Responsibilities of SOADs

The visiting SOAD has the following responsibilities:

- satisfy themselves that detention papers are in order
- interview the patient in private if possible
- consult with two people (statutory consultees). One must be a nurse; the other must not be a nurse or a doctor. Both must have been professionally concerned with the patient's medical treatment but neither may be the clinician in charge of the proposed treatment or the responsible clinician
- be prepared where appropriate to consult other concerned people (e.g. the GP, family, carers, and advocates)
- consider the clinical appropriateness of the treatment and its appropriateness in the light of all the other circumstances of the patient's case
- provide written reasons in support of their decisions to approve specific treatments and an indication whether, in their view, disclosure of these reasons to the patient would be likely to cause serious harm to the patient's physical or mental health or that of any other person
- inform the clinician in charge of treatment as soon as possible of any disagreement with the treatment plan.

Responsibilities of Clinicians

- Approved clinicians should ensure that the SOAD is informed whether the hospital knows that the patient has an attorney or deputy authorised under the MCA to make decisions about medical treatment on the patient's behalf. Details of any relevant advance decisions or advance statements of views, wishes or feelings should already be recorded in the notes and drawn to the attention of the SOAD
- It is the personal responsibility of the clinician in charge of the treatment to communicate the results of the SOAD visit to the patient and to record their actions in providing (or withholding) this information. A record should also be made of any disagreements and the patient's responsible clinician (if different) should be informed.

- Staff administering the treatment or directing its administration must continue to satisfy them that it is appropriate and take reasonable steps to ensure that the treatment is authorised by the certificate. It is bad practice for clinicians to prescribe 'as required' or PRN medication that is not written on the certificate. Such medication would be unlawful
- Original signed certificates should be kept with the detention papers and a copy kept in the patient's notes and with the patient's medicine chart.

Responsibilities of Consultees

In discussion with the SOAD consultees may wish to comment on:

- the proposed treatment and the patient's ability to consent to it;
- their understanding of the patient's past and present views and wishes;
- other treatment options and the way in which the current treatment plan was arrived at;
- the patient's progress;
- the views of carers;
- the implications of imposing treatment on a patient who does not want it.

Review of Certificates

The clinician in charge of any treatment given in accordance with a SOAD certificate must provide a written report on that treatment and the patient's condition at any time if requested to do so by the Care Quality Commission under s61.This is in addition to the reports on the CQC Section 61 Review of Treatment Form which are required at various points during a detained patient's section.

If the SOAD visits and decides not to give a certificate, the treatment must end immediately.

It also cannot continue against the wishes of a patient who has the capacity to refuse treatment because, in those cases there is no prospect of obtaining a new certificate.

Staff administering treatment on the basis of a certificate should always take reasonable steps to satisfy themselves that the certificate remains applicable to the circumstances.

There are no statutory timescales for how long a T2 is valid for. However the Code at 25.76 says *'although the Act does not require the validity of certificates to be reviewed after any particular period, it is good practice for the clinician in charge of the treatment to review them (in consultation with the responsible clinician, if different) at regular intervals'.*

It is suggested organisations should have robust procedures for ensuring these reviews take place. It may be that the patient has lost capacity and/or is no longer consenting to the treatment.

Circumstances where certificates cease to authorise treatment

- Certificate issued by approved clinician under s58 or s58A when the approved clinician changes.
- SOAD certificate under s57 when the patient no longer consents to treatment or no longer has the capacity to consent
- SOAD certificate under s58 or s58A when: the patient ceases to be detained (except in the case of s58A patients aged under 18 years)
- the SOAD specified a time limit which has expired
- the certificate was given on the basis that the patient consented but the patient no longer consents or has lost the capacity to consent
- the certificate was given on the basis that the patient lacked capacity to consent but now has capacity
- (s58 only) The certificate was given on the basis that the patient had capacity to consent but was refusing and either is now consenting or has lost the capacity to consent
- (s58A only) The certificate was given on the understanding that the treatment would not conflict with an advanced decision to refuse treatment or the decision of an attorney, a deputy or the Court of Protection but the person giving treatment has become aware of such a conflict
- (s58A only) An attorney, deputy or the Court of Protection makes a new decision that the treatment should not be given.

Urgent Treatment under section 62

Sections 57, 58 and 58A do not apply in urgent cases where treatment is immediately necessary to:

- *'save the patient's life'*
- *'prevent a serious deterioration in the patient's condition'*
- *'alleviate serious suffering in the patient'*
- *'prevent the patient behaving violently or being a danger to himself or others and the treatment represents the minimum interference necessary for that purpose'.*

With the exception of treatment covered in the first bullet point the treatment must also not have unfavourable physical or psychological consequences which cannot be reversed. In the case of the final two bullet points it must also not entail significant physical hazard.

If the treatment is ECT (or medication administered as part of ECT) **only the first two categories apply**. Urgent treatment under this section can continue only for as long as it remains necessary. If it is no longer immediately necessary, the normal requirements for certificates apply. It is suggested that organisations develop a form for the use of s62 and monitor its use.

Note the additional criteria within s62 (2) which gives the authority to treat in circumstances where discontinue of treatment would cause 'serious suffering to the patient.' In circumstances when the RC is awaiting a SOAD visit this has been commonly interpreted too cover any medication which is of therapeutic benefit to the patient.

Common questions about Part 4 and Part 4A

How is the three month rule calculated?

The MHA calculates the three month period as beginning when medication is first administered but - to avoid confusion - 'custom and practice' is often to calculate the three months from when the period of detention began (discounting s5, s135 and s136). If someone is detained under s4 which is then converted to s2 the three months begins from when the s4 had begun.

What are examples of treatment other than medication or ECT which fall within Part 4?

The following is an extract from the lead case of B v Croydon Health Authority case (1995) in which Judge Lord Hoffman's ruling defined 'ancillary treatment'. This case concerned a patient with borderline personality disorder who was being fed by naso-gastric tube. He ruled that this treatment did fall within the scope of the MHA.

He said:

- *'a range of acts ancillary to the core treatment that the patient is receiving fall within the term "medical treatment" as defined in s145(1)'*
- *'treatment is capable of being ancillary to the core treatment if it is nursing and care which is concurrent to the core treatment or as a necessary prerequisite to such treatment or to prevent the patient from causing harm to himself or to alleviate the consequences of the disorder'*
- *'relieving the symptoms of the mental disorder is just as much part of treatment as relieving the underlying cause'.*

It is suggested that the following are examples of interventions which do fall within the meaning of ancillary treatment:

- use of seclusion
- taking blood to accompany administering Clozapine or Lithium
- treating the side effects of medication given under Part 4
- assisting a detained patient to attend to their personal hygiene if they are refusing to do so
- treating wounds inflicted by the patient on him or herself and a result of their mental disorder
- preventing a patient assessed as having suicidal tendencies from attempting to commit suicide.

It is stressed however that organisations do need to seek legal advice especially where cases are particularly complex or unusual.

What are the implications of administering medication without statutory authorisation?

Anyone administering medication without statutory authorisation is acting unlawfully. It would be expected that organisations should inform detained or CTO patients if this happens.

Note that such an action is still unlawful even if the patient is consenting to the medication or in some cases actually asking for it to be given. Section 62 will cover some situations but not all where there is no statutory form.

Can a patient have concurrent statutory forms?

A number of different views have been expressed. The most recent guidance from the CQC to their own SOADs says that it is permissible to have concurrent forms. An example would be where the patient is giving informed consent to all the medication except one.

PART FOUR SUMMARY

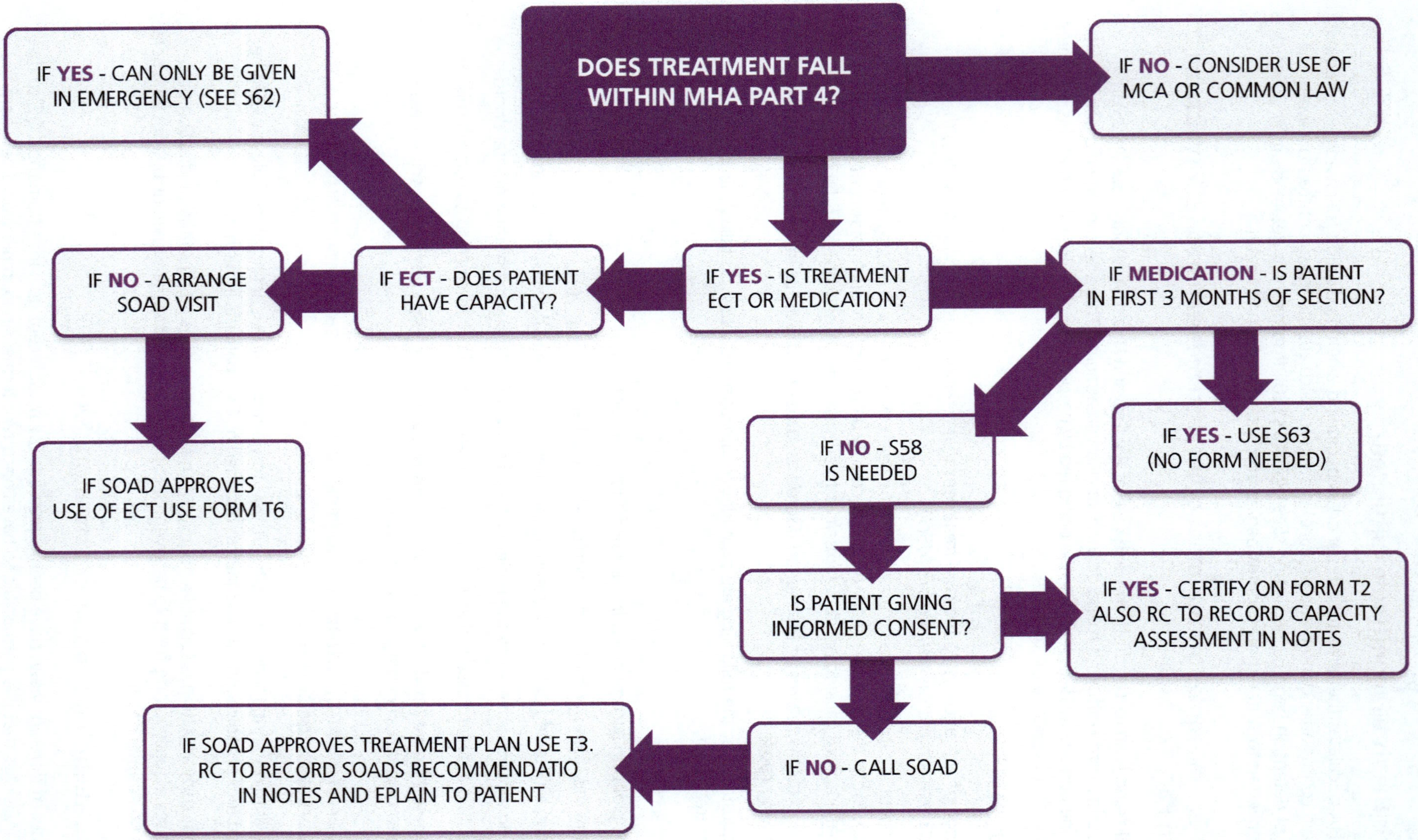

NOTE THIS FLOW CHART EXCLUDES ISSUES FOR UNDER 18'S. FOR PART 4A(CTO) PATENTS SEE CHAPTER 21

Chapter 11 Leave, Absence Without Leave and Transfers

Summary of s17 leave

MHA s17 enables detained patients to be granted leave of absence to leave the hospital in which they are detained. MHA s18 deals with absence without leave referred to in this Guide as AWOL.

What is Leave of Absence?

The MHA s17 (A) defines leave of absence as *'leave to be absent from the hospital.'* The Code 27.5 suggests *'no formal procedure is required to allow patients to move within a hospital or its grounds'* which implies that what the Code terms 'ground leave' is not technically s17 leave at all.

Organisations will need to devise operational procedures which make clear the parameters for leave within hospital sites or premises. This will be especially important for hospital sites with buildings or sets of buildings shared by different organisations. An example of this would be a site which is occupied by two NHS trusts e.g. where there is both a general acute hospital and a mental health trust.

To Whom Does Leave of Absence Apply?

S17 leave can be granted by the patient's Responsible Clinician (RC) for patient's detained under s4, s2, s3 or s37 (without restrictions). Though ward based nurses and junior doctors may have responsibilities for the day to day management of leave the final responsibility for the authorisation of leave rests with the patient's RC.

S17 leave cannot be granted to patients detained under s5 (2), s5 (4), s135 or s136. This is because the patients detained under these sections do not have a RC.

The procedures for granting leave for patients detained under Part 3 of the MHA (forensic sections) are dealt with in Chapter 26 of this Guide.

Processes for granting leave of absence should work on a cyclical basis including the following elements:

- the planning of leave for individual patients
- documentation of any leave granted
- implementation of any leave granted
- reviewing of any leave granted
- revoking (if necessary) any leave granted.

Legal and best practice points

Purpose of leave

The granting of leave should always be placed in the context of the patient's care plan. It can include the granting of leave for specific occasions or for specific or indefinite periods of time. Examples are the use of leave to the community or to attend medical appointments in a particular hospital.

Note that if a patient is being sent on 'extended leave' for more than seven consecutive days the RC has the legal requirement to consider whether the application of a Community Treatment Order (CTO) is a more appropriate alternative. Reasons for use of s17 over CTO should be clearly documented.

Conditions of leave

It is lawful for the RC to attach conditions to a patient's leave. Examples include the following:

- as part of 'trial leave' requiring the patient to live at a named address
- as part of short periods of leave requiring the patient to do particular things (e.g. collecting belongings from their place of residence)
- as part of short or extended periods of leave requiring the patient to do particular things (e.g. continue to take medication) or not do particular things (e.g. not to take illicit drugs or use alcohol).

Involvement of patients and carers in planning leave

As much as practicable the patient should be fully involved in the planning of their leave. Subject to the normal rules of patient confidentiality, carers and other relevant people should be consulted before leave is granted - especially if the patient is going on leave to where the carers reside.

The patient should be given a copy of their leave form.

Escorted or custodial leave

When leave is granted to any detained patient the decision will need to be made as to whether the person should be 'escorted' or not. The word escort is not used within the Act but in many circumstances it will be necessary for the patient to be escorted by professional staff.

Leave forms should always make clear the number of escorts required and may indicate that - for example - the escort should be a registered rather than unregistered nurse.

Professional staff who escort detained patients should be aware of risk issues and there will need to be a contingency plan to deal with untoward situations. An example is if the patient runs away from the escort(s) or refuses to return to the hospital at the agreed time. The main role of an escort is to provide support and supervision to the patient; in an extreme situation however the 'duty of care' may require the use of force. An example would be if the patient became suicidal and was attempting to kill themselves by running onto a busy road or jumping off a bridge.

In many situations there will be a preference for the patient using leave to be accompanied by family members, friends or maybe a worker from a voluntary sector organisation. If this happens it should be made clear to those people that they are not expected to have 'professional' responsibility for the patient. In a very small number of cases the RC may wish to give to either professional or non-professional staff a custodial role (see next section).

Custodial Arrangements

It is possible for the RC - in deciding to grant leave - to give to particular people custodial powers. These powers are contained in s17 (3) and effectively make available to the custodian the powers within s137 and s138 of the Act. S137 gives to the custodian the same powers as a police constable to detain and/or convey the detained patient.

S138 gives to the custodian the legal authority to 'retake' a patient who has escaped from being in custody - again these are the same powers as are available to police constables.

Note however that neither s137 nor s138 gives the authority to enter private premises with force; entering private premises in that way would require a s135 (2) warrant to have been obtained - see Chapter 7.

If there are significant risk issues it may be appropriate for organisations to develop protocols in which - for example - they contract a private security firm - to convey a patient from a hospital unit to a court or to a medical hospital if the patient needs to receive medical treatment.

It is very rare but permitted under s17 (3) for the RC to specify that the detained patient - while on leave - should be in the custody of someone who is not employed by the organisation which detains the person. Examples are:

- those managing a hostel where the patient is going on trial leave
- a friend or carer of the patient
- where a patient goes for treatment to an acute hospital.

If such custodial arrangements are made the person who is to be custodian must understand the role and accept the consequent responsibility it entails.

Revocation of leave

In many cases the day to day management of patients on leave will be delegated by the RC to nursing staff or junior doctors. This might mean that - due to concerns about the patient's mental state - the decision is made not to allow a particular patient to use their authorised leave. It may also mean that - if leave is not used appropriately - ward based staff may 'suspend' future leave.

If this happens on a regular basis it is necessary to review more formally the leave status for that patient - this might happen at the next ward or management round. This review is vital because there has been a change in circumstances in which decisions previously made by the patient's RC have had to be overridden.

If a patient is on s17 leave the RC has the authority under s17 (4) to recall them. The criteria for doing so under s17 (4) are that recall is necessary in the *'interests of the patient's health or safety or for the protection of others.'* If a patient refuses to respond to a lawful request for them to return to hospital their status becomes that of being absent without leave.

Renewal of section for patients on extended leave

In a number of cases since 1983 judges have considered the lawfulness of the practice of renewing a patient's section while they are on extended s17 leave. A summary of the current legal position is:

- a patient does not need to be an in-patient if consideration is being given to renewing their section
- if not an in-patient there must be some element of hospital-based assessment or treatment within their treatment plan
- it is not helpful to attempt to define how little or how much the treatment is hospital-based as each case must be judged on its merits, the term 'hospital' has been interpreted to be broader than an in-patient facility.

It is suggested that the onus should always be on the RC to demonstrate that continued liability to detention is necessary. It is bad practice to have open-ended periods of extended leave with no intention of exploring other alternatives. Such alternatives could be the use of a Community Treatment (CTO) or guardianship or to work with the patient without any legal framework at all. In many case the RC may hold the view that the 'history' of the patient suggests that ending the section may lead the patient to stop taking medication and/or disengaging from contact with the care team.

A key role in deciding whether a renewal is lawful is given within the MHA to the Tribunal (either following a referral or appeal) and the Hospital Managers when they review detention.

Transfers of Detained Patients

Summary of transfers

The Act allows for the transfers of detained patients from one hospital to another. If the two hospitals are managed by the same organisation no formal legal processes are needed to allow this to happen. If the two hospitals are managed by different organisations formal MHA procedures - including documentation - are required.

Transfers between hospitals managed by the same organisation

The following are examples of when this might occur:

- safety or security issues mean that the patient needs to be transferred - e.g. they might need to be moved from an acute to an intensive care facility
- the needs of the patient have changed or a more appropriate ward has been identified
- bed pressures require a patient to 'sleepover' on another ward.

Chapter 37 of the Code contains material giving guidance on the factors which should be taken into account when transfers are being considered. If such transfers occur then there should be clear procedures in place for the way the patient is to be conveyed from one hospital to another.

Transfers between hospitals managed by different organisations

The reason that a formal transfer process is needed is because the different organisations will have different 'hospital managers'.

If the transfer is of a patient detained under s2, s3 or s37 the transfer needs to be formally authorised by the hospital sending the patient and then formally received by the hospital to which the patient is sent. This is done by completion of form H4. The first part of the form must be completed by someone from the hospital transferring the patient out and the second part by someone from the hospital receiving the patient.

When the transfer takes place the original section papers normally would go with the patient. If the original papers are not available (e.g. if an urgent transfer takes place in the middle of the night and nursing staff cannot access the original papers) it may be that the receiving hospital will accept copies of the original papers if they know that the original papers are to follow. If the original papers are not available it should be checked with the receiving hospital to see if they are willing to take the patient without the original papers. A copy of the H4 form signed by the receiving hospital should be returned to the original hospital.

Patients detained under s4, s5 (4) or s5 (2 cannot be transferred in this way. Issues concerning the transfer of s5 (2) patients are dealt with in Chapter 3 of this Guide.

If the transfer is for someone under s35, s36 or s38 the court concerned in the case must be consulted. If transfer is for someone detained under a restriction order (s41 or s49) the Ministry of Justice must be consulted.

If transfer is of a patient under s135 (1) or s136 organisations need to have local protocols enabling such transfers both to be documented and monitored. If the patient is sent to another hospital for a short period of leave, a Form H4 need not be completed.

Section 17 Leave of absence as an alternative to transfer under Section 19

In some situations there will be a choice between a formal transfer under the Act and the use of s17 leave to move the patient.

These issues are dealt with in the CQC Guidance Note Leave of absence and transfer under the Mental Health Act 1983(18W). An example where s17 leave would probably be a preferable alternative to transfer would be if the patient on a mental health ward had a pressing medical need requiring treatment on a medical ward for a few days. If s17 leave was used then the patient's RC would remain responsible for the care and treatment of the patient's mental disorder.

Transfers between hospital in different jurisdiction

The MHA has sections to enable such transfers to take place which are summarised in the following table for transfers from England or Wales to Scotland, Northern Island or Isle of Man/Channel Islands.

From	Scotland	Northern Ireland	Isle of Man/Channel Islands
Detention in hospital	S8OB	S80B	S84 and S85
CTO	S80C	N/A	S85ZA
Conditional Discharge	S80D	S82A	S85A
Guardianship	N/A	S82	S85

The mechanisms for these transfers are complex in many cases and also vary according to the laws within the other jurisdiction. The Department of Health Reference Guide Chapters 34-37 deal in detail with all aspects of the processes of transfers between England and Wales and Scotland, Northern Ireland and the Isle of Man/Channel Islands.

Transfers from England or Wales of foreign patients

S86 gives the Secretary of State the power to authorise the removal from the UK of someone who is neither a British nor Commonwealth citizen with the right of abode within the United Kingdom who is detained under the Act.

Before authorising removal the Secretary of State needs to be satisfied of the following:

- that removal is in the patient's best interests
- that proper arrangements are in place both for the removal and for care and treatment of the patient in the place to which they are to be removed.

S86 enables the Mental Health Tribunal to consider the case and then for the Secretary of State to make the final decision. Though this might be considered the 'normal' process for removal the Reference Guide does point out some of the practical difficulties involved in following this process.

In some cases a patient who has no legal right to remain in the UK may be repatriated using powers such as immigration legislation.

Note that for the removal of a Part 3 patient it is the Ministry of Justice rather than the Department of Health which should be contacted.

Alternatives to the use of s86

In many cases it may be more appropriate for someone who has no legal right to remain in the UK to be removed (i.e. repatriated) using immigration legislation. In the case of R (on the application of X) v Secretary of State for the Home Department (2002) it was found to be lawful to have removed the patient from the UK even though they were detained under the MHA. The UK Border Agency within the Home Office offers advice on this issue to clinical staff.

Other transfers - CTO and guardianship

CTO patients

CTO patients can be transferred from one set of Hospital Managers to another. An example of where this might happen would be if the patient was moving from one part of the country to another. The clinical aspects of transferring care and treatment would normally be done in the context of CPA/ s117; the legal mechanism for the transfer would require the completion of form **CTO10**. If the transfer followed recall to hospital form **CTO6** would need to be completed.
If a patient was being transferred to England form **CTO9** would need to be completed.

Guardianship patients

Although guardianship can be applied to a patient who is informal or not in hospital at all, in some cases the patient will already be detained under the Act. Section 19 allows the transfer from hospital to guardianship with the agreement of the responsible local social services authority (or where applicable the proposed private guardian). In such cases form **G6** must be completed.

If a guardianship patient needs to be admitted to hospital this can happen in several ways. They may be admitted informally or under s2 or s4; in these circumstances the guardianship order remains in place. If however the admission is under s3 the guardianship order ceases to exist. A final way in which admission to hospital can occur is if the guardianship order is changed to a treatment order. This requires two medical recommendations and an application to be made using the forms for s3. Once these forms have been filled in the completion of form G8 provides the authority to admit the patient under s3.

Summary of s18 absence without leave (AWOL)

A patient becomes AWOL in a number of ways. Examples are:

- where a patient has no authorised s17 leave but chooses to abscond from a hospital ward
- where a patient did not return to the ward by the time that they were meant to be back
- where a patient has been recalled to hospital (either from s17 leave or under CTO) but does not return as lawfully requested.

Organisations need to be familiar with the procedures for reporting certain cases of AWOL to the Care Quality Commission.

A patient who is AWOL and who is liable to be detained or under CTO may be retaken by a police officer, an officer on the staff of the hospital, or an AMHP. If the patient is on private premises and entry is barred then the procedures contained in s135 (2) to obtain a warrant must be followed, see Chapter 7.

Under s128 it is an offence to induce or knowingly assist a detained person to go AWOL. It is also an offence under this section to knowingly harbour a patient who is AWOL or hinder his/her return to hospital.

The provisions detailed below apply to patients detained under s2, s3 or s37 and those subject to guardianship or CTO. They do not apply to:

- restricted patients who, if they are AWOL, can be returned to hospital or to court at any time
- patients detained under sections lasting 72 hours or less - s5 (2), s5 (4) or s4 - who can only be 'retaken' before the section expiry time.

AWOL under s2

If the detained patient returns or is brought back to hospital with more than seven days of the s2 to run the s2 continues as before.

If the patient returns with less than seven days of the s2 to run the s2 can be extended for up to seven days.

The seven days starts from when the patient returns so - for example - if they returned with five days left on the s2 two days would be added to make a total of seven days.

This enables the s2 assessment (which was disrupted by the patient being AWOL) to be completed. If the s2 has already run out there is no authority to retake the patient - if there are concerns, the patient would need to be reassessed under the MHA.

AWOL under s3, s37, guardianship or CTO

Patients under s3, s37, guardianship or CTO (described here as an 'order') can be returned at any time up to six months from the date they went AWOL or until the expiry date of the order (whichever is later).

There are particular procedures summarised in the flow chart below which depend on the stage in the order they are at and whether the period of being AWOL is more or less than 28 days. It is suggested that organisations have a form recording the date when a patient goes AWOL and when they return so that there is a clear record for how long a patient has been AWOL.

AWOL GUIDELINES

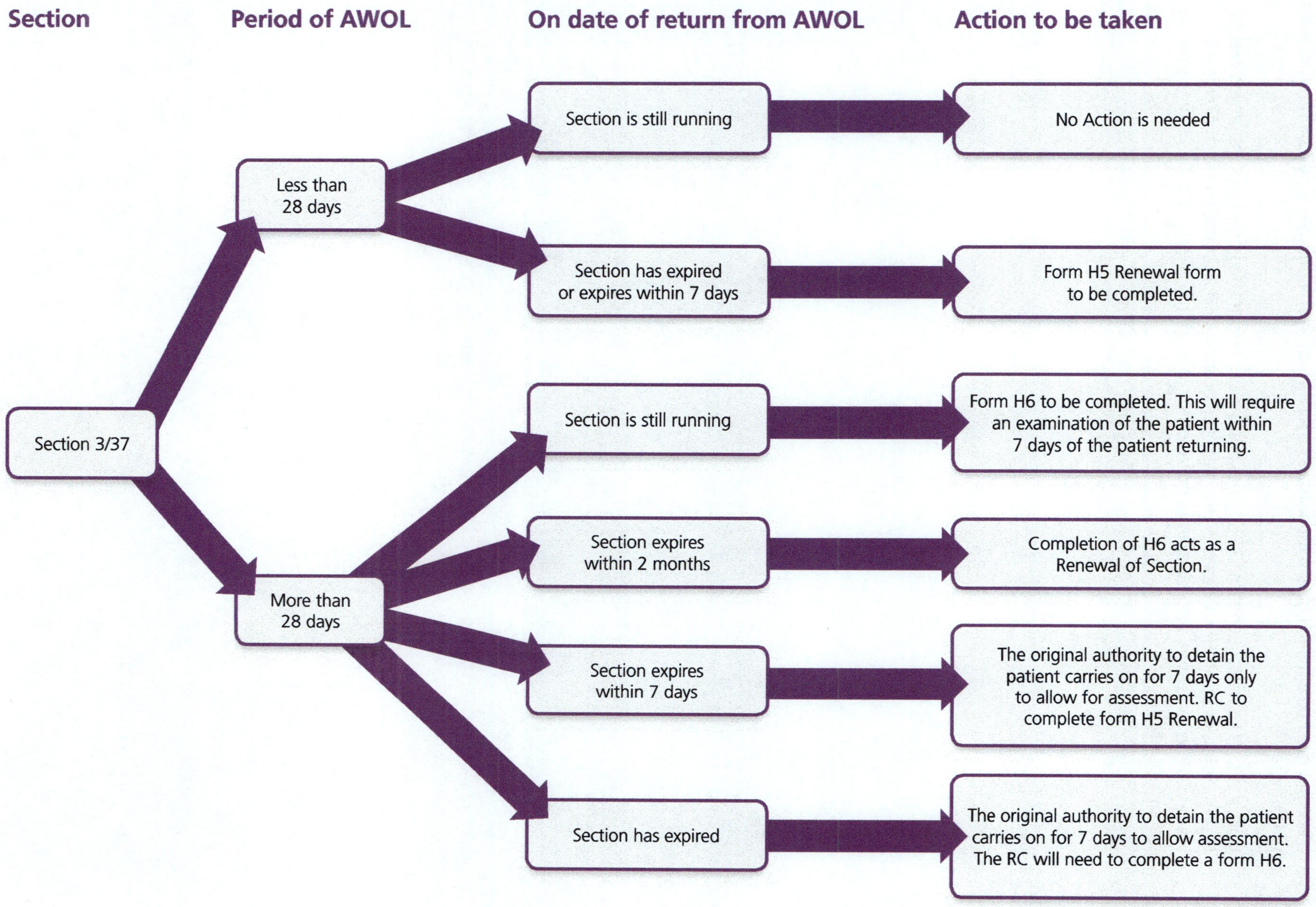

Section 135(2)

This section is to enable private premises to be entered to 'retake' a patient who is AWOL. To do this a warrant must be obtained from a Magistrate's court which then authorises a police officer to enter the premises.

Unlike s135 (1) a warrant under s135 (2) does not have to be obtained only by an Approved Mental Health Professional (AMHP). Officers on the staff of a hospital or police officers can apply for the warrant. When executing the warrant the police officer does not in law need to be accompanied by a doctor or AMHP.

Chapter 12 Ending and Renewing Sections

Ending of civil sections by the Responsible Clinician

The patient's Responsible Clinician (RC) has the authority to end the following sections at any time if he or she no longer believes the statutory criteria to be met:

- s2
- s3
- s4
- CTO
- s37 (without restrictions).

To end the section the RC needs to do this in writing. It is recommended that organisations use an end of section form - to be completed by the patient's RC -so everyone is clear that the patient is no longer detained under the Act.

Sections should not normally be ended without the RC seeing the patient or when the patient is AWOL.

Following discharge from section a patient may remain in hospital informally or leave hospital. Best practice is that patients are informed verbally and in writing that they are no longer detained. If the patient has a nearest relative they should be informed that the section has ended but only if the patient agrees to this.

Renewing civil sections

Renewal of s3 or s37

This applies to s3 and s37 (without restriction). The powers to renew Community Treatment Orders (CTO) and s7 Guardianship are dealt with respectively in Chapters 21 and 22 of this Guide.

The first renewal of s3 or s37 is for up to six months and subsequent renewals are for up to one year at a time.

S20 requires that the patient's RC should examine the patient during the two months preceding the day on which the authority for detention is due to expire. The RC can only renew the section if they believe the following legal criteria are met:

- *'the patient is still suffering from mental disorder of a nature or degree which makes it appropriate for him to receive medical treatment in a hospital'* and
- *'it is necessary for the health or safety or the protection of other persons that he should receive such treatment and that it cannot be provided unless he continues to be detained'* and
- *'Appropriate medical treatment is available to him.'*

An additional requirement is that the RC has to obtain the agreement to renewal of 'someone who has been professionally concerned with the patient's medical treatment'. Assuming that the RC is a doctor this 'someone' cannot be a doctor by professional background. This person does not need to be an Approved Mental Health Professional. Note more than one person can be consulted. Guidance is given in the Code about the role of this 'second professional'.

Paperwork for s20 renewals

The Form for renewing a section is form H5. This form is divided into four parts and can only be completed by the patient's RC.

Part 1 requires the RC to confirm their belief that the patient still meets the criteria for detention (see above) and to give reasons the section renewal is needed. The reasons are divided into three parts.

- The first requires the RC to describe the patient's symptoms and behaviour and explain why these symptoms and behaviour lead to the conclusion that the patient requires 'treatment in hospital'
- The second requires an explanation as to why continued detention is needed to ensure this treatment is given
- The final part requires the RC to be satisfied that 'taking into account the nature and degree of the mental disorder from which the patient is suffering and all the other circumstances of the case, appropriate medical treatment is available to the patient'.

The RC must then sign and date Part 1.

Part 2 is completed by a person who is 'professionally concerned' with the patient. They are confirming that they agree with the RC's view that the patient meets the statutory criteria for continued detention. This person then signs and dates Part 2 including which profession they belong to.

Part 3 is completed by the RC and requires them to say how they are 'furnishing the report' (i.e. the form). Furnishing means to deliver it to the people responsible for processing the renewal (this is normally a MHA Office). The form gives the option of saying whether or not they have used the 'internal mail system' to deliver the form. To avoid forms being lost it is suggested organisations always require the form to be hand-delivered to a MHA Office. The RC needs to sign and date Part 3.

Part 4 is completed 'on behalf of the hospital managers' and would normally be completed by MHA Administration staff. Note that this form no longer requires Hospital Managers to sign after they have reviewed detention at a hearing - a record of that hearing and the decisions made would be recorded on separate paperwork.

Good practice suggests that renewal forms should be medically scrutinised.

Good Practice Issue

It is not unknown for there to be cases where a CTO /treatment order does need to be renewed but the RC fails to complete the necessary paperwork. There are serious implications if this happens – not least if a patient is treated as being on a CTO/treatment order when they are not. Robust procedures are needed to ensure that RC's are aware of expiry dates and ensure that they meet with the patient in question before the current period of CTO/detention ends For patients living in the community under CTO's a special meeting may need to be arranged or a CPA review brought forward. 32.10 of the Code highlights the seriousness of this failure including the need to notify the CQ and service commissioners and the need to carry out an internal review - within a month - of why this happened.

Other actions following renewal

Repeating of information to the patient

The patient needs to be informed verbally and in writing that their section has been renewed. Organisations should devise a form on which repeating of rights is recorded. This could be electronic where health records are stored electronically.

Tribunals

Chapter 13 of this Guide deals with the appeal rights by detained patients following renewals and also the circumstances in which patients would be referred for Tribunals.

Review of detention by Hospital Managers

The Hospital Managers' review of detention is covered in Chapter 16 of this Guide.

Managers Hearing

Under s20 of the Act the Hospital Managers must consider all renewals of section and s20A requires them to consider all CTO renewals. The Code suggests a number of ways in which renewals are considered by Managers and these are dealt with in Chapter 16.

In law it is the completion of the form by the RC which renews the section.

Expressions explaining the role of Managers as to 'renew sections' or 'uphold or ratify renewals' are not helpful; the only power which Managers have during the renewal process is that they can choose to exercise their powers of discharge or not.

CQC Section 61 Review of Treatment Form

If during the previous period of detention a SOAD completed a form T3 (for medication) the patient's RC must complete CQC Section 61 Review of Treatment Form and send it to the Care Quality Commission. A copy of this form should be given to the patient and also put with the section papers.

Part Three Patient Rights and MHA Safeguards

Chapter 13 Role of the Mental Health Tribunal

Introduction

The Mental Health Tribunal (MHT) provides an important safeguard within the MHA. It also enables the MHA to be compatible with the Human Rights Act (HRA) as it enables clinical decisions to detain people of 'unsound mind' to be reviewed by an independent court of law.

Summary of Structures

A number of important changes to the structure and role of the MHT came into force in November 2008. These changes follow the implementation of the Tribunals, Courts and Enforcement Act 2007. This Act provides the judicial and legal framework in which the MHT operates alongside other statutory tribunals. Within this there are two levels of Tribunal; the First-tier Tribunal and the Upper Tribunal. The First-tier Tribunal is the body which deals with applications by detained patients.

The term application includes appeals by patients and referrals on their behalf. The Upper Tribunal will hear appeals against any decisions made by the First-tier Tribunal. Such appeals to the Upper Tribunal will be need to be on points of law.

The MHT sits within the Health Education and Social Care (HESC) chamber of the First-Tier Chamber. The practical implication of this change will be that the MHT procedural rules will now be exercised within the generic procedural rules for all First-tier Tribunals within the Tribunal Service.

The MHT website includes information for patients, family members, legal representatives and health and social care professionals about all aspects of the Tribunal process.

Summary of Role

The MHT role is usefully summarised in the following extract from the R v Canons Park Mental Health Tribunal ex parte A, Sedley J which described the MHT as *'a body charged with reviewing the operative decisions of the responsible authorities to detain the patient, and its functions are to reappraise the patient's condition at the time of the hearing, and in the light of its findings do one of three things - to direct discharge as of right, to direct discharge in exercise of its discretion, or to do neither.'*

Note that the Tribunal is not adjudicating on the original decision to detain a patient but on the day of the hearing is determining whether the criteria for justifying detention continue to be met.

At all Tribunals the burden of proof is on the detaining authority (or those responsible for CTO) to show that continued detention is justified rather than on the patient to prove why he or she should be discharged.

Summary of procedures

Before a Tribunal

Making an application

Information about how to make an application is contained within the rights leaflets given to patients. Copies of the form for making an application should be made available to patients on hospital wards and in community settings. The application should be written or signed by the patient or someone authorised to do so on their behalf. The Tribunal office will acknowledge receipt of the application made by the patient.

Entitlement to Hearings

The following three tables summarise

1. Application rights by patients against Part 2 and Part 3 sections and CTO
2. Referral procedures for Part 2 and Part 3 patients and CTO patients
3. Application rights by nearest relatives against Part 2 sections and against CTO and following displacement

More detailed information is contained in the Department of Health Reference Guide about a number of aspects of Part 3 applications and applications where the patient had been transferred in from other jurisdictions or subject to other legislations - such as the Criminal Procedure (Insanity) Act 1964.

Table One-Applications by patients - s67, s69 and s70

Section	Application Rights	Other Notes
S4	No application rights	If the s4 is superseded by s2 an application made while the patient was under s4 would be accepted.
S5(4)	No application rights	
S5(2)	No application rights	
S135(1)	No application rights	
S136	No application rights	
S2	One application during 28 day duration of this section	▪ Application must be made within first 14 days. This means that if the patient was placed on section on the 1st February they must make their application by the end of the day on the 14th February. ▪ If patient's status changes to s3 before the Tribunal takes place the Tribunal goes ahead (considering s3 criteria) but the patient can still make their own application against s3 if they wish to.
S3	One application during each period of detention	This means one application permitted within first 6 months of s3 and one application during second 6 months if section renewed and one application during each year for subsequent renewals.
CTO	One application during each period of detention	This means one application permitted within first 6 months of s3 and one application during second 6 months if section renewed and one application during each year for subsequent renewals. The 2009 decision by the Upper Tribunal in the case of A.A. determined that an appeal by a patient against s2 or s3 prior to their being placed under CTO still stands.

Section	Application Rights	Other Notes
CTO (following revocation)	If a s3 patient, one application in the period of six months following revocation. If a Part 3 patient the point at which the application can be made depends on the length of time on the hospital order prior to the beginning of the CTO. Chapter 6 of the Reference Guide gives more information.	Note that this is in addition to automatic referral if CTO revoked (see Table Two).
S35	No application rights.	
S36	No application rights.	
S37	No application rights during first 6 months of detention but one application right during first period of renewal and one application right during each subsequent yearly period(s) of renewal.	
S37/41	No application rights during first six months of detention but one application right during second 6 months and one application right during each subsequent yearly period.	
S38	No application rights.	
S45A (if patient is detained in hospital under both hospital and limitations directions and has never been conditionally discharged)	If patient is detained in hospital under a restriction order and has never been conditionally discharged they have one right of application after the first six months of the order having been made and before the second six months have ended and one application during subsequent twelve month periods.	

Section	Application Rights	Other Notes
S45A (if patient had been conditionally discharged and then recalled)	One right of application after the first six months of recall and before the first twelve months of recall have ended and then one application during each subsequent period of one year.	Note the date of recall is calculated as the day on which the patient arrived in the hospital to which they had been recalled.
S46	One right of application during first six months and then one right of application in subsequent periods.	
S47 or S48 (with S49 restriction order) and if never having been conditionally discharged	One right of application during the first six months from which the transfer direction was made and one further application during subsequent six months and one further application during subsequent yearly periods.	
S47 or S48 (with S49 restriction order)) if recalled to hospital	One right of application after the first six months of recall and before the first twelve months of recall have ended and then one application during each subsequent period of one year.	■ Note the date of recall is calculated as the day on which the patient arrived in the hospital to which they had been recalled. ■ Note also the duty of the Secretary of State to refer the case to the Tribunal if a patient has been recalled.

Table Two Referrals under s67, s68, s71 and s75

Note the changes included within the 2012 Tribunal Procedures (Amendment) Rules which permit a 'reports only' Tribunal to be held following a CTO referral. For such a Tribunal to be held there must be clear evidence that the patient does not wish to attend a full Tribunal (or to be represented at a hearing) or that the patient's legal representative has indicated that the patient wants neither to attend or to be represented at a full Tribunal.

- Sections 67 and s68 deal with all patients (except restricted ones) and s71 and s75 deal with restricted patients
- Note that the organisation detaining the patient is responsible for making the referral (unless as indicated in the table that it is the Secretary of State's responsibility). In organisations which employ 'MHA Officers' those staff would take charge of this and have robust systems to ensure referrals are made within the statutory timescales
- S68A enables the Secretary of State (or Welsh Ministers for Wales) to reduce the periods in the future before automatic referrals are made
- If patients make applications (see Table One above) and then withdraw them (and the withdrawal is accepted) their cases are still referred in the same way as for any other patient.

Section	Referral	Other Notes
S3	■ If patient did not make an application during first six months of detention they are referred for a Tribunal under s68. ■ If they do not make an application during subsequent periods of detention they must next be referred before three years has past since their case was last considered by the Tribunal. ■ If the patient is under 18 the subsequent referral must be before one year has past rather than the three years applicable to adults referred for automatic Tribunal under s68. ■ If the patient's nearest relative had made an application to the Tribunal during the first six month period then referral would not take place at the six month point. ■ Another circumstance in which the patient would not be referred at the six month point would be if a Tribunal had been held during the first six month period following an s67 referral (see below). ■ The final circumstance in which a referral would not be made would be if the s3 patient was one whose CTO had been revoked. Because revocation would automatically be followed by a referral no additional referral would need to be made.	If the patient had been detained under s2 without a gap before that section was changed to s3 the period of detention under s2 is subtracted from the six months calculation of when referral takes place. In other words if the patient was detained under s2 for 20 days and re-graded to s3 and did not appeal against the s3 the referral would be made on the date which was six months minus 20 days. ■ Note if the patient has made an appeal whilst detained under s2 this should be disregarded in calculating the point of referral.

Section	Referral	Other Notes
S37	If patient did not make an application a referral should be made after three years from the date of the hospital order or transfer direction (or one year if the patient is under 18)	The reason that s37 patients are not referred in the same way as s3 patients is that there has been review of their case by the sentencing Court which placed them under s37.
CTO	■ If patient did not make an application during first six months of CTO they are referred for a Tribunal under s68. ■ If they do not make an application during subsequent periods of CTO they must next be referred before three years has passed since their case was last considered by the Tribunal. ■ If the patient is under 18 the subsequent referral must be before one year has past rather than the three years applicable to adults referred for automatic Tribunal under s68. ■ In calculating the point of referral this take into account any time spent on s3. In other words if a patient was detained under s3 for four months (and they had not appealed) they would be referred after two months of being placed under CTO.	These timescales are the same as for s3.
CTO (if Revoked)	The case should be referred as soon as possible to the Tribunal by the detaining authority.	The referral should always be made regardless of whether the patient has made their own application while under CTO.
Secretary of State For Health's power to make referrals (for unrestricted patients)	■ S67 enables the Secretary of State for Health to refer a particular case at any time for a Tribunal. This request can be made by either the patient, nearest relative or the detaining/local authority. ■ The referrals can be made for anyone detained under s3, s7 or for CTO patients.	■ The circumstances in which this discretionary power might be used are where it is felt that the patient's rights under the ECHR are being or might be jeopardised. ■ An example would be where s29 has been used to seek displacement of the nearest relative and the s2 of the patient has been extended; particularly if the patient had not yet had a Tribunal or it had been a significant period since the Tribunal last considered the case.

Section	Referral	Other Notes
Secretary of State for Justice's power to make referrals **(for restricted patients)**	▪ The Secretary of State for Justice can refer the cases of restricted patients (including those of conditionally discharged patients) at any time to the Tribunal. ▪ Referrals must always be made if the three years have passed since the Tribunal last considered the case and in all cases where a conditionally discharged patient has been recalled to hospital.	

Table Three - Nearest Relative Applications

Section	Application Rights	Other Notes
S3 if discharge by nearest relative is barred	If the patient's RC has barred discharge by the nearest relative the nearest relative can make one application.	The application must be made within 28 days of the nearest relative being informed that the RC has barred discharge.
Other Part 2 sections	With the exception of the circumstances described in the above row nearest relatives have no other rights to make applications where the patient is detained under Part 2. This is because the nearest relative can themselves exercise the power of discharge (including against s7 Guardianship).	
Part 3 sections (where there are no restriction directions)	One application in the period following the first renewal after six months and then one application during subsequent period(s) of renewal	
CTO if discharge by nearest relative is barred	If the patient's RC has barred discharge by the nearest relative the nearest relative can make one application.	The application must be made within 28 days of the nearest relative being informed that the RC has barred discharge.
Displaced nearest relatives - covering CTO, s3 and s7	One application during the period of 12 months starting from the day of the county court's order and subsequently once during each 12 month period that the order is in force.	Applications to the Tribunal by a displaced nearest relative can only be if the grounds for displacement by a county court were contained in s29(3)(c) or (d). The criterion in s29(3)(c) is that the nearest relative had *'unreasonably objected to an application for admission for treatment or a guardianship application'* and for s29(3)(d) is that they. *'have exercised or are likely to exercise their power of discharge without due regard to the welfare of the patient or the interests of the public'.*

Preparation by organisations

In preparation for Tribunals the organisation detaining the patient need to prepare statements and reports. These requirements are contained in Practice Directions of which the most recent came into effect in October 2013. These contained guidance for those producing reports which were followed during 2017 by templates for report writers. Though not obligatory to use it is suggested organisations form a view as to whether to use them or not. There are a number of other templates those organising Tribunals need to be familiar with. All these templates can be found on the MHT website. Organisations may wish to produce templates and guidelines for their staff; if they do they must be broadly compatible with the MHT Directions.

Before a Tribunal - Legal Representation for the patient

All patients who make an appeal or are referred for a Tribunal have a right to legal representation through legal aid.

Lists of solicitors who are able to represent patients should be available in both hospital and community settings. Patients can also access solicitors from the Tribunal Office or from the Law Society.

It is very important that staff employed by any organisation do not choose solicitors for patients in order to preserve the independence of the Tribunal. In a small number of cases – most likely to be where a patient lacks capacity - the Tribunal itself may decide to appoint a solicitor to represent the person.

Before a Tribunal - Withdrawal of appeals

If a patient wishes to withdraw an appeal they must do so in writing and it should be supported by a letter from their solicitor (if they have one). It will be for the Tribunal to decide whether to accept the withdrawal. It is possible for the patient to reinstate their appeal but the Tribunal rules stipulate that the patient would need to do that within 28 days of their withdrawal being accepted.

Before a Tribunal - non disclosure of reports

Any report not for disclosure to the patient should be clearly indicated and a written explanation attached giving reasons for requesting non-disclosure. The Tribunal will consider carefully the request for non-disclosure and all the issues involved before deciding whether to override the wishes of the author of the report. The Tribunal will only agree to non-disclosure where there are compelling reasons to do so, and where they are convinced that *'disclosure would be likely to cause that person or some other person serious harm.'* The Tribunal may give direction that the reports be made available to the patient's representative.

Examination by doctor

Note the changes introduced in 2014 about the role of the 'preliminary examination' by the MHT doctor. For s2 MHT's in all cases the doctor will conduct a pre-hearing examination (unless the patient declines this). For all other hearings the pre-hearing examination will only take place if requested by the patient (or their legal rep) or the MHT itself.

Before the hearing, the Tribunal doctor will need to examine the patient and see their records.

At The Tribunal Hearing

Panel Membership

The three members of the Tribunal will normally be:

- a legal member who will also chair the Tribunal - for restricted cases this will be a judge
- a medical member
- a 'lay' member.

Tribunal Procedures

The hearing is conducted in private unless the patient requests a public hearing and the Tribunal accepts the request.

Attendance

Normally the patient will be present throughout the hearing, unless one of the parties requests otherwise. If the Tribunal agrees, and accepts that the presence of the patient at a particular stage will adversely affect their health or the welfare of the patient or others, the patient will not need to remain in the Tribunal. The patient's representative will however be entitled to be present throughout the hearing.

The Tribunal will expect the patient's RC or their deputy to attend the hearing. If the RC does send a deputy the RC is responsible for ensuring that they have both sufficient psychiatric expertise and adequate knowledge of the case concerned.

If a nurse attends they should be the person who prepared the nursing report or a suitably briefed deputy.

The person who attends to present the Social Circumstances Report needs to be able to present further, up to date information about the patient, including information on their home circumstances and after-care facilities in the event of a decision to discharge.

If the Tribunal have been provided with full details about the patient's nearest relative or their next of kin that person will be invited to attend the hearing.

Powers of discharge

Section 72 gives the power to the Tribunal to discharge patients detained under s2 or s3. There is a general discretion to discharge but an obligation to discharge in the following circumstances.

For s2 they must discharge the patient if they are not satisfied:

- *that the patient is then suffering from mental disorder of a nature or degree which warrants detention in hospital for assessment (or assessment followed by medical treatment) for at least a limited period:'* **or**
- *'they are not satisfied the patient's detention is justified in the interests of the patient's own health or safety or with a view to the protection of other persons'.*

For s3 they must discharge the patient if they are not satisfied:

- *'that the patient is then suffering from mental disorder of a nature or degree which makes it appropriate for the patient to be liable to be detained in hospital for medical treatment'* **or**
- *'that it is necessary for the health or safety of the patient or for the protection of other persons that he should be receive such treatment;'* **or**
- *'appropriate treatment is obtainable for the patient'.*

If the MHT is being held following a s3 nearest relative application for discharge which has been barred the MHT must discharge if they are not satisfied that the *'patient, if released, would be likely to act in a manner dangerous to other persons or themselves.'*

The discharge criteria in effect mirror the admission criteria. **Note that *'then suffering'* has the same meaning as now suffering.**

CTO Tribunals

The MHT must discharge a CTO patient if they are not satisfied that:

- *'the patient is then suffering from mental disorder of a nature or degree which makes it appropriate for the patient to receive medical treatment',* **or**
- *'that it is necessary for the patient's health or safety or for the protection of other persons that the patient should receive such treatment',* **or**
- *'that it is necessary that the responsible clinician should be able to exercise the power under section 17E (1) to recall the patient to hospital',* **or**
- *'that appropriate treatment is available for the patient'.*

If the MHT is being held following a CTO nearest relative application for discharge which has been barred the MHT must discharge if they are not satisfied that the *'patient, if released, would be likely to act in a manner dangerous to others or themselves.'*

Other Powers Available to the Tribunal

Power to defer discharge

This means the discharge comes into place at a specified future date. Note this power is not available when the MHT is considering applications concerning CTO or guardianship.

Power to make recommendations

Though any recommendations are not binding the RC or Hospital Managers must consider them. Recommendations could be that the patient is granted s17 leave of absence or transferred to another hospital as part of preparation for future discharge. The MHT has no power to place a patient under CTO but may make a recommendation that the RC considers this as an option.

The MHRT has the power to reconsider a patient's case if any of its recommendations have not been put into practice.

After the Tribunal

The decision will normally be made on the day of the Tribunal and communicated to the patient and their solicitor. Copies of the written decision will either be given to the parties concerned or sent to them within a few days. The Tribunal will leave a short decision form (Form P6) for the patient on the day of the Tribunal.

Chapter 14 Role of the Care Quality Commission (CQC)

Overview of its role

The Care Quality Commission (CQC) is the independent regulator of health and social care services in England. . The CQC was created by the 2008 Health and Social Care Act and takes over (in England) the functions previously undertaken by the Mental Health Act Commission (MHAC). The CQC website includes information about all aspects of its role. The functions of the CQC are very broad and contain within them the specific responsibilities contained within MHA s120.

Note the CQC remit now includes DOLS.

Key Functions of the CQC

Visits

S120 enables the Secretary of State to delegate to the CQC the responsibility for reviewing the way the MHA's powers and duties are being exercised with both detained and CTO patients. The CQC's remit has been extended to monitor the use of Deprivation of Liberty Safeguards.

A very important element of this review is that the CQC is authorised to visit and interview detained and CTO patients. These visits can take place to hospitals, care and children's homes and to other facilities. Detained and CTO patients must be made aware of when such visits are to take place. Visits will deal with both statutory and non-statutory issues (e.g. environmental, care and safety issues) Examples of the statutory issues which visiting Commissioners will deal with are:

- legality of detention papers
- compliance with the consent to treatment provisions
- giving of information to detained patients
- use of s17 leave
- use of seclusion
- complaints.

S120 also provides the authority for the CQC to investigate complaints made by patients or former patients or by anyone with an interest in these matters. Detained and CTO patients must be told of their right of complaint to the CQC; 4.53-4.68 of the Code describes the support someone may be given if needed.

Review of withholding of correspondence

Where the managers of high security psychiatric hospitals have made decisions to withhold patients' correspondence s134 gives the CQC responsibility - if requested to do so - for reviewing those decisions.

Appointment of Second Opinion Appointed Doctors (SOADs)

S118 gives the authority for the Secretary of State to delegate to the CQC responsibility for appointing Second Opinion Appointed Doctors (SOADs) for the specific role of issuing certificates under Part 4 and Part 4A. More information about the role of the SOAD is contained in Chapters 10 and 21 of this Guide.

Review of Code

S121 also gives the CQC responsibility for submitting to the Secretary of State the following:

- its views about what should be included in the Code of Practice
- its concerns about any particular forms of treatment which might benefit from being subject to scrutiny by SOADs. Note this would be in addition to treatments currently covered by s57.

Publications

The CQC publish a number of documents including:

Policy Briefings and Guidance Notes going back to October 2002.

People are advised to regularly check the CQC website for changes and updates. All these Guidance Notes can be downloaded from the website. Forms which need to be completed in particular circumstances are summarised in the table below.

Name of Form	Circumstances when it needs to be completed and returned to the CQC
CQC Section 61 Review of Treatment Form (previously MHAC-1)	As described in s61 when the patient's RC is using s58(3)(b), 58A(4) or (5) or 62A (in accordance with a Part 4A certificate).
SOAD Report Form (previously MHAC - 2)	Form to be completed by SOAD following a visit to see a patient.
Death of a Detained Patient Notification Form (previously MHAC-3)	When a detained patient dies - to be completed by hospital.
CQC Second Opinion Request Form	There are different forms to be completed depending on whether the request is for a CTO or non-CTO patient.

Chapter 15 Role of the Code of Practice

The MHA can be described as saying what needs to be done and the Code of Practice (referred to as the Code) as to 'how to do it'. The Code is intended to be a source of guidance for professional staff in how to use the MHA and also gives more general guidance concerning the treatment of mental disorder. The new Code seeks to be more accessible to patients,carers and others seeking to protect and enhance the rights of detained and CTO patients. The CQC have made clear that the benchmark for it's visits will be to check compliance with the Code.

This means that - properly applied - the Code offers a number of significant safeguards for patients. Patients should have access to copies of the Code on wards where they are detained and in the community if under CTO.

The legal status of the Code has often been a source of confusion and clarification was given by the Law Lords following the 2005 Munjaz case. Though the judgement of the Law Lords rejected the view that organisations and the staff working for them had a legal duty to follow Code guidance it made clear the expectation that any departure from following guidance in the Code could only be for reasons which were 'cogent'. One helpful part of the new Code is the explanation of what key terms used within it mean and to what audience particular parts are addressed.

Terminology	How it is to be understood	Exceptions
Must	Reflects legal obligations which it is essential to follow.	No exceptions.
Should	For those to whom this is statutory guidance.*	Any exceptions should be documented with reasons.
May/could/came	Reflects guidance to be followed where possible.	Good practice but exceptions permissible.

*Clinicians (AMHP's, AC's etc) working with the Act and local authority staff

S118 (2A) and (2B) says that the Code should include a statement of principles and states what matters should be addressed by them. Chapter One of the Code contains these five guiding Principles which are reproduced below.

Least Restrictive option and maximising independence	'Where it is possible to treat a patient safely and lawfully without detaining them under the Act, the patient should not be detained. Wherever possible a patient's independence should be encouraged and supported with a focus on promoting recovery where possible.
Empowerment and involvement	'Patients should be fully involved in decisions about care, support and treatment. The views of family, carers and others, if appropriate, should be fully considered when taking decisions. Where decisions are made which are contradictory to views expressed, professionals should explain the reason for this'.
Respect and dignity	Patients, their families and carers should be treated with respect and dignity and listened to by professionals'.
Purpose and effectiveness	'Decisions about care and treatment should be appropriate to the patient, with clear therapeutic aims, promote recovery and should be performed to current national guidelines and/or current, available best practice guidelines'.
Efficiency and equity	'Providers, commissioners and other relevant organisations should work together to ensure that the quality of commissioning and provision of mental health services are of high quality and are given equal priority to physical health and social care services. All relevant services should work together to facilitate timely, safe and supportive discharge from detention'.

Chapter 16 Role of the Hospital Managers

Summary

Section 145 of the MHA confers upon the managers of hospitals (referred to in this guide as 'hospital managers') various powers and duties which should not be confused with tasks undertaken by individuals employed by organisations in managerial roles.

Definition of Hospital Managers

The identity of the 'hospital managers' depends upon the nature of the organisation concerned. Within an NHS Trust or NHS foundation Trust the hospital managers will be the Trust or Foundation Trust as a body. For an independent hospital the hospital managers are the person of persons in whose name the hospital is registered.

Delegation and Accountability

In practice many duties within the Act for which 'hospital managers' are responsible will be delegated. Delegation is authorised within the MHA Regulations and - in the case of discharge powers – within MHA s23. Many of the functions will usually be delegated to MHA Administration. Organisations may delegate the s23 role to a group of people sometimes referred to as Associate Hospital Managers of Mental Health Act Managers. It is important to stress that the Hospital Managers retain overall responsibility for any delegated duties.

Organisations should have review and monitoring mechanisms in place so that they are satisfied that those exercising duties on their behalf are competent to do so. This includes staff with MHA responsibility and any groups referred to above who hold the delegated powers of discharge under s23.

The next section of this Chapter summarises these functions. The final section of the Chapter deals with the distinctive role of the hospital managers in 'reviewing detention' in the context of what is often known as a Hospital Manager 'hearing'. Note that the power of discharge contained within s23 cannot be delegated to employees within an organisation.

Functions of hospital managers

Overall responsibilities

Chapter 37 of the Code identifies the overall responsibilities of the hospital and describes the specific functions mentioned in the Act.

Admission (37.12-37.13)

This requires that detention papers are valid and in order. Chapter 8 of this Guide deals with the processes for receipt, scrutiny and rectification of detention papers.

Note that if the application to detain a patient under s2, s3 or s4 is made by the nearest relative rather than an Approved Mental Health Professional (AMHP) the hospital managers must request a social circumstances report from the relevant local social services authority. In practice it is often staff working in the MHA Administration team who make this request.

Information about independent mental health advocates (IMHA's) (37.14-15)

In practice this will be done when the s132/s132A rights are given (see Chapter 9 of this Guide).

Transfer between hospitals (37.16-31)

Note this section of the Code also covers transfers to guardianship and the transfer and assignment of responsibility for CTO patients. Chapter 11 of this Guide gives more information about the processes involved in transferring patients.

Information for patients and carers (37, 32 - 33)

The responsibilities which the hospital managers have for giving information to detained and CTO patients and their nearest relatives are dealt with in Chapter 9 of this Guide.

Duties in respect of victims of crime (37.34-36)

These paragraphs deal with the processes for liaising with victims in relation to certain Part 3 (unrestricted) patients who have committed sexual or violent crimes. These duties are a legal requirement under the Domestic Violence Crime and Victims Act 2004. A brief summary of the implications of this legislation is contained in Chapter 26 of this Guide.

Patients' correspondence (37.37-38)

These paragraphs deal with the procedures for withholding outgoing correspondence from detained patients contained in s134 including the specific procedures for patients detained in high-security psychiatric hospitals. More information about the issues concerning patient correspondence is contained in Chapter 19 of this Guide.

Duties to refer cases to Tribunal (37.30)

These paragraphs deal with referrals by hospital managers (using s68 powers) and by the Secretary of State (using s67 powers). Chapter 13 of this Guide presents, in table form, the information as to when it is a requirement (under s68) or an option (under s67) for such referrals to be made. In practice referrals will normally be made by staff working in MHA Offices.

The next section of this Chapter deals with the distinctive role of Hospital Managers in terms of review of detention and discharge powers.

Powers of Hospital Managers

MHA s23 of the MHA gives to the hospital managers powers to discharge most detained patients and any Community Treatment Order (CTO) patients. They have no powers to discharge patients detained under s35, s36 or s38. They do have the powers to discharge restricted patients but only if the Secretary of State for Justice authorises them to do so. This could only happen following submission of a recommendation by the Hospital Managers that a person be discharged made to the Secretary of State for Justice after a hearing.

Review of detention

Chapter 38 of the Code deals with the powers of Hospital Managers to discharge from detention in the context of a Hearing. MHA s23 confers upon managers the power to discharge particular categories of patients. This power applies to s2, s3 or s37 (without restriction) patients and CTO patients.

Note the wording in s23 is 'three or more.' In practice panels of managers usually contain three people only. Case law has clarified that - if a panel of three wishes to discharge the patient - it must be a unanimous decision whereas a decision not to discharge would not need to be unanimous.

When to review detention

The Code describes four sets of circumstances in which detention can be reviewed for a particular patient.

- where a request as has been made by a patient (often termed an appeal). In the case of an appeal there is a discretion not to hold a hearing if the case has recently been considered by a MHT or will be in the near future.
- following the submission of a renewal report by the Responsible Clinician (RC) for the patient. Note the wording in the Code that a review must take place. Thorough in law the CTO or section is renewed by the RC organisations need to be familiar with the guidance contained in 38.50 of the Code.
- following barring by the patient's RC of discharge by the patient's nearest relative In this set of circumstances there is a discretion not to hold a hearing if the case has recently been considered by a MHT or will be in the near future.
- a discretionary option to review detention of any patient at any time.

In this set of circumstances no further guidance is given as to when and the reason panels should conduct 'discretionary reviews'. Some organisations have the practice of 'managers' initiated reviews'. An example of when this might be conducted would be if clinical staff believed a patient was 'appealing' against detention but due to a lack of capacity was not able to cooperate with the process of making an appeal and instructing a solicitor.

How to review detention

Note also that - in contrast to Tribunals - there is no statutory guidance as to how hearings are conducted. This means that there will be variations as to how hearings are conducted between different organisations. The following material is based on the guidance in the Code Chapter 38. It is recommended that all organisations develop their own protocols.

Whatever approach is adopted it is important that hearings are conducted in a way the Code at

38.24 describes as satisfying the 'fundamental legal requirements of fairness, reasonableness and lawfulness'. Though a Managers' hearing is generally considered to be less 'formal' than a Tribunal it is important to stress the features they have in common which include:

- the necessity for the panel to obtain and consider reports from the appropriate professionals. The guidance from the Tribunal (see Chapter 13) on report content could be adapted for use by Hospital Managers for use when they review detention.
- the need for the hearing to gather evidence in order for a decision to be made as to whether the patient continues to meet the statutory criteria
- the need for all parties including the patient (if they wish to) to have the opportunity to put their 'case' to the panel.

Hearing Preparation Reports

Before the hearing begins the panel need to have available to them written reports. A report should always be available from the patient's RC. If this report is prepared by someone else best practice (as for Tribunals) would be that the RC should counter-sign it.

The Code at 38.27 describes the other reports which should be available to the panel as being by such people as *'the patient's care co-ordinator, named nurse, social worker, occupational therapist or clinical psychologist.'*

Local practice may vary but the minimum requirement should always be that nursing and 'social circumstances' reports are provided. A nursing report - for an in-patient - is invaluable as it provides important evidence as to 'how the patient is' on the ward. For all patients a 'social circumstances' report is invaluable as it provides important evidence as to what the community based resources would be were the panel to discharge the patient (and the author's views on the likelihood of those resources being accessed by the patient).

For some groups of patients there might be advantages in reports being provided by other professionals. Examples might be on a Rehabilitation Unit or a Forensic Ward where occupational therapists or psychologists might have significant involvement in the care of particular patients.

It is suggested that the guidance on Tribunal reports (referred to in Chapter 13) could be adapted for use at Managers hearings. This should include a report on risk and any relevant probation service reports. If a previous Tribunal report is used it should be sufficiently updated.

*If a patient is discharged on CTO with an outstanding s3 renewal hearing case law has clarified that the panel should consider the CTO criteria at the hearing.

Other pre-hearing actions

Choice of Venue

For in-patients a hearing is normally held away from the patient's ward unless there are security reasons or the patient's own lack of mobility which require it to be ward-based.

For CTO hearings and hearings where the patient is on leave from hospital best practice is for the hearing to be on a non-hospital site. Some patients may prefer to have the hearing at a hospital. For this reason it is good practice to offer the patient a choice.

Reports

The panel members need to spend time before the hearing reading the reports which will assist them to decide what questions to ask of the patient and professionals during the hearings.

The reports should be made available to the patient and their legal representative or advocate (if they have one).

Professionals may submit reports which they believe should not be disclosed to the patient but it is for the panel to decide whether disclosure should take place. . The Code at 38.28 gives guidance on non-disclosure.

The hearing itself

Neither the MHA itself or the Code are prescriptive as to how a hearing should be conducted. It is suggested that organisations develop protocols for how hearings are conducted; the Code at 38.34 says the procedures should *'balance informality against the rigour demanded by the importance of the task'*. The Code suggests procedures should be based on the following guiding principle.

Empowerment and involvement	*'Patients should be fully involved in decisions about care, support and treatment. The views of family,carers and others, if appropriate, should be fully considered when taking decisions. Where decisions are made which are contradictory to views expressed, professionals should explain the reason for this'.*

Post-hearing actions (including recording the decision and communicating this to the patient and others)

Organisations need to develop protocols which include paperwork in which the Managers record their decisions and reasons. It is suggested that a summary of 'evidence' presented by all parties should be included within the paperwork. It is also suggested that the paperwork should focus on consideration of the statutory criteria for the section concerned.

The patient and (if applicable) the nearest relative and the professionals concerned need to receive copies of the written decision. If the decision is to discharge the patient it is advisable that the patient's RC and either the care co-ordinator or ward staff are immediately informed of the decision.

Issues relating to 'hearings' for renewals

The Code 38.26-38.46 suggests a procedure - for renewal hearings only - which organisations might wish to adopt whereby a distinction is made between contested and uncontested hearings. The definition of 'uncontested' used in 38.41 is *'if the patient has indicated that they do not wish to challenge the renewal or extension.'*

If organisations choose to adopt this approach the Code gives guidance as to how an uncontested hearing should be conducted; this is paraphrased here.

- The Managers consider the renewal report (H5 or CTO-7 form) plus reports from professionals
- If at the paper hearing there is prima facie evidence that the statutory criteria are not met a full hearing should be arranged as soon as possible

If the 'paper' or 'report only' hearing format is adopted it is important that the patient is aware of all aspects of the role of the Hospital Managers in the renewal process and of their right to challenge the renewal if they wish. This requires a robust but also flexible system which would acknowledge:

- that some patients may lack the capacity to make decisions
- that some patients may be ambivalent about being on a section or on a CTO
- that some patients may feel or be disempowered by the 'system' which means despite their lack of apparent 'objection' to renewal that they are not actually in agreement with the renewal.

Issues relating to 'hearings' after nearest relative discharge has been barred

The legal issue for this type of hearing is whether the Managers should base their decision on the 'dangerousness' criteria or on the 'usual' criteria for s2, s3, s37 or CTO. The Code suggests that at such a hearing the 'usual' criteria should first be considered and then the Managers should consider the issue of 'dangerousness'. If the Managers decide that the usual criteria are met but that the 'dangerousness' test is not met the advice in the Code is that the Managers should *'usually'* discharge the patient. 38.22 recognises that the Managers have what is described as *'a residual discretion not to discharge in these cases, so panels should always consider whether there are exceptional circumstances why the patient should not be discharged.'*

Other powers - deferred or conditional discharge?

A number of commentators have argued that at a hearing Managers have the power to defer discharge (i.e. the discharge to come into effect on a specified future date) or to conditionally discharge (i.e. the discharge comes into effect on a future date when particular conditions have been met). This power is not explicitly mentioned in MHA s23 and is notable that the new Code makes no reference to it.

Chapter 17 Human Rights Act

This Guide does not attempt to provide comprehensive information about all aspects of the Human Rights Act (HRA) but gives a brief summary of the main articles and focuses on aspects of the HRA which impact on patients detained under the MHA and staff working with them.

Summary of the HRA

The 1998 HRA became law within the UK on 2nd October 2000. It incorporated the 1950 European Convention on Human Rights (ECHR) into UK law. Before the HRA was passed the UK had been bound by the Convention but had not incorporated Convention articles into UK legislation.

Why is the HRA important?

The HRA requires public authorities and their employees to act compatibly with convention rights. Failure to act compatibility may apply to both positive acts and omissions. The HRA enables the UK citizen (known as the 'victim' or 'potential victim') to bring a stand-alone legal action if they believe that their Convention Rights have been or are about to be breached. Note also that from December 2008 the HRA has been extended to cover private sector care homes which provide services under contract from any local authority.

It is important to emphasise that when Approved or Responsible Clinicians and Approved Mental Health Professionals are carrying out their statutory functions their actions can be scrutinised under the HRA.

The HRA is important for organisations and individuals working with detained (and informal) patients as it offers a framework to assist staff to ensure that patients receive quality care.

The Department of Health document 'Human Rights in Healthcare A Short Introduction' suggests the following as the key benefits of a 'human rights based' approach.

- *'It helps ensure experience and outcomes for patients, service users and staff by approaching services and decisions in a person centered way.'*
- *'It supports the delivery of wider NHS priorities such as the Next Stage Review and Commissioning.'*
- *'It improves compliance with the Human Rights Act and reduces complaints and litigation.'*

How can staff best work within this framework?

The Department of Health document suggests that in their day to day interventions clinical staff should be conscious of the following questions:

- *'does this intervention impact on anyone's human rights?'*
- *'if so, what rights and who do they belong to?'*
- *'how should my practice, decision or response reflect this?'*

What are these rights?

The rights of the citizen are enshrined within the Articles of the HRA.

The main Articles are as follows:

2 **Right to Life**

3 **Prohibition of torture or inhuman or degrading treatment/punishment**

5 **Right to liberty and security**

6 **Right to a fair trial**

7 **No punishment without law**

8 **Right to respect for private and family life**

9 **Freedom of thought, conscience and religion**

10 **Freedom of expression**

11 **Freedom of assembly and association**

12 **Right to marry**

14 **Prohibition of discrimination**

Which articles are most relevant in a mental health setting and how to they relate to the MHA?

The key articles are 3, 5, 6 and 8.

Article 3 Prohibition of torture or inhuman or degrading treatment/punishment

Note this is an absolute right.

Even though there is broad compatibility between the MHA and HRA it is perfectly possible for the ways in which the MHA is used to be scrutinised by a court of law and for that court to decide that in a particular case a patient's Article 3 rights had been breached., An example is the use of seclusion (which the courts have decided is a form of s63 treatment). A breach could occur if – for example - if there was evidence that the patient was being secluded for punitive reasons or because the conditions within a seclusion room fell below acceptable standards.

Within the MHA compulsory treatment (with a number of safeguards) is permitted but it should be stressed that decisions to force a patient to have treatment they do not want is a decision that should not be taken lightly.

Articles 5 & 6 Right to liberty and security of person and the right to a fair trial

Note this is a limited right as there are circumstances in which someone – a convicted prisoner for example - has had their rights removed.

In a broad sense the two pieces of legislation are compatible. This is because detention with compulsion (which is at the heart of the MHA) is recognized as a lawful option within Article 5 of the HRA. This Article permits a nation state to have such legislation - specifically in Article 5.1 which says: *'everyone should have the right to liberty and security of person. No one shall be deprived of their liberty save in the following cases and in accordance with a procedure prescribed by law'*. The following cases include in Article 5.1(e) *'the lawful detention of persons for the prevention of spreading infectious diseases, of persons of unsound mind, alcoholics or drug addicts or vagrants.'*

Article 5.4 says that *'everyone who is deprived of his liberty by arrest or detention shall be entitled to take proceedings by which the lawfulness of his detention shall be decided speedily by a court and his release ordered if his detention is not lawful.'* A further indication of the compatibility of the HRA and the MHA is that - within the MHA - the role of the Mental Health Tribunal fulfils the requirement within the HRA that patients have access to an independent court of law to decide whether continued detention is justified.

Note that the HRA issues first raised in the Bournewood Case have been addressed by the introduction of Deprivation of Liberty Safeguards (DOLS) which are dealt with in Chapter 24 of this Guide.

6 right to a fair trial

The procedures used by the MHT must be consistent with this Article – note the importance of the MHT being completely independent of the detaining authority.

- Article 8 Right to Family and Social Life Right to respect for private and family life

Note this is a qualified right.

The decision – for example – to place someone on a section and remove them from home (and possibly family) constitutes a huge intrusion into their Article 8 rights. The concept of proportionality is helpful here-the intrusion may be justifiable if a valid societal aim – the protection of others – is met by the use of the MHA

The following are examples of actions which raise issues about the human rights of patients (or groups of patients). They are included as a way of raising awareness and encouraging debate.

- due to bed pressures a detained patient being transferred many miles away from their family with no consideration of the needs of the person to continue to be visited by their family
- blanket prohibition of a patient having access to their mobile phone in the absence of any evidence that they would use it inappropriately and in fact would benefit from having regular conversations with family and friends
- using control and restraint on a patient when there was time to have explored other ways of managing their 'behaviour' in a less intrusive way
- subjecting a female patient with a history of sexual abuse to admission to a mixed ward or being searched by male nurses
- not assisting a detained patient – where there is evidence that they will find a Manager's hearing distressing – to be supported by an advocate or lawyer.

Chapter 18 Role of the Independent Mental Health Advocate

The role of Independent Mental Health Act Advocate (IMHA) was introduced in April 2009 and is contained in s130A of the Act. In December 2008 the Department of Health published the regulations for this new role. These regulations specify the competencies, training and accreditation processes for anyone taking up the role of an IMHA. At the same time NIMHE published 'Independent Mental Health Advocacy: Guidance for Commissioners'.

Summary of Role

This new role does not replace the role provided by other advocacy or support services but is intended to be an additional safeguard for patients who are subject to the Act. The IMHAs are specialist advocates with specific training to work within the framework of the Act to assist to meet the needs of patients.

Scope of role

The services of an IMHA will be available to the following groups of patients-referred to in the Act as *'qualifying patients'*.

- All patients detained under the Act with the exception of patients detained under s5, s4, s135 and s136
- All Community Treatment Order (CTO) patients and patients subject to guardianship
- All conditionally discharged restricted patients.

A number of informal patients will also have access to IMHAs if they fall into one of the following two categories.

- Patients being considered for treatment under s57
- Patients under 18 who are being considered for Electro-Convulsive Therapy (ECT).

Purpose of the IMHA role

SS130B(1)(a)-(f) outlines the help the IMHA is intended to give the patient in order gain understanding of and information about the following:

- *'the provision of this Act by virtue of which he is a qualifying patient'*
- *'any conditions or restrictions to which he is subject by virtue of this Act; what (if any) medical treatment is given to him or is proposed or discussed in his case'*
- *'why it is given, proposed or discussed'*
- *'the authority under which it is, or would be given':* **and**
- *'the requirements of this Act which apply, or would apply, in connection with the giving of the treatment to him' and then in S130B (2) (a) and (b);*
- *'that the help available under the arrangements to a qualifying patient shall also include '*
- *'help in obtaining information about, and understanding any rights which may be exercised under the Act by or in relation to him',* **and**
- *'help (by way of representation or otherwise) in exercising those rights.'*

There is some overlap with the role of clinical staff who have statutory responsibilities to give information to patients. Examples are where a nurse gives s132 information to a detained patient or a Responsible Clinician (RC) gives information and seeks to elicit informed consent about treatments under Part 4 of the Act.

One valuable aspect of the role of the IMHA is not just to give information themselves but to ensure that clinical staff do in fact give information to patients and do so in the best possible way to elicit understanding and empowerment. Another valuable aspect of the role of the IMHA is that they are completely independent of those responsible for the care and treatment of patients.

Though s130B does refer to representation, the role of IMHA is not intended to replace the role of a legal representative when a patient is appealing either the Hospital Managers or to the Tribunal.

It would be anticipated that on a number of occasions patients attending hearings will be supported before, during and after the hearing by both an IMHA and a legal representative.

How the IMHA exercises the role

In order to exercise their role effectively the IMHA has a number of 'rights' which are summarised in s130B (3) (a)-(d) as being that they may:

- *'visit and interview the patient in private'*
- *'visit and interview any person who is professionally concerned with his medical treatment'*
- *'require the production of and inspect any records relating to his detention or treatment in any hospital or registered establishment or to care services provided for him by section 117 above'*
- *'require the production of and inspect any records of, or held by, a local social services authority which relates to him'.*

How the patient accesses an IMHA

All qualifying patients must be given information as soon as practicable about the IMHA role. If the patient is detained under the MHA the responsibility to give information and to assist access to the IMHA service rests with the hospital concerned. Organisations may wish to incorporate this into their s132 giving of rights policy and should add this to the Department of Health rights forms.

If a patient is subject to guardianship the responsibility will rest with the responsible social services authority.

In many cases it is likely that the patient themselves will wish to have access to an IMHA. They may do so directly or staff may assist them to do so.

The law also permits a nearest relative, an AMHP or an RC to make a request the attendance of an IMHA. .

If such a referral is being considered, if practicable, the patient should be involved in the decision. If the patient does not wish to be interviewed by or accept help from an IMHA who visits they cannot be made to. The patient also has the right to choose to end any support they are receiving from an IMHA.

Access to records and confidentiality issues

When the IMHA visits a patient and has conversations with the patient the normal rules of confidentiality apply. The same rules apply also to any conversations the IMHA has with members of the care team.

If the patient consents (which presumes capacity) then the IMHA will have the right to see any records held by the detaining authority or the local social services authority - see s130b (3)(d) above.

The criteria for the disclosure of records to an IMHA where the patient lacks capacity is according to s130B (4) (b) (i) & (ii):

'the records may be relevant to the help to be provided by the advocate: and the production or inspection is appropriate.'

The Code suggests that this person should not grant access automatically but should always ask the IMHA to give reasons why they believe access to be both relevant and appropriate.

6.30 – 6.38 of the Code gives guidance on granting access of records to IMHA's.

More information about the role of an IMHA is contained in Chapter 6 of the Code.

Chapter 19 Miscellaneous Issues

This chapter deals with a number of issues which can loosely be described as concerning 'patient rights'. For some of the issues there is clear guidance within the MHA, its Code or other legislation. For other issues professionals required to make decisions about particular interventions with or for patients will often need to balance the 'duty of care' (or 'best interests') with the 'autonomy' or 'civil liberties' of the patient.

The issues dealt with are the following:

- common law
- informal patients
- discrimination
- voting
- marriage
- correspondence
- searches of patients and/or their property
- rights to travel.

Common law

Within the UK statutory law exists under common law. The MHA and MCA (which includes DOLS) are examples of statutory law which has been passed by parliament which must be followed. Common law is 'judge made law' which cover aspects of everyday life not specified in statutory law. Within mental health settings statutory law should always be used in preference to common law. An example is if an informal patient tells nursing staff they wish to discharge themselves and there are immediate risk concerns. Rather than rely on 'duty of care' to prevent the person leaving the nurse should consider the use of s5 (4).

The most valuable definition of the scope of common law as applicable to someone of 'unsound mind' is to be found in the judgment in the case of Black v Forey (1987) where Lord Griffiths said the power is 'confined to imposing temporary restraint on a lunatic who has run amok and is a manifest danger to himself or to others - a state of affairs as obvious to a layman as to a doctor. Such a common law power is confined to the short period of confinement necessary before the lunatic can be handed over to the proper authority'.

The common law (or judge made law) exists to fill the gaps which statutory law does not cover.

The MHA and MCA (which includes DOLS) are examples of statutory law passed by Parliament and a sound understanding of the MHA and MCA and DOLs and the law of consent is essential so that clinicians can identify the legal framework which applies to care and treatment and which authorises detention/deprivation of liberty in hospital.

In a hospital setting, the MHA and MCA provide the statutory legal framework for deprivation of liberty and care and treatment in a hospital.

An example for use of the MHA would be if an informal patient tells a member of nursing staff they wish to leave and there are immediate risk concerns if the patient were to leave hospital. If the patient is willing to stay for a review then a MHA assessment for admission under section 2 or 3 of the MHA should be considered. Where there is an immediate risk the person will leave then, in this case, the nurse should consider use of section 5(4) MHA or ask a doctor to exercise powers under s 5(2) MHA to stop the patient from leaving.

If the MCA is the legal framework being used care needs to be taken to identify the point at which any intervention moves beyond being a restriction of liberty which is permissible under the MCA to become one where the person is deprived of their liberty, which is not permissible, unless authorised under DOLS or by the court.

Only where there is a gap in statutory law and immediately necessary steps are required to protect a patient or others from immediate risk of significant harm is the 'common law duty of necessity' available to staff. An example would be to prevent a person from leaving an Emergency Department where the holding powers of MHA sections 5(2) or 5(4) are not available and it is not possible to assess the patient's capacity; or to prevent an immediate assault or harm to others.

The common law is not an alternative to the use of the MHA or MCA and should only be relied on for the shortest possible time until either the MHA or MCA is applied. If it is believed the person meets the criteria for detention under the MHA the process of assessing them under the MHA should begin as soon as possible.

In a small number of cases the response to a crisis might be that the police are called and the patient is arrested.

If the person lacks capacity the intervention - rather than be regarded as made under 'common law' - could be seen as falling within the remit of s5 and s6 of the 2005 Mental Capacity Act (MCA) but only if the restraint was intended to prevent harm to the patient. More information about the MCA is to be found within Chapter 23 above.

Where the patient lacks capacity the use of the MCA or DOLS are possibilities which are dealt with in Chapters 23 and 24 above.

Informal Patients

Informal admission to hospital is the preferred approach to admission to hospital. Section 131 of the MHA authorises admission where the patient consents to admission or, if unable to make a decision, where the patient does not object to admission to hospital and is not deprived of their liberty in hospital. If a DOL then detention under the MHA or a DOLS authorisation under the MCA must be considered and a decision made as which legal framework should be applied to authorise the deprivation of liberty. If a patient has been admitted informally it is important that they are made aware of their legal rights and done so in a way which makes clear the distinction between their legal status and that of anyone on the same ward who is detained under the MHA.

The legal rights of an informal patient can be summarised as being:

- their right to come and go from the ward (subject to reasonable expectations that being an inpatient requires 'rules' be followed and to be available to participate in ward-based activities. The term 'rules' is used here to mean – for example – that a ward would not normally let any patient out in the middle of the night to go for a walk.
- their right to decline to receive treatment
- their right to discharge themselves at any time.

It is not uncommon for informal patients to be asked to agree to a care plan (or 'contract') which places restrictions on their freedom of movement or choice of treatment. Wards are likely to have rules. If such 'contracts' are made it is important that the patient is aware that they are entitled to withdraw their consent to what they have agreed to previously. It is also important that informal patients are not told they will be detained if they do not wish to agree to restrictions on either their freedom of movement or choice of treatment.

If an informal patient wishes to discharge themselves from hospital (and the team do not agree that this is in their best interests) then there is no barrier to that person being assessed for detention under s2 or s3 of the MHA. In many cases this assessment will be preceded by detention under either s5(2) or s5(4).

Care should be taken to avoid using MHA terminology with informal patients in such a way that it implies the person is detained. Examples are terms such as 'absent without leave' or 'escorted leave'.

Discrimination

Clinicians need to be familiar with the Equalities Act 2010. This Act makes it unlawful to discriminate (directly or indirectly) against a person on the grounds of a protected characteristic or combination of protected characteristics. Protected characteristics include age, disability, reassignment, marriage and civil partnership, pregnancy and maternity, race, religion or belief, sex and sexual orientation. The protected characteristic of disability includes a mental impairment that has a substantial and long-term adverse effect on the person's ability to carry out normal day to day activities. People who are or have been 'mentally disordered' suffer discrimination in many aspects of their lives. The discrimination is added to by the stigma associated with being 'sectioned'.

The 1995 Disability Discrimination Act makes unlawful in a number of situations discrimination against someone because of their 'disability'. This Act includes 'mental illness' and 'mental impairment' as falling within the scope of the meaning of disability. Examples of the areas covered by this Act are: insurance, employment and buying or renting land or property.

Changes to strengthen the rights of 'disabled' people were introduced in the Disability Discrimination Act 1995 (Amendment) Regulations 2003 which came into effect in 2004. Further changes were introduced in the Disability Discrimination Act 2005. These changes imposed on public authorities a duty both to prevent discrimination and to promote equality. It also contained in s1 a revised definition of disability which is a *'physical or mental impairment which has a substantial and long-term adverse effect on his ability to carry out normal day-to-day activities'.*

Voting

The Representation of the People Act 2000 (RPA) allows patients detained under civil sections to register to vote in the same way as any other citizen of the UK. Patients remanded to hospital under either s35, s36 or s48 can also register to vote. The only group of patients not able to register is those who are detained in hospital as a result of criminal activity.

In order to be placed on the electoral register a patient needs to contact either the Electoral Registration Office or their local council. Once their name has been registered it will appear on the electoral register enabling them to vote in a forthcoming election. It is suggested that organisations should take an active interest in reminding detained (and informal) patients of their rights to register and vote and offering assistance if patients need it.

It is possible for a detained (or informal) patient to put down a hospital as their place of residence. There is no further guidance within the RPA as to how long a patient needs to have been in hospital before they can be regarded as a 'resident' of the hospital. Note that the definition of hospital used within the RPA excludes someone living in a residential care home.

If at the time of registration the patient is unsure for how much longer they will be in hospital it is possible for them to register at their home address. If the patient does not have a current home address the RPA allows them to put down as their address the place where they would be residing if they were not in hospital or an address they lived at in the past.

Someone (who may or may not have 'mental disorder') may be actually prevented on the day of election from casting their vote if the presiding officer at a polling station decides the person wishing to vote does not understand what they are doing. The test the presiding officer would need to apply is whether the person has a broad understanding of what voting meant and what the consequences of voting were. Note that there is no provision within the MCA for anyone to vote on behalf of someone else.

Applying for a postal vote is an option for a detained or informal patient as it would be for any other person. If it seemed likely that a particular patient on the day of an election would not be allowed to have s17 leave to go to vote arranging for them to vote by post would be a sensible option.

Marriage

Section 1 of the 1983 Marriage Act provides for detained patients to get married in the same way as anyone else. In some situations there might be concerns about the level of a patient's capacity to get married; the test from the case of Park v Park (1954) is that a patient must have a broad understanding of the marriage contract and the duties and responsibilities normally involved in getting married.

Section 12 of the Matrimonial Causes Act 1973 lays down conditions making particular marriages 'voidable'. Examples are if one of the two parties had not consented to the marriage or if one of the parties was suffering from 'mental disorder' (as defined within the MHA) where the disorder was *'of such a kind or to such an extent as to make the person unfitted for marriage.'*

This Section of the Matrimonial Causes Act 1973 would enable anyone (possibly a professional) to lodge what is called a 'caution' with the Registrar or 'clergyman' who was to perform the ceremony.

This law enables the Registrar or clergyman to decide not to perform the marriage ceremony or to 'put it on hold'. In the context of mental health it is suggested that the raising of a caution should be planned in advance as the issuing of a caution does put an obligation on the registrar or clergyman to investigate the concern. They might want to get the views of professionals such as doctors or social workers as to the patient's mental capacity. Note also that the MCA does allow a 'marriage' already made to be declared void.

If a care team had concerns about a patient's capacity to consent to getting married the onus would be on that team to prove that the patient lacks capacity.

Correspondence

MHA s134 deals with the circumstances in which the mail of a detained patient can be inspected and possibly withheld. This applies to both outgoing and incoming mail.

The powers within s134 are quite limited: in a number of situations staff will have other legal powers to prevent patients (both detained and informal) from receiving and keeping certain items. An example is s3 (1) of the Criminal Law Act 1967 which authorises staff to withhold items such as weapons or explosives from patients. These powers can also be seen as having a basis in 'common law'. Note also that the Malicious Communications Act of 1988 allows for the prosecution of anyone who sends or delivers letters or other articles if their intention is to cause anxiety or distress.

If a detained patient wishes to send mail to someone who has requested that they not receive that mail s134 (1) allows the hospital to stop it being sent.

There are special provisions within s134 for patients detained in Special Hospitals.

In other situations where the 'duty of care' suggests staff should restrict letters being sent out by any patient or restrict letters coming in, it is suggested that organisations obtain legal advice.

Rights to travel

If a patient is detained under the MHA s17 leave could be granted for a patient to leave the

United Kingdom. An example would be where the patient wanted to attend the funeral of a family member taking place in a foreign country. The patient's section does not end if they leave the UK: but there will be no powers to 'retake' them if they decide not to return to the UK. If a patient is detained under the MHA and the patient's RC suspects that the patient may try to leave the UK (and this is not considered desirable) the RC could put as a condition of s17 leave that the patient does not leave the UK but there would be no 'sanctions' if the patient ignored the condition.

Sometimes a past or current diagnosis of mental disorder (including having in the past been detained under the MHA) will adversely affect someone's application for permission to enter another country. Anyone who is or has been detained will need to acquire information from the embassy or high commission of the country they wish to visit as to what that country's requirements are.

The most common example mentioned is of the USA but in fact there is no barrier to someone who has been or is currently detained from visiting that country.

Searching of patients and their property

There are no powers explicitly in the MHA which authorise the searching of a patient or their property. It is recommended that organisations should have operational policies for both the searching of patients and their property. These policies should give staff clear guidelines on what the legal authority for such searches are.

It is important to obtain if possible informed consent to any proposed searches. If a patient is detained but refuses to be searched or to have their possessions searched the situations in which the search could take place can be summarised in the following way:

- where a search is necessary to prevent a crime being committed
- where a patient is suspected of possessing an offensive weapon or articles/substances that could be used to harm himself/herself or others or to aid his/her escape from hospital.

Part Four Compulsion in the Community

Chapter 20 Care Programme Approach and s117

Note that flow charts summarising various aspects of the CTO processes can be found at the end of this chapter.

Overview

The term Care Programme Approach (CPA) describes the system used to co-ordinate care for people with mental disorders. It is a framework for making arrangements to assess, plan and review their care. Someone subject to CPA must have a named care co-ordinator.The 1983 MHA introduced s117 which applied mainly to patients detained under treatment orders and gives to those patients a statutory entitlement to aftercare. In practice many patients will be subject to both CPA and s117. This Chapter summarises the way in which CPA works and also describes the distinctive features of s117.

Note the terminology in this Chapter used the phrase 'patient' and 'mental disorder' as these terms are used in the MHA Code.

What is the CPA?

The term CPA describes the system for co-ordinating the care for someone with a mental disorder. Central to the CPA is the CPA care plan. This plan should identify all aspects of the patient's need and how they will be met. Examples of what the care plan should cover are:

the patient's treatment plan which describes the nursing, medical, psychological and therapeutic support the person needs to promote recovery and prevent deterioration

- details on any medication and any physical health problems
- support needed for social needs such as housing, occupation and finances
- guidance and actions to respond to any crisis or deterioration
- support provided for carers

Use of the term CPA

Since the CPA was introduced there have been a number of policy changes in who exactly should or should not receive it. The Code at 34.7 describes them as those in need of:

- multi-agency support
- active engagement
- intense intervention and/or
- support with dual diagnoses

This will include most people who are entitled to s117 aftercare and everyone under a CTO or guardianship.

Best practice in care planning is described in Chapter 34 of the Code.

Section 117

Overview

Prior to 1983 no statutory provision was made for after-care of patients discharged from hospital. Section 117 introduced and defined formal after-care. S117 (2) states:

'It shall be the duty of the Clinical Commissioning Group or Local Health Board and of the local social services authority to provide, in co-operation with voluntary agencies, after-care services for any person to whom this Section applies, until such time as the Clinical Commissioning Group or Local Health Board and of the local social services authority are satisfied that the person concerned is no longer in need of such services; but they shall not be so satisfied in the case of a community patient.'

NB: Health Authorities should now be understood to mean Clinical Commissioning Groups.

Section 117 of the 1983 Mental Health Act applies to patients who have been detained under s3, s7, s37/41, s47/49, s48/49, s17A (CTO). Note the entitlement to s117 aftercare applies to s37,s47 and s48 patients irrespective of whether a restriction order or transfer direction accompanies the section.

As described above CPA provides the framework by which s117 aftercare is provided to patients. The vast majority of patients subject to s117 will be receiving care within the CPA. The next section of this Chapter describes the distinctive aspects of s117 aftercare including several important legal judgements.

The duty to provide after-care services lasts so long as such services are required because of the patient's mental condition. Section 117 applies until such time as the responsible Authorities have undertaken an assessment and are jointly satisfied that the person concerned is no longer in need of such services.

Definitions of After-Care

In the case of Clunis v Camden & Islington Health Authority (1994) the judge gave the following definition of after-care: *'They would normally include social work support in helping the ex-patient with employment, accommodation or family relationships, the provision of domiciliary services and the use of day centre or residential facilities.'*

CCG's and local authorities should interpret the definition of aftercare broadly to cover the following:

- health care, social care and employment services
- supported accommodation (if applicable)
- services to meet someone's broader social,cultural and spiritual needs (if the needs relate to the person's mental disorder and help to prevent a deterioration in their condition)

Charging for after-care

Patients who are subject to s117 and who have assessed social care needs that form part of their after-care plan cannot be charged for the costs of this social care. This may include:

- domiciliary services for Home Care
- meals on wheels
- day centre services
- residential services.

Patients who are subject to s117 and who have assessed **health care needs** that form part of their after-care plan cannot be charged for the costs of this health care. This may include:

- prescription medication
- provision of a care home or independent hospital including care, board and other services, facilities and amenities
- nursing care
- psychotherapeutic and psychological interventions

Note the importance of providers having systems to ensure someone entitled to after-care services to receive them as 'direct payments'.

In the case of R v Manchester City Council ex parte Stennett 2002 the House of Lords confirmed that no charges can be made for any services wherever these are provided as part of an after-care plan under s117. This includes services provided by both Local Authority (e.g. residential, day care) and NHS (e.g. prescription medication).

Discharge from s117 and Authorisation

A patient can only be discharged from the after-care provisions of s117 once designated members of both the CCG and Social Services have agreed that the patient no longer requires after-care for their mental health needs.

If the responsible consultant psychiatrist and care co-ordinator are satisfied that the person is now equipped to cope with life outside hospital, and, the purpose of any further services will be to support the person in the community through the provision of health and social care services, but that those services are not needed to prevent readmission for treatment for mental disorder, they will recommend that s117 after-care be ended. This can only take place following a re-assessment of the patient's needs.

In the case of R -v - Richmond LBC Ex p Watson (1999) it is noted that there may be situations where a patient no longer requires after-care for their mental illness but does require social care for physical disability. In such cases care must be taken before deciding to discharge a patient and consideration will need to be given to what condition the care required is directed at alleviating.

Need for s117 register

In addition to there being a register of CPA patients it is suggested that organisations need to have a s117 register. Such a register would need to have a clear mechanism for patients entering and then exiting the register.

It is suggested that clear procedures are needed for the level of staff within both health and social services that would make the decision to end s117. The patient and carers would need to be involved in this process.

Chapter 21 Community Treatment Orders

Note the term Supervised Community Treatment (SCT) is obsolete as it is not used in the new Code

This chapter concludes with flow charts summarising various aspects of the CTO process.

Purpose of a Community Treatment Order (CTO)

A CTO is a power allowing certain detained patients to leave hospital and to continue with an agreed treatment plan while living back in the community. The power to bring this about is a CTO which is contained in MHA s17A-G.

Patients eligible for CTO

The power is available to be used with only some detained patients. These are:

- patients detained under s3
- patients detained under Part 3 unrestricted hospital orders (s37 or s51)
- patients detained under Part 3 hospital or transfer directions (s45A or s47 or s48) (without limitation or restriction directions).

Note it cannot be used for any patient detained under s2 or s4 or any restricted patients. Nor can it be retrospectively applied to any patient living in the community who were previously under a Section which has now ended.

Legal Criteria for CTO

The criteria for making a CTO are:

- *'The criteria for making a CTO are:*
- *'patient is suffering from mental disorder of a nature or degree which makes it appropriate for the patient to receive medical treatment'*
- *'it is necessary for the patient's health or safety or for the protection of other persons that the patient should receive such treatment'*
- *'subject to the patient being liable to be recalled as mentioned below, such treatment can be provided without the patient continuing to be detained in a hospital'*
- *'it is necessary that the responsible clinician should be able to exercise the power under section 17E(1) to recall the patient to hospital', and*
- *'that appropriate treatment is available for the patient'.*

The first two and the last one of these five criteria are very similar to the s3 criteria for detention. The only difference is that the reference to medical treatment excludes the phrase *'in a hospital.* The third of the five criteria suggests that the use of CTO would not be appropriate if necessary treatment could only be given in a hospital setting. The fourth criteria suggests that - if there were no concerns as to whether a patient would continue with agreed treatment plans after leaving hospital - no purpose would be achieved by placing them under CTO.

The following tables are reproduced from the Code giving guidance as to whether CTO, s7 guardianship or extended s17 leave should be used with a particular patient.

Comparison of CTO and use of s17 leave (from Code Chapter 31)

Factors suggesting longer-term leave	**Factors suggesting CTO**
▪ Discharge from hospital is for a specific purpose or a fixed period ▪ The patient's discharge from hospital is deliberately on a 'trial' basis ▪ The patient is likely to need further in-patient treatment without their consent or compliance ▪ There is a serious risk of arrangements in the community breaking down or being unsatisfactory - more so than for CTO.	▪ There is confidence that the patient is ready for discharge on an indefinite basis ▪ There are good reasons to expect that the patient will not need to be detained for the treatment they need to be given ▪ The patient appears prepared to consent or comply with the treatment they need - but risks as below mean that recall may be necessary ▪ The risk of arrangements in the community breaking down, or the patient needing to be recalled to hospital for treatment, is sufficiently serious to justify CTO, but not to the extent that it is very likely to happen.

Comparison of CTO and guardianship (from Code Chapter 31)

Factors suggesting guardianship	**Factors suggesting CTO**
▪ The focus is on the patient's general welfare, rather than specifically on medical treatment ▪ There is little risk of the patient needing to be admitted compulsorily and quickly to hospital ▪ There is a need for enforceable power to require the patient to reside at a particular place	▪ The main focus is on ensuring that the patient continues to receive necessary medical treatment for mental disorder, without having to be detained again ▪ Compulsory recall may well be necessary, and a speedy recall is likely to be important

Procedures for using a CTO

The process starts by the patient's current Responsible Clinician (RC) completing form CT01.

The form has three parts and Parts 1 and 3 are completed by the RC who indicates that the legal criteria are met and specifies any conditions with which the patient is expected to comply. Part 2 of the form must be completed by an Approved Mental Health Professional (AHMP) who is acting on behalf of a local social services authority.

The role of the AMHP is to decide whether to endorse the RC's view that all the legal criteria are met and that it is appropriate that the patient to be placed under CTO. This AMHP has to agree with all the conditions (see next section) which the RC proposes.

The completed form is then returned to the 'Hospital Managers' of the hospital where the patient is liable to be detained. In practice this will normally be to a MHA Administration Office. As there is no mechanism under s15 to rectify errors on this form it is suggested that the form is scrutinised by the MHA Administration Office before the RC completes Part 3 of the form. The date of the RC's signing is the date from when the CTO begins. This requirement is written on the CTO1 form.

Conditions for a CTO

There is only one condition which applies to all CTO's. This condition is that the patient makes themselves available for 'examination' if their RC is considering whether to renew the CTO (see s20A). This condition is explicit on the CTO1 form.

All other conditions – which should be clearly written on the CTO1 form are what the RC considers are **necessary and appropriate** to achieve one or more of the following purpose:

- ensuring the patient receives medical treatment
- preventing risk of harm to the patient's health or safety or for protecting other people.

The conditions must never deprive the person of their liberty and it is suggested that they need to link clearly with the care and recovery plan for the patient in question. For the vast majority of patients conditions are likely to focus on concordance with medication and continued engagement with the community mental health team. Note that the condition to reside at a particular place should only be stipulated if there are reasons to suggest the patient might want to live elsewhere or live as a homeless person. It should not be put down simply to record where somebody lives.

Variations of conditions

The RC has the authority during the period of the CTO to either vary conditions or suspend them on a temporary basis. The agreement of the AMHP is not required for this. Any variations of conditions must be recorded on form **CT02** which will need to be sent to the relevant MHA Administration Office. Note that the suspension of any conditions does not need to be recorded on Form CT02.

After the first month the patient's RC should complete form CT0-12 but only if the patient both has capacity to consent and is consenting. If the patient is not giving informed consent a Second

Opinion Approved Doctor must certify the appropriateness of treatment and any conditions attached to it, not whether the patient has or lack capacity or is refusing the treatment. The certificate certified by the SOAD will include that which can be given if the patient is recalled to hospital.

Effects of a Community Treatment Order

A Community Treatment Order (CTO) discharges the patient from detention in hospital subject to the possible recall of that patient to hospital for further medical treatment if necessary. Though the patient's previous section remains in place the commencement of the CTO means the authority to detain the patient is suspended.

This means the patient can leave hospital and the CTO comes into effect. However, the patient might remain in hospital as an informal patient for a limited period of time (e.g. if the discharge and aftercare plan was not yet finalised).

If the patient is on s17 leave of absence at the time the CTO comes into effect their detention under s3 would be suspended from that point onwards.

Length of Community Treatment Order

As for s3 the duration of a CTO is up to six months and can be extended for another six months, and then at yearly intervals. Examination of the patient by their RC with a view to extending the CTO can take place at any time in the final two months of the CTO which are the same timescales as for s3 or s37 renewals.

Information about CTO

S132A requires statutory information to be given to the patient in the same way as for any other patient. If the patient is currently in hospital a nurse would normally give the information whereas if the patient was on extended s17 leave in the community the patient's care co-ordinator might be the best person to give the information.

The information must be given both verbally and in writing. Written information should be given to the nearest relative unless the patient requests otherwise, using either leaflet **CTO-Pt2** or **CTO-Pt 3**.

The information given to the patient should focus on the following areas:

- the provisions in the MHA that apply to a CTO patient. This would include the condition applicable to the patient; the consent to treatment provisions and how and why recall might occur
- the rights of appeal to the MHT and the Hospital Managers
- the availability of independent mental health advocacy (IMHA).

Appeal rights against CTO

The patient has the right to make one appeal to the Tribunal during each period of detention. This means one appeal to the Tribunal during the first six months and then one appeal during the next six months (if CTO is renewed) and then one appeal during each subsequent yearly period.

If CTO patients do not appeal they are referred for Tribunals in the same way as s3 patients.

Note also that the patient must be referred for a Tribunal if the CTO is revoked (see below). Patients also have the right of appeal to Hospital Managers.

The rights leaflet for CTO is **CTO-Pt2** or **CTO-Pt 3**. The difference is whether the patient went onto CTO from a Part 2(civil) or Part 3(forensic) section.

Recall Procedures

Grounds for recall

These are dealt with in s17E. The patient's RC can decide to recall the patient if they believe the patient needs medical treatment - in a hospital - for their mental disorder and - if they were not recalled - there would be a risk to the health or safety of the patient or others. Recall can also be activated by the RC if the patient breaches any of the mandatory conditions described above.

The RC must give the patient written notice of recall using form **CT03**.

Processes for recalling a patient

There are three methods by which notice of recall is served on the patient:

- by delivering the recall notice by hand to the patient. As soon as the notice is given to the patient notice is deemed to have been served
- by delivering the notice by hand to the patient's usual or last known address. The notice is deemed to be served at the start of the following day
- by sending by pre-paid first class post the notice to the patient's usual or last known address. The notice is deemed to have been served at the start of the second business day after it has been posted.

If at all possible the first of these three methods should be used.

Recall paperwork

A copy of the CTO3 form must be delivered to the 'Hospital Managers' (usually the MHA Administration Office) for the hospital to which the patient is to be recalled. The hospital to which they are recalled could be any hospital (not just the hospital from which they were discharged) but the RC must first have established that that hospital is able to accept the patient.

There is nothing in the law requiring the place of recall to be an in-patient facility - it could for example be an out-patients clinic. Organisations will need to develop their own protocols as to where patients might be recalled to. It is possible for a CTO patient to be admitted informally to a hospital. If during that admission there are concerns about their mental health they can be recalled at that point. Form CTO3 to recall the patient must be completed and the full recall process followed.

The recall period begins from the time when the patient arrives at the place to which they have been recalled, not from the time at which the recall notice was served. Form CTO4 must be used to record the start of the patient's period of detention. Failure to complete this will render the recall invalid. As the arrival of the patient at the recall place may be outside 'office hours' organisations will need to have protocols as to who should complete the CTO4. It is also suggested that organisations should devise a form to record when the period of recall ends as there is no statutory form for this.

Information for recalled patients

As soon as practicable the CTO patient should be given verbal and written information about the provisions of the Act under which they have been recalled and the effect of those provisions.

The rights leaflet for a recalled patient is **CTO - Recall.**

Failure to comply with recall requirements

If the patient does not comply with the recall requirements they are deemed to be absent without leave and the processes contained within s18 apply to them in the same way as for detained patients. Absence without leave means either the situation where the patient does not comply with the requirement to go to the place of recall or absconds from the place to which they have been recalled.

Period of recall

The period of recall is for **up to 72 hours**. During that period it is lawful to transfer the patient from one hospital to another. If the transfer is between hospitals under different management form **CTO6** must be completed. Those authorising the transfer must be satisfied that arrangements are in place for the new hospital to receive the patient. If the transfer is between sites within the same hospital or between hospitals under the same management no formal procedures are needed.

Outcome of recall

There are two possible outcomes for the recalled patient.

Revoking the CTO

The first possible outcome is that (following assessment during the 72 hours) the patient's RC can revoke the CTO. The RC can do this if they believe the patient meets the s3 criteria. This revocation is subject to the approval of an AMHP and is recorded on form **CT05**. The AMHP must both believe the patient meets the s3 criteria and that it is appropriate for the RC to revoke the CTO.

Revoking means that the patient becomes detained again (or liable to be detained again) under the section they had been on immediately before they became a CTO patient. The only difference is that the period of detention under the 'reactivated' section begins all over again and does not take into account any period for which the patient had already been detained. If the CTO has been revoked the detaining authority must refer the patient for an MHT.

If a patient's CTO is revoked they should be given rights leaflet **CTO-RevPt2** or **CTO-RevPt3**.

Release from recall

The second possible outcome is that the patient's RC can decide to release the person from the recall power at any point during the 72 hour period. Note that the patient might agree to remain in hospital as an informal patient. If they leave hospital and return to the community they continue to be a CTO patient as before.

Note that particular conditions might be varied or suspended following assessment during the 72 hour period.

Treatment of CTO patients

The next part of this Chapter is divided into three parts. These are:

- CTO patients who have left hospital and not been recalled
- CTO patients who have been recalled to hospital and covers the time during the period of recall (up to 72 hours)
- CTO patients where the CTO has been revoked.

Treatment of non-recalled CTO patients

The treatment of CTO patients who have not been recalled to hospital is dealt with under Part 4A of the Act. Section 64, A-K deal with their treatment and detailed guidance on treatment issues is dealt with in Chapters 24 and 25 of the Code.

For medication a certificate is not required immediately but must in general be in place within one month from when a patient leaves hospital under the CTO. However, if the patient had been receiving medication under section for a relatively brief period before the CTO was made, there will be a total of three months from the start of receiving medication, in or out of hospital before the certificate is required.

After the first month, a Second Opinion Approved Doctor (SOAD) must certify that such treatment is appropriate on a Part 4A certificate (form CTO11). The SOAD certifies the appropriateness of treatment and any conditions attached to it, not whether a patient has or lacks capacity or is refusing the treatment. The treatment certified by the SOAD will include that which can be given if the patient is recalled to hospital.

Treatment of non-recalled CTO patients - capacity issues

There are different rules for Part 4A patients who have capacity to consent to specified treatments and those who do not. Anyone who has capacity can only be given treatment in the community that they consent to unless s64 applies. Treatment without consent for someone with capacity could only occur following recall to hospital.

The capacity threshold for treatment of CTO patients means there is an interaction between Part 4A of the MHA and the Mental Capacity Act (MCA). The rules within Part 4A recognise the role of advance decisions and persons appointed to make surrogate decisions under the MCA (i.e. court appointed deputies and those with Lasting Power of Attorney or Court of Protection derived powers).

If a CTO patient lacks capacity treatment could be given to them in the community by or under the direction of an approved clinician (normally this would be the patient's RC) unless:

- the treatment - for a patient 18 or over - was contrary to a valid and applicable advance decision by the patient
- the treatment - for a patient 16 or over - was contrary to someone authorised under the MCA to refuse treatment (i.e. attorney, deputy or court of protection)
- force was needed to administer the medication and the patient was objecting to the treatment (this applies to patients of any age).

Treatment of non-recalled CTO patients - issues of objection

Guidance on the meaning of 'objecting' is given in 24.21 of the Code. This guidance makes clear that in many cases the patients will be able to state their objection (either verbally or by their dissenting behaviour). But - where patients are unable to communicate fully or partially their 'objection' - the guidance is that *'clinicians will need to consider the patient's wishes, feelings, views, beliefs and values, both present and past, so far as they can be ascertained'.*

Treatment of non-recalled CTO patients - emergency treatment

The use of force is only lawful if the treatment is authorised under s64G the criteria of which are reproduced in the next paragraph. Such emergency treatment can be given by anyone (i.e. does not need to be an Approved Clinician or the patient's RC). If such treatment is to be given it must meet one or more of the legal criteria reproduced in the next section of this chapter.

- *'save the patient's life'*
- *'prevent a serious deterioration of the patient's condition, and the treatment does not have unfavourable physical or psychological consequences which cannot be reversed'*
- *'alleviate serious suffering by the patient and the treatment does not have unfavourable physical or psychological consequences which cannot be reversed and does not entail significant physical hazard'*
- *'prevent the patient behaving violently or being a danger to themselves or others, including children, and the treatment represents the minimum interference necessary for that purpose, does not have unfavourable physical or psychological consequences which cannot be reversed and does not entail significant physical hazard.'*

If the treatment is Electro-convulsive Therapy (ECT) or medication administered as part of ECT, only the **first two** of the above apply.

Treatment of non-recalled CTO patients - use of force

If force is used - whether or not the patient objects - the treatment must be necessary to prevent harm to the patient and the force must be proportionate to the likelihood of the patient suffering harm and to the seriousness of that harm.

The guidance in 24.28 of the Code makes clear that the usual circumstances in which treatment with force would be given would be following recall to hospital. It describes exceptional circumstances as being *'where the situation is so urgent that recall is not realistic, or where taking the patient to hospital would exacerbate their condition, damage their recovery or cause them unnecessary anxiety or suffering.'*

In an emergency where treatment is immediately necessary as above, it may be given even if it goes against an advance decision or a decision made by a person authorised on the patient's behalf under the MCA.

These are the only exceptional circumstances in which force can be used to treat an objecting CTO patient without first recalling them to hospital. In non-emergency situations (excluding ECT)) a patient may lack capacity and object to treatment but where physical force is not required he or she can be treated with medication for mental disorder in the community during the first month following discharge on a CTO.

When completing the certificate requirement the SOAD will consider what treatments (if any) should be approved in the event that the patient is recalled to hospital and to specify any conditions that will apply.

Form **CTO11** should be kept with the original CTO and detention papers but a copy must be kept in the clinical records which might include a scanned copy where the primary record is electronic.

It is suggested that organisations develop a form for the use of s64 and monitor its use.

SOAD visits to CTO patients

The arrangements surrounding these visits will be complicated by the fact that the patient is in the community so an appropriate person should be asked to confirm arrangements with the SOAD and coordinate the process. This may be the patient's care co-ordinator. Note that the stipulations as to which groups of clinical staff can and cannot be 'consultees' is less prescriptive for CTO than for other categories of detained patients. The following are examples of combinations of 'consultees' that can be used:

- care co-ordinator (nurse) plus ward based nurse
- care co-ordinator (social worker) plus ward based nurse
- care co-ordinator (social worker) plus AMHP (e.g. AMHP who made s3 application or ward based AMHP)
- care co-ordinator (social worker or nurse) plus patient's general practitioner
- care co-ordinator (social worker or nurse) plus pharmacist, psychologist or occupational therapist.

Other than in exceptional circumstances SOAD examinations will be arranged in a hospital or clinical setting. If the RC agrees that it is necessary to visit a CTO patient in a hostel or home, the SOAD will always be accompanied by an appropriate member of the care team.

CTO patients - issues for children and young people

Parents (or other people with parental responsibility) may not consent on a child's behalf to treatment for mental disorder (or refuse it) while the child is on CTO. However, if CTO patients under the age of 18 are living with one or both parents, the person giving the treatment should consult with the parent(s) about the treatment (subject to the normal considerations of patient confidentiality), bearing in mind that if there is something that the parents would not accept,

it would make it very difficult for the patient to live with their parents while on CTO. This dialogue should continue throughout the patient's treatment on CTO.

If a parent is unhappy with treatments or conditions attached to CTO (where the child is not competent to give consent) the care team needs to consider whether the treatment and care plan (and CTO in particular) is still appropriate for that child.

Part 4A patients over the age of sixteen who lack capacity may be given specified treatments on the authority of an Attorney or court appointed Deputy or by order of the Court of Protection. If over sixteen, treatment cannot be given when an Attorney or Deputy refuses on the patient's behalf. If the patient is over eighteen, treatment cannot be authorised if it would contravene a valid and applicable advance decision made under MCA.

Treatment on recall

There is no barrier in law to an old CTO12 being used during the recall period but it is unlikely that a patient in reality will be giving informed consent to any medication needed during the recall period.

When a patient on CTO is recalled, they will become subject to the provisions of those sections of the Act governing treatment for detained patients, i.e. subject to s58 and s58A of the Act.

There are three exceptions to this general rule:

- a certificate under s58 is not required if less than one month has passed since the patient became an CTO patient;

- if a SOAD has approved any treatment (on form **CTO11**) in the event of the patient's recall to hospital, such treatment may be given as approved subject to any conditions that may have been specified. Unless the SOAD has indicated otherwise, the certificate will authorise treatment (other than ECT) whether the patient has or does not have capacity to refuse it; and
- on recall treatment, that was already being given, as described on form **CTO11**, but has not been specifically approved by the SOAD for treatment on recall, may continue to be given if the approved clinician in charge of the treatment considers that stopping it would cause the patient 'serious suffering'. However, steps must be taken at the earliest opportunity to obtain a new certificate to authorise treatment by another SOAD.

In the absence of form **CTO11**, treatment during the recall period can only be given if forms **T2** or **T3** are completed. If the situation is urgent, s62 should be used. If treatment is ECT, only the first and second of the s62 legal criteria apply. Note that s64g does not give authority to treat a recalled patient as it only covers treatment prior to recall for patients who lack capacity.

Treatment on revocation of CTO

If the decision is made to revoke the CTO during the 72 hour recall period, a **CTO11** form (if it had been completed) no longer provides the authority to treat the patient as the patient is now subject to Part 4, rather than Part 4A of the Act.

The treatment of the patient can be found in one of the following ways:

- If the patient is believed by their RC/AC to be giving informed consent by the completion of form T2 (if the combined period on the s3 and the time on the CTO exceed three months)
- If the patient is not giving informed consent by the completion of form T3 by a visiting SOAD (if the combined period on the s3 and the time on the CTO exceeds three months)
- In the absence of either a T2 or T3 b the use of s62. Note that if the treatment is ECT, only the first two of the four legal categories apply.

Because s62 provides the authority to treat, using the old form T2 or T3 should not be relied upon (Code of Practice 24.81).

Treatment of CTO patients who have been informally admitted

If the decision is made to revoke the CTO during the recall period a CTO11 or CTO12 form (if either had been completed) no longer provides the authority to treat the patient is now subject to Part 4 rather than Part 4A of the Act.

In the absence of a form **CTO11** or **CTO12** the authority to treat can be found in one of the following ways.

- The RC completes a new form **T2** (if the combined time on the s3 and the time on CTO exceed three months and the patient consents)
- A visiting SOAD completed a form **T3** (if the combined time on the s3 and the time on CTO exceeds three months and the patient does not consent)
- In the absence of either forms **CTO11** or **CTO12**, **T2** or **T3**, treatment could be given if the patient lacks capacity (and has been assessed as such) and the treatment is immediately necessary using s64G. However, if an informal patient required treatment in these circumstances it would be best practice to recall the patient and follow the process described above.

THE PATIENT'S JOURNEY – COMMUNITY TREATMENT ORDER

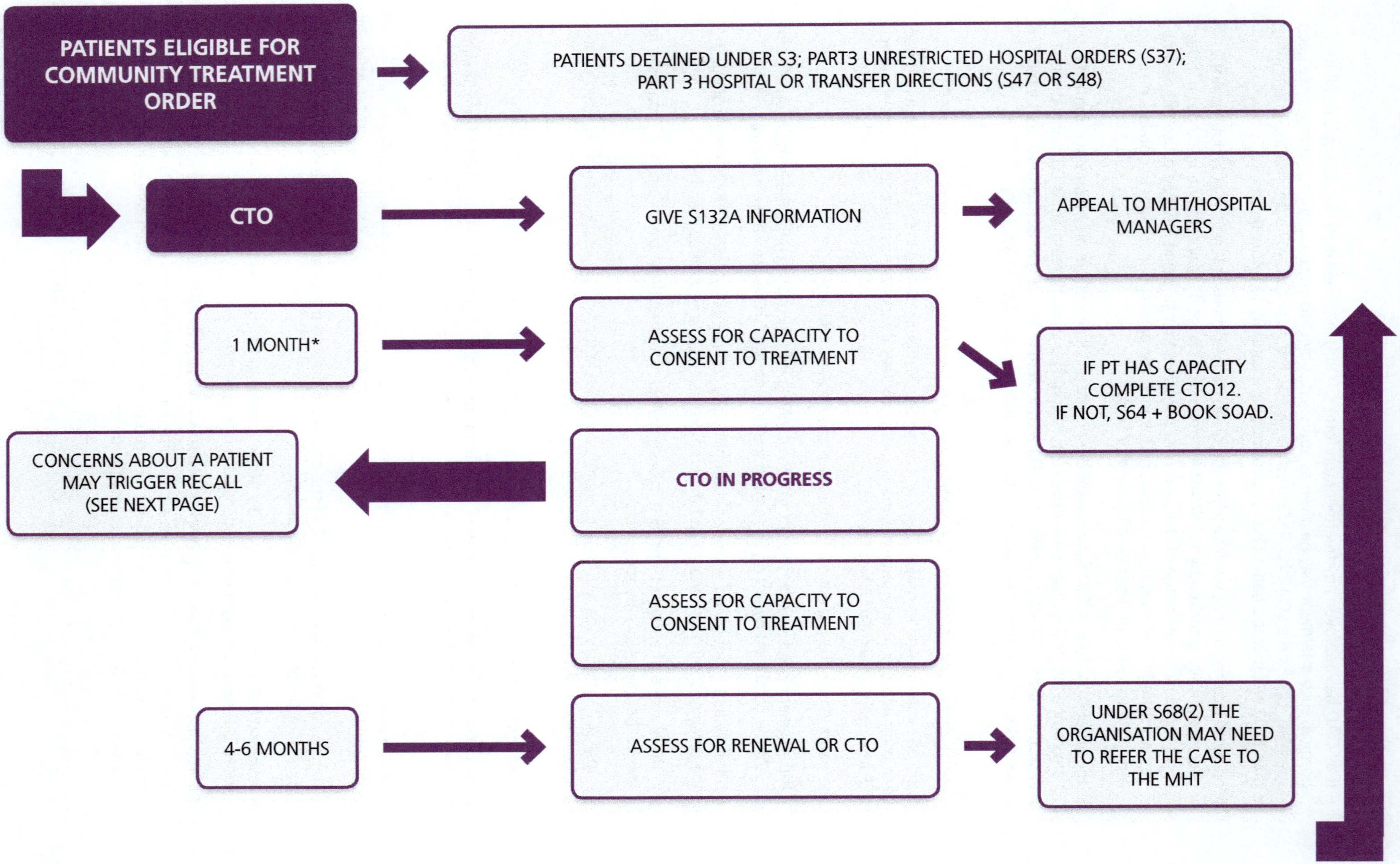

*** If the end of the 3 months Consent to Treatment date is further than the 1 month date, the later date is used.**

THE PATIENT'S JOURNEY – RECALL TO REVOCATION

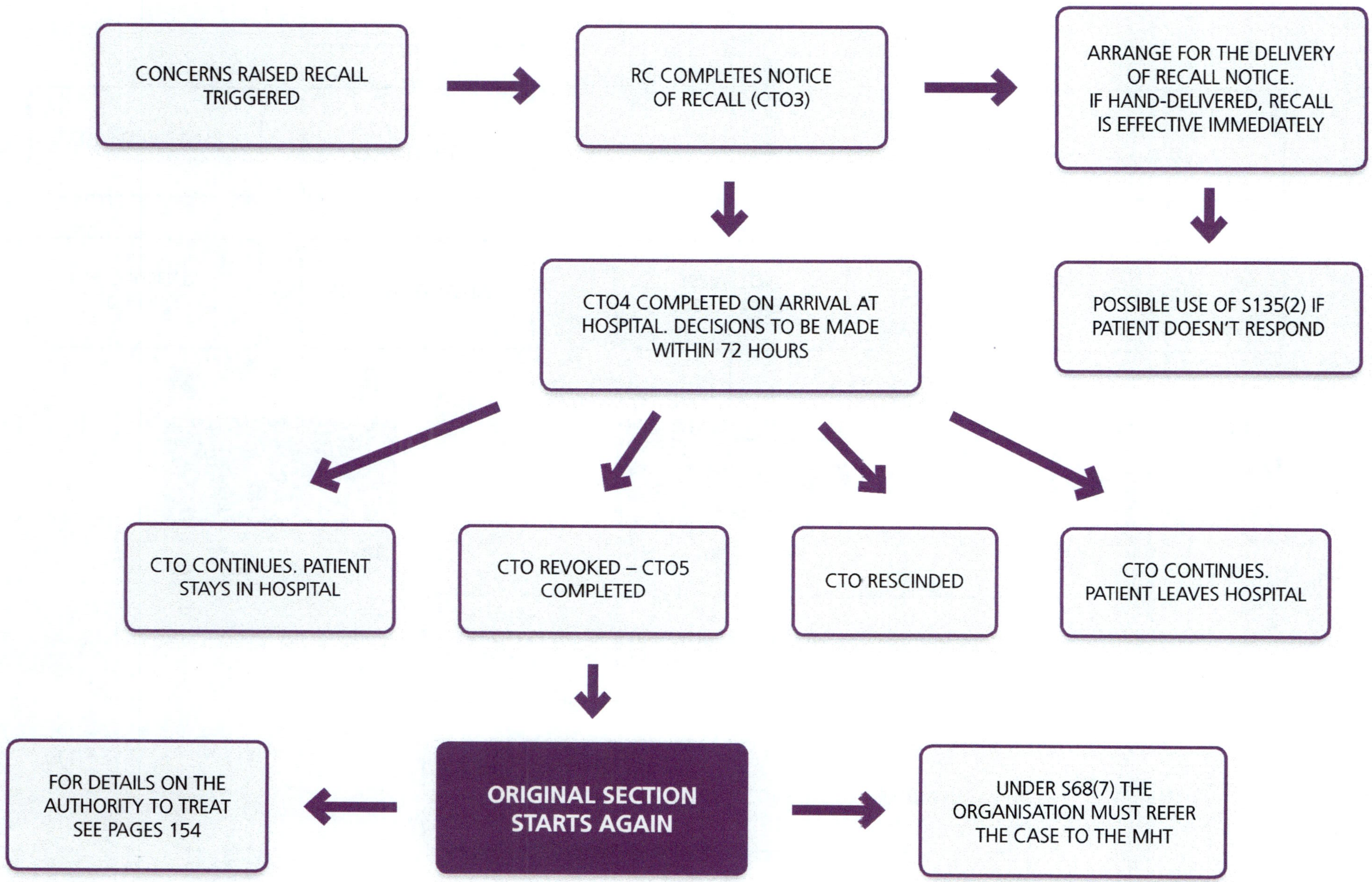

CONSENT TO TREATMENT – PART 4A

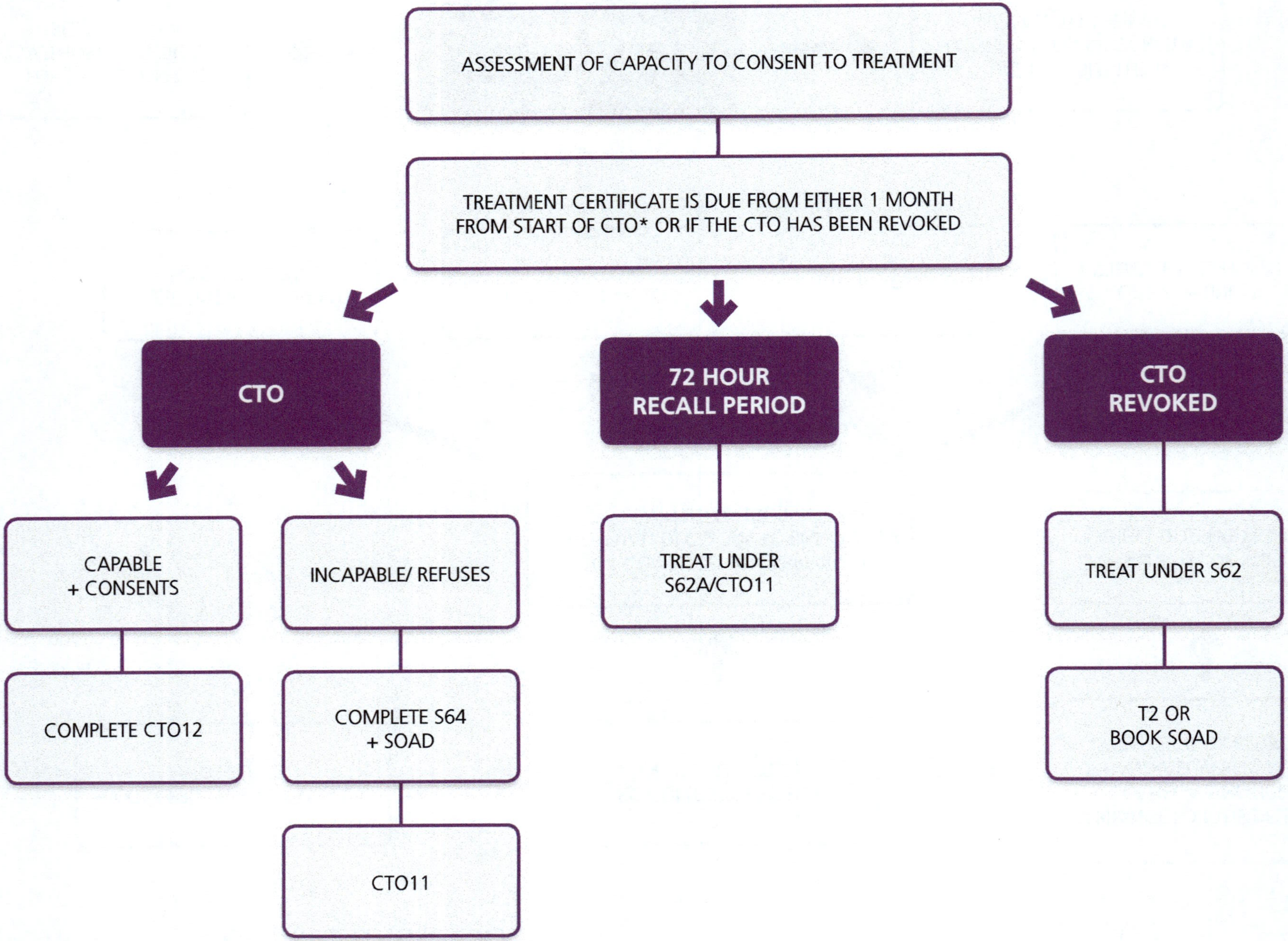

* If the end of the 3 months CTT date is further than the 1 month date, the later date is used.

Chapter 22 Guardianship

Purpose of Guardianship

30.2 of the Code summarises its purpose as *'to enable patients to receive care outside hospital when it cannot be provided without the use of compulsory powers. Such care may or may not include specialist medical treatment for mental disorder.'*

Legal criteria for Guardianship

To be received into guardianship s7 states the patient must:

- *'have attained the age of 16 years'*
- *'be suffering from mental disorder of a nature or degree which warrants his reception into guardianship under this section' and*
- *'it is necessary in the interests of the welfare of the patient or for the protection of others that the patient shall be so received.'*

Paperwork for Guardianship

Two medical recommendations are required on one form **G3** or two separate Forms **G4**. One must be completed by a doctor who is s12 approved. As with s3 the two doctors if submitting separate forms must have personally examined the patient within five days of each other.

Following this an Approved Mental Health Professional (AMHP) or the nearest relative can make an application for guardianship. If an AMHP is making the application they must complete form G2 or if the nearest relative is making the application they must use form G1.

The applicant must have personally interviewed the person within 14 days of the date of the last medical recommendation. The application has no effect until it is accepted by the local social services authority responsible for the guardianship order. The person within the authority to accept it must complete Form G5.

If the nearest relative objects to the order it cannot be completed unless the relative is put aside by the County Court following displacement procedures (see Chapter 6 of this Guide for more information about displacement procedures).

Note however that if s37 (4) is used to instigate s7 the nearest relative cannot object.

Length and renewal of Guardianship

Guardianship operates in the same way as s3, initially for six months and renewable for a further six months and then for a year at a time. The Responsible Clinician (RC) renews this order by completing form **G9** in the period of up to two months before the expiry of the order.

The criteria for renewal are the same as described above. The RC completes Part 1 of the form and someone from the Local Social Services Authority (LSSA) will complete Part 2. Note there is no statutory requirement - unlike for s20 renewals -for the RC to formally get the approval of a colleague. Note also that a 'nominated medical attendant' instead of the RC can renew the order.

Administration and Monitoring of Guardianship

The main difference between guardianship and civil sections such as s2 or s3 is that the LSSA is responsible for the administrative and legal processes.

It is suggested that each LSSA should have a policy including the following:

- receiving and scrutinising applications
- monitoring the use of this power
- ensuring that private guardians are suitable for the role and able to understand and carry out their duties under this power
- ensuring a robust system is in place for giving the patient written and verbal information (in a similar way to how s132 and s132A information is given and assisting patient to appeal if they wish to)
- ensuring each patient has an RC
- having mechanisms for ensuring that consideration is given to renewing guardianship if appropriate
- discharging patients from guardianship as soon as it is no longer required.

Powers of Guardianship

A guardianship order can be made in civil cases under s7, and in criminal cases under s37. In both cases the effects of such an order are the same.

The powers of the guardian are contained in s8 and can include:

- *'the power to require the patient to reside at a place specified by the authority or person named as guardian'*
- *'the power to require the patient to attend at places and times so specified for the purposes of medical treatment, occupation, education or training'*
- *'the power to require access to the patient to be given, at any place where the patient is residing to any registered medical practitioner, approved mental health professional or other person so specified.'*

Enforcement of these powers

It is lawful not just to require someone to live at a particular place but also to take that person into legal custody if they leave the place in which they are required to live without permission. Note also that the power can be used to take the person for the first time to the place where they are to live.

Though the consent of the patient should always be sought - and hopefully given - it is possible to use force to ensure that the person either goes to the place of residence for the first time or is retaken and returned to that place.

In deciding whether to use and enforce such powers the Code at 30.30 gives examples of the use of powers to discourage the patient from:

- *'living somewhere the guardian considers unsuitable'*
- *'breaking off contact with services'*
- *'leaving the area before proper arrangements can be made'* **or**
- *'sleeping rough'.*

Note that paragraph 30.37 of the Code says *'if a patient consistently rejects exercise by the guardian of any of their powers, it can normally be concluded that guardianship is not the most appropriate form of care for that person, and the guardianship order should be discharged.'* Note also the importance of ensuring that the patient is not being 'deprived of their liberty' or being effectively detained while subject to this power. The most recent ruling NL v Hampshire Council case of 2014) concluded that guardianship -in itself – cannot deprive someone of their liberty. If the care plan necessitates deprivation a guardianship order may need to be supplemented by a DOLS authorisation or a MCA s16 Court of Protection order.

30.4 of the Code say that guardianship 'provides an authoritative framework for working with a patient, with a minimum of constraint, to achieve as independent a life as possible within the community.'

If an adult lacking capacity has been assessed as needing residential care an alternative to the use of guardianship might be to move the person to the place of residency using powers under the MCA s5 or (from April 2009) using DOLS. Note that a DOLS authorisation can only be made out to a care home as defined in the 2000 Care Standards Act.

The Guardian

The guardian can either be a named individual or a named local authority.

Consent to Treatment for guardianship

A patient under guardianship is in the same position as an informal patient and therefore can refuse treatment. Unless there is separate authority under the MCA no one has the right to make decisions about treatment on the patient's behalf.

Appeal Rights against Guardianship

The patient has the right of appeal to the Mental Health Tribunal against guardianship. There is no right of appeal to the Hospital Managers.

The rights leaflet is G-7 or for an order made under s37) (4) **G-37**.

The nearest relative has a right of appeal to the Mental Health Tribunal only if the guardianship order has been made under s37 (4).

Ending of Guardianship

The RC, social services authority and nearest relative can discharge the order at any time (the nearest relative cannot do this for orders made by a court).

Part Five Mental Capacity Act and Deprivation of Liberty Safeguards

Chapter 23 Mental Capacity Act

Introduction

The Mental Capacity Act 2005 (MCA) was fully implemented in October 2007. It provides a statutory framework for making decisions on behalf of people aged 16 and over who lack the mental capacity to make a decision, or decisions, for themselves. The aim of the MCA is to enhance individual autonomy, whilst making sure that individuals who lack capacity have decisions made for them in a way that protects their rights and freedoms. Though MCA s5 and s6 do allow for the liberty of a person to be restricted they can never deprive that person of their liberty. The next Chapter of this Guide deals with Deprivation of Liberty Safeguards (DOLS).

The MCA is important for staff working with a number of client groups, particularly those with learning disabilities, dementia and brain injuries. Because the MCA defines capacity in relationship to specific decisions it may also apply in particular situations to patients on psychiatric wards.

The terminology used throughout this Chapter to describe someone who lacks capacity is person rather than patient as many of these people will not be hospital in-patients.

Direct quotes in this Chapter from the MCA or its supporting Code of Practice are in italics.

Principles and values within the Act

MCA s1 contains five core principles which are reproduced here in italics with comments on their meaning in **bold** below.

'A person must be assumed to have capacity unless it is established that he lacks capacity' - s1 (2)

It should be presumed that someone has the capacity to make a specific decision unless there is reason to think the person lacks capacity.

'A person is not to be treated as unable to make a decision unless all practicable steps to help him to do so have been taken without success'. - s1 (3)

Anyone working with a person should do as much as they can to assist them make any decision for themselves. Examples of how this can be done are:

- simplifying information
- presenting in non-verbal form (if that helps)
- giving the person time to understand.

'A person is not to be treated as unable to make a decision merely because it is considered to be unwise.' - s1 (4)

Staff should never decide someone lacks capacity because they do not agree with the choice or decision the person wants to make.

'An act done or decision made, under this act for or on behalf of a person who lacks capacity must be done, or made, in the persons best interests'. - s1 (5)

The decision made on someone's behalf must be what the best is for that person.

'Before the act is done, or the decision is made, regard must be had to whether the purpose for which it is needed can be as effectively achieved in a way that is less restrictive of the person's rights and freedom of action'. - s1 (6)

Any act done for, or any decision made on behalf of, someone who lacks capacity should be an option that is less restrictive of their basic rights and freedoms - as long as it is still in their best interests.

Other key principle in the MCA are;

- the MCA is decision-specific i.e the statement 'Mr X or Ms Y lacks capacity is meaningless - the lack of capacity can only relate to a specific matter. Just because someone has a mental disorder or a particular diagnosis does not mean they lack capacity.
- it is possible for somebody to have capacity to make one decision but lack the capacity to make another. It can be said that in general the level of capacity needed to make a simple decision is less than for a more complicated one.
- For some people - especially if they are mentally unwell. - their capacity can fluctuate. If at all possible capacity should be assessed at the point in time when the person is most likely to have capacity. An example is if someone with a diagnosis of dementia has times of day when they are most lucid that is when the assessment should take place. Other factors - the presence of relative or familiarity of venue - can assist in overcoming what may appear to be a lack of capacity.

When to carry out mental capacity assessments

The following guidance is intended to assist those making clinical decisions.

Because the MCA starts with the presumption of capacity there may be circumstances when a mental capacity assessments does not need to be carried out or it may not be in the person's best interests to keep repeating assessments.

General points are:

- with less invasive treatments (e.g psychology or OT interventions) mental capacity assessments may not need to be repeated;
- if mental capacity was assessed in the context of the admission to hospital (and the intended treatment plan) there may not be a need to repeat it if the clinical view is that mental capacity has not changed. If there is no intention to repeat the assessment it could be documented that the previous assessment remains valid. If it remains clear that the person has capacity it could be stated that the presumption of capacity within the MCA rules out the necessity for repeating a MCA assessment;
- as a general principle clinicians should always document something about mental capacity document circumstances in which it is decided not to carry out an assessment.

Specific points are:

- at the point of admission to hospital – and the associated treatment plan – a mental capacity assessment should be carried out on all patients
- if there is a change in circumstances the assessment should be repeated. Examples of such changes are: change in legal status/informal patient wishing to discharge themselves/any significant change in the patient's mental state.

For detained patients capacity should be assessed:

- when the person is first detained;
- after three months of detention;
- If any new medications are commenced which are not on a SOAD certificate
- If covert medication is commenced.

For informal patients capacity should be assessed as best practice:

- at the point of admission for medication to be given;
- repeated every time new medication is given;
- if covert medication is commenced.

Other interventions which an assessment of capacity should be considered are the following:

- when a major treatment intervention is being considered;
- when restraint is needed e.g taking bloods or changing dressings;
- when social care decisions are to be made e.g care package being introduced or moving into a placement;
- when financial decisions need to be made.

Definition of incapacity

The MCA gives a statutory definition for lack of capacity, and these criteria must be fulfilled before staff can make decisions on behalf of someone else.

There is a two-stage test as follows:

The first stage is s2 (1) that the person must be *'unable to make the relevant decision for himself in relation to the matter because of an impairment of, or a disturbance in the functioning of, the mind or brain.'* Note also that s2 (2) says *'it does not matter whether the impairment or disturbance is permanent or temporary'.*

The second stage is to be found in s3 (1) which defines a person as being unable to make a decision if he or she is unable:

- 'to understand the information relevant to the decision'
- 'to retain that information'
- 'to use or weigh that information as part of the process of making the decision' or
- 'to communicate his decision (whether by talking, using sign language or any other means)'.

N.B: if a person is unable to do any one of the four requirements above then they are deemed to lack capacity.

It is suggested that all organisations should have a standardised form on which capacity assessments are recorded. Where a service user has fluctuating capacity it is best practice to attempt to find out what that person's choice or decision is at a time when they have capacity.

Best interests - decisions and choices

If staff or others are making decisions or choices on behalf of a service user establishing what is in that person's 'best interests' is at the heart of the process.

The MCA provides a statutory checklist of factors which need to be considered when making decisions on behalf or someone who lacks capacity. Some of these factors are paraphrased below as being:

- ensuring that options are not being limited because the person lacks capacity
- trying to improve the capacity of the person to make the decision for themselves or
- considering whether or not the person might regain capacity in the future
- considering what their wishes might have been and consulting other people.

It also requires that best interests are considered in a broad sense rather than only focus on the person's medical needs. Examples of broader factors which should be considered are:

- how it will it affect their welfare
- how will it impact on them emotionally
- what impact it will have on their social circumstances.

5.13 of the MCA Code of Practice provides a useful checklist for those responsible for making best interest decisions or choices.

How to make a best interests decision – key principles

Before starting on the process, it is worth remembering the some of the central principles of the Mental Capacity Act. The Mental Capacity Act was brought into force to help empower clients who lack the mental capacity to make decisions, so this means we need to do all we can to help the individual make the decision themselves, but if they are not able to we need to continue putting the client at the centre of decision making. This means taking into account their current and past wishes and choosing the option which will give them the most freedom and rights possible in the light of the risks (least restrictive principle). It means thinking about what is the right thing to do for this particular person (and their family) at this particular time, including any views or advance decisions the person had prior to lacking capacity.

How to make a best interests decision – processes and suggested template

A more formal best interests meeting may be required if the decision is very complex or if there is a dispute about what is in the patient's best interests. If there is a dispute between the clinical team and relatives, then consideration should be made to inviting an independent chair. If an IMCA is involved, they must be present at the meeting.

The following is a suggested outline for the meeting:

1 Record those present at the meeting and the chair.

2 Confirm the decision that is to be made.

3 Confirm the person lacks the capacity to make the decision. The date and record of this capacity assessment should be provided and who carried it out.

4 What is the expressed wish of the person?

The person may not be able to make a capacitous choice, but their current wishes and opinions must be considered and evidence and rationale recorded as to why their view was set aside if their view presents a significant risk to their own best interest or a safeguarding risk.

5 What were the person's previous wishes?

What have they said about the particular circumstances during their life? What are their lifelong values which may be relevant to the decision?

6 Confirm who is the principal decision maker under the MCA.

For medical decisions the principal decision maker would be the consultant, social care decisions e.g funding/commissioning of services the social worker would be the principal decision maker. The decision maker can also be a family member or carer if they are managing the patient's finances.

7 Confirmation that no person present is acting with prejudice.

8 Presentation of information about the person as a person and his or her life.

The purpose of this is so that everyone in the room is able to build up a picture of the person and take this into account when making the decision. Families should be invited to prepare information about the person and their life prior to the meeting and this should be discussed and presented at the meeting. Photographs are often helpful here and should be passed round to everyone present.

9 Presentation of information about the person's condition from their clinical team.

10 Completion of table regarding decision:

This is an opportunity to consult and weigh up risks and benefits in a more formal way and all present should be encouraged to contribute to the table. When making a best interests decision it is important to consider the advantages and disadvantages of both options available and a helpful way of doing this is using the table below. It is important that those present know that they can express anything that they think/feel for the table and that it doesn't have to be "clinically right" or even sensible. Difficult decisions can often lead to irrational thoughts and feelings and it is important that everything is recorded and taken into account. The aim is that all options should be presented and a clear rational recorded as to why each decision was discarded or agreed upon The table can sometimes be helpful visually, if there is a much longer list in one or two of the boxes, it can be a guide for making the decision.

Advantages of alternative A	Disadvantages of alternative A
Advantages of alternative B	Disadvantages of alternative B

1.Each person present to give their decision

Each person after considering all the information presented and opinions expressed at the meeting should give their decision.

Scope of the MCA

A key term within the MCA is 'acts' used to describe interventions which staff working with service users who lack capacity undertake on a daily basis. Examples of such 'acts' are:

- attending to someone's personal care
- providing some form of healthcare treatment
- shopping or paying bills on behalf of someone.

Staff undertaking such tasks would often describe themselves as doing so under their 'duty of care'. The MCA gives protection to the person carrying out the acts.

These interventions are given a statutory authorisation under s5 and it is recognised that for some service users it is not possible to get that person's permission to touch them or to interfere with their property. The need for this authorisation is because it departs from the 'normal' legal requirement which makes it unlawful to touch someone or to interfere with their property without their consent. In legal terms s5 provides protection from liability for the member of staff intervening in that way.

Staff are not expected to do capacity assessments and hold best interests meetings about these matters on a daily basis, as this would clearly be unworkable. For routine decisions, it will be sufficient for the judgements about capacity and best interests to be made and documented as part of the care planning process. This is summarised in 6.25 of the MCA Code in the following way:

'Decisions about a person's care or treatment are often made by a multi-disciplinary team (a team of professionals with different skills that contribute to a person's care), by drawing up a care plan for the person. The preparation of a care plan should always include an assessment of the person's capacity to consent to the actions covered by the care plan, and confirm that those actions are agreed to be in the person's best interests. Healthcare and social care staff may then be able to assume that any actions they take under the care plan are in the person's best interests, and therefore receive protection from liability under section 5. But a person's capacity and best interests must still be reviewed regularly.'

Limits to the scope of the Act

Use of Restraint

Section 6 of the MCA recognises that in some situations it may be necessary for 'restraint' to be used in order for an intervention to be made. The intervention can only be if the person both lacks capacity and if it is believed the intervention is in the person's best interests (see above).

One example of an intervention would be to prevent harm to a person who was running out into the road or trying to hurt themself. Unless it is an emergency it may be that some interventions can be anticipated and the use of restraint should be agreed within the person's care plan.

Another example of the use of restraint might be to prevent a serious deterioration in a person's health. In such cases the use of restraint is lawful providing the restraint is proportionate to the risk of harm presented by the person. In making that judgement both the likelihood and/or the seriousness of the harm need to be assessed. Note that in both these examples the harm is to the person themselves. If the person is likely to harm others staff still have powers under 'common law' to take appropriate and necessary action to prevent them from doing this. Common law is dealt with in Chapter 19 of this Guide.

The amount of restraint used may amount to a restriction of that person's liberty but should never amount to that person being deprived of their liberty. The next Chapter of this Guide deals with Deprivation of Liberty Safeguards.

Other Roles within the MCA

Staff working with any person who lacks capacity need to be aware whether someone has been appointed to make decisions on behalf of that person. The following part of this Chapter summarises these roles.

Donees

While a person has capacity they may have made a Lasting Power of Attorney (LPA), which names people (donees) who have authority to make decisions for them. The LPA has to be made while the person still has capacity, and they have to be over 18 years of age. There are two types of LPA: one to manage personal welfare decisions (including health and residence) and one to manage money and finances. The LPA can specify whether the donees can make decisions separately or whether they have to make them jointly and can also specify which decisions they can or cannot make.

Decisions made by a donee of an LPA have to be made in the person's best interests and they must have regard to the MCA Code of Practice.

Deputies

Deputies are appointed by the Court of Protection to make decisions on behalf of someone who lacks capacity. The Court of Protection can specify which decisions the deputy can make. The deputy also has to act in the person's best interests and must have regard to the MCA Code of Practice.

Staff need to make sure they know whether or not there is an appointed decision-maker (either donee or deputy) and what decisions they are allowed to make. The appointed decision-maker has authority to make those decisions, even if staff do not agree with them.

If staff believe that an appointed decision-maker is abusing their position, and not acting in the best interests of the person, then they should be reported through the Safeguarding Adults procedure. It should also be reported to the Office of the Public Guardian (OPG).

The OPG might refer to the Court of Protection, which has the power to remove the appointed decision-maker and make urgent decisions instead.

Independent Mental Capacity Advocates

The Act requires that an Independent Mental Capacity Advocate (IMCA) is appointed in situations where a person lacks capacity and has no relatives, friends or appointed decision-makers to speak up for them or otherwise safeguard their interests. They are not instructed for every decision, but in significant ones, as follows:

- where a decision needs to be made about serious medical treatment
- long-term admission to a hospital (which will last for more than 28 days) or to a care home (where the admission is to be for more than eight weeks)
- moving to different long stay accommodation.

They are also instructed if there is a safeguarding adults issue, and may be instructed to participate in the care reviews, when there is no one else to represent them. If there is a family but they have no contact, are unable or unwilling to be consulted, or it would not be reasonable to consult them (for example if they lived a very long way away) it may be appropriate to instruct an IMCA. Staff will need to document who they have tried to consult, why it was unsuccessful and why it is reasonable not to continue to attempt to consult them.

Advance decisions

The MCA also allows for advance decisions, which make it possible for a person to refuse a specific treatment. An advance decision has to specify what treatment is being refused, and under what circumstances. If it is valid, then healthcare staff must respect it. If they do not, they could be liable to either civil or criminal action.

In order to be valid and applicable, the advance decision has to meet certain requirements, as follows:

- the person making it is aged 18 or over
- they had the capacity to make the advance decision when they made it
- they now lack capacity to make the decision about their treatment
- they have specified the treatment that is not to be carried out
- they have specified the circumstances in which they do not want to be treated
- they have not withdrawn (either verbally or in writing) the advance decision
- they have not given authority to a donee of a LPA to give or refuse consent to the treatment specified (this authority would need to have been given after the advance decision had been made)
- they have not indicated by their behaviour, or in any other way, that they have now changed their mind about the advance decision
- an advance decision can be valid and applicable, even if it is expressed in layman's terms, rather than medical terms.

S25 (4) (c) of the MCA(c) defines circumstances in which the decision-maker might question the applicability of an apparently valid Advance Decision. These would be if *'there are reasonable grounds for believing that circumstances exist which P did not anticipate at the time of the advance decision and which would have affected his decision had he not anticipated them.'*

It is not possible to make a legally binding advance decision to demand a certain treatment. However, expressions of the patient's preferences should be considered when assessing best interests. If the advance decision involves refusing 'life-sustaining' treatment, then it has to follow certain rules as laid out in the MCA. These are:

- that it is in writing
- that is signed by the person (or under the person's direction if they are unable to sign for themselves and in their presence)
- that it is witnessed and signed by the witness
- there has to be a statement by the person that the refusal of treatment is to apply even if their life is at risk.

An advance decision cannot override any proposed treatment for someone detained under the Mental Health Act (MHA) where the treatment falls within the scope of MHA Part 4. In this sense the MHA can be seen as 'trumping' the MCA. Note however that within the MHA 'capacity thresholds' are of relevance if the proposed treatment is Electro-Convulsive Therapy (ECT) or for patients subject to Community Treatment Orders. More information about the consent to treatment provisions for ECT and CTO are contained respectively in Chapters 10 and 21 of this Guide.

If the person has attempted suicide, has written a note saying they do not wish to be treated and they now lack mental capacity, two matters will need to be considered:

- if they will die without treatment, any advance decision will need to meet the requirements as laid out in the *'advance decision to refuse life-sustaining treatment requirements'* (see above)

- if the treatment is not life-sustaining, and they have not specified the treatment to be refused in their suicide note, this will not meet the requirements of a valid and applicable advance decision. If treatment is specified, the note should only be acted upon if there is evidence that the patient had capacity at the time it was written.

Ill-treatment or neglect

This is dealt with in s44 of the MCA. If a carer, a donee or a deputy ill-treats or willfully neglects a person who lacks capacity, then they can be charged with a criminal offence. If convicted, they can face up to 5 years imprisonment or a fine. Ill-treatment can be broader than physical ill-treatment and need not result in harm. Neglect is not well-defined, but must be willful (which could consist of knowing the correct course of action and choosing not to intervene or having refrained from acting because of not caring about the risk to the person).

The Court of Protection and the Public Guardian

Court of Protection

The Act provides for a new Court of Protection to make decisions in relation to the property, affairs, healthcare and personal welfare of adults (and children in a few cases) who lack capacity. The Court also has the power to make declarations about whether someone has the capacity to make a particular decision.

The Court has the same powers, rights, privileges and authority in relation to mental capacity matters as the High Court. It is a superior court of record and is able to set precedents.

The Court of Protection has the powers to:

- decide whether a person has capacity to make a particular decision for themselves;
- make declarations, decisions or orders on financial or welfare matters affecting people who lack capacity to make such decisions;
- appoint deputies to make decisions for people lacking capacity to make those decisions;
- decide whether an LPA or Enduring Power of Attorney (EPA) is valid; and remove deputies or attorneys who fail to carry out their duties
- hear cases concerning objections to register an LPA or EPA and make decisions about whether or not an LPA or EPA is valid.
- to make declarations a person is deprived of their liberty in a supported living or home setting.

Referring to the Court of Protection

There are also some decisions which will require a ruling from the Court. They are situations considered to be requiring 'serious medical treatment' and are cases involving the following:

- decisions about the proposed withholding or withdrawal of artificial nutrition and hydration from a person in a permanent vegetative state or a minimally conscious state
- cases involving organ or bone marrow donation by a person who lacks capacity to consent
- cases involving non-therapeutic sterilisation of a person who lacks capacity to consent. An example of when a ruling would be needed would be where the proposed intervention would not have an explicit and positive effect on the physical or mental health of the individual.

This list is not exhaustive and other situations such as certain terminations of pregnancy, medical procedures for the purpose of donation to another person, having to use a degree of force to restrain the person, experimental or innovative procedures or those raising ethical dilemmas in an area which is untested will also need a ruling from the Court before they can proceed.

Sometimes it is not possible to get agreement as to what is in the best interests of a person. In these cases, when the decision will have serious consequences for the person, application should be made to the Court of Protection. This must be done through the administrative office for the MCA in the particular organisation.

The Public Guardian

The Office of the Public Guardian (OPG) has a supervisory function in relation to donees and deputies, and also reports to the Court of Protection on matters related to the MCA.

The Public Guardian, supported by the OPG has the following powers:

- setting up and managing a register of Lasting Powers of Attorney (LPA);
- setting up and managing a register of Enduring Powers of Attorney (EPA);
- setting up and managing a register of court orders that appoint Deputies;
- supervising Deputies, working with other relevant organisations (for example, social services, if the person who lacks capacity is receiving social care);
- instructing Court of Protection Visitors to visit people who may lack mental capacity to make particular decisions and those who have formal powers to act on their behalf such as Deputies;
- receiving reports from Attorneys acting under LPAs and from Deputies; and
- providing reports to the Court of Protection, as requested, and dealing with cases where there are concerns raised about the way in which Attorneys or Deputies are carrying out their duties.

The Public Guardian is also personally responsible for the management and organisation of the OPG, including the use of public money and the way it manages its assets. A separate Public Guardian Board publicly scrutinises the work of the Public Guardian and then reports to the Lord Chancellor.

Relationship with the MHA

When a person is detained under the MHA other than section 4, 5, 35, 135, 136 or 37(4) or 45A (5), and they lack capacity, treatment of their mental disorder is under the provisions of the MHA. Even if detained, treatment for a physical disorder is under the MCA.

Chapter 13 of the MHA Code gives guidance as to whether the MCA or MHA should be used. Figure 5 on P106 and Figure 6 on P109 of the Code provide useful tools to apply when thinking whether to use MHA or MCA. The flow charts are replicated at page 170 of this book.

The Public Guardian is also personally responsible for the management and organisation of the OPG, including the use of public money and the way it manages its assets. A separate Public Guardian Board publicly scrutinises the work of the Public Guardian and then reports to the Lord Chancellor.

Relationship with Children Act

Chapter 19 of the Code of Practice provides helpful guidance in relation to Children under the MHA, see also Chapter 26 of the MAZE.

There may be disputes about placement relating to young people aged 16 or 17. The Family Court may transfer these cases to the Court of Protection, depending on circumstances.

A young person under the age of 18 cannot make an advance decision to refuse medical treatment or make a Lasting Power of Attorney

Chapter 24 Deprivation of Liberty Safeguards

Overview

The 2005 Mental Capacity Act (MCA) provides a statutory framework for making decisions in England and Wales for people who lack the capacity to decide matters for themselves.

These decisions range from small ones, for instance what kind of food to request on a menu card to choose to more important decisions, for example whether it is best to remain at home despite increasing frailty. The 2007 Mental Health Act amended the MCA by adding Deprivation of Liberty Safeguards (DOLS).

April 2015 has seen the publication by the Law Society of 'Identifying a deprivation of liberty: a practical guide.' It is recommended that all those involved in issues concerning potential / actual deprivations use this guide.

Why DOLS were introduced

The European Court of Human Rights (ECHR) had identified a gap in English and Welsh Law in the case of HL versus UK - often referred to as the Bournewood Case. In this case the ECHR concluded against the UK government as it decided that HL had been unlawfully deprived of his liberty. It also found that his rights under Article 5 (1) and 5 (4) of the European Convention of Human Rights had been breached.

ECHR Article 5(1) states *'Everyone has the right to Liberty or security of Persons. Nobody shall be deprived of his liberty except in the following cases and in accordance with Procedures prescribed by law'. ECHR Article 5(4) states 'Detainees have a right to speedy access to a court to review the lawfulness of their detention.'*

The safeguards were introduced because decisions about care for an individual who lacks capacity can lead to depriving that person of their liberty in their best interests. It is essential to be sure that the patient (referred to under DOLS as the 'relevant person') has a voice and that the proposed treatment or care is indeed in their best interests and not in the interests of convenience or financial benefit of others however well meaning. These safeguards apply to persons who lack capacity to consent to treatment or care in a hospital or care home, but who are not detained under the Mental Health Act 1983 where their care can only be provided in circumstances amounting to a deprivation of liberty.

The legislation for DOLS consciously did not provide a definition of what a deprivation actually was. The Supreme Court judgement made in 2014 (commonly referred to as the 'Cheshire West case') do now provide a definition. This definition is generally agreed to have lowered the threshold for what a deprivation is and at the time of the publication of this Guide the implications of the rulings are still being worked through by organizations.

Purpose of the safeguards

The safeguards exist to provide a proper legal process and suitable protection in those circumstances where deprivation of liberty appears unavoidable in the person's best interests. The law applies to people 18 and over in England and Wales who lack capacity to give consent to being treated in care homes (A care facility registered under the Care Standards Act 2000) or hospitals, but this huge step can only be justified if it can be shown to be in the person's best interests.

It is important for everyone involved in commissioning or providing care or treatment to try to prevent deprivation of liberty. This could be by modifying the care plans that have been drawn up for that person. If deprivation of liberty is essential to provide necessary care it should be for no longer than is necessary.

Ideally a DOLS authorisation should only be considered in advance of admission to a care home or a hospital if it is anticipated that this is likely to cause a deprivation of liberty. Sometimes authorisations will apply to individuals already resident in such circumstances that amount to a deprivation of liberty. The safeguards do not apply to anyone currently detained under the Mental Health Act (MHA) in a hospital. It is important to note that people under 18, if deprived of a liberty as a result of treatment or care, are covered by the Children Act or the MHA. In all cases it is essential for those staff involved to be clear whether the MHA would be more appropriate than applying for a DOLS order.

The Cheshire West judgement

On 19th March 2014 there was a Supreme Court judgement regarding Deprivation of Liberty which has implications for when it is applied. One of the main conclusions of the ruling is that an incapacitated person may be deprived of their liberty independent of whether or not they object to their living or care arrangements and regardless of the reason or purpose behind their placement. In effect this means that a person may be happy and fully compliant with their care plan and admission to hospital, or their care in the community, but the nature of that care plan means that they are deprived of their liberty. If the patient is deprived of their liberty in hospital (i.e. cannot consent to admission and is under continuous supervision and control and is not free to leave) then the patient cannot be admitted informally and the patient must either be detained in hospital under the MHA or their admission authorised under MCA DOLs.

The Cheshire West 'acid test'

A person is being deprived of their liberty if the following applies.

The person is under continuous supervision and control AND is not free to leave, AND the person lacks capacity to consent to these arrangements.

Implications of the Cheshire West case

The following flow chart suggests how anyone admitted to a mental health unit should be assessed.

Note that – although MCA s1 starts with the presumption of capacity – the expectation is that the person's capacity should be assessed.

Summary of DOLS process

If it is agreed that a DOLS may be occurring the next step is for DOLS form 1 (urgent Authorisation Form) and DOLS form 4 (standard Authorisation Form) to be completed. These will be sent to the relevant local authority 'DOLS Office'. At the time of publication of this Guide an ADASS commissioned DOLS project group has been working on new forms which are now available for use. The project was set up in response to widespread criticism of the existing forms. These forms are available from a number of sources including **www.mental healthlaw.co.uk**

Use of DOLS or the MHA?

This is considered below in the material on the DOLS eligibility assessments.

Summary of the DOLS Processes

The DOLS process involves two key bodies.

Firstly: the Managing Authority i.e. the hospital or care home in which the person is or may be deprived of their liberty. This could be an NHS hospital or the authority responsible for running the hospital, an independent hospital or care home.

Secondly: The Supervisory Body. i.e. the local authority commissioning the care of a person in hospital or the local authority for the area in which the person is normally resident in a registered care home or where the care home is situated. The Managing Authority, having recognised that a DOLS order is required, must request a standard authorisation from the Supervisory Body in advance, if possible, of the deprivation of liberty.

If there is a need for an urgent authorisation this can be granted by the managing authority for a period of 7 days. The period can be extended by the supervisory body for a further 7 days.

The supervisory body must then arrange the assessments for a standard authorisation within a period of 21 days. If all assessments agree the Supervisory body can issue a deprivation of liberty authorisation.

At the heart of the DOLS processes are the following six assessments

Age

This is a check to ensure that the person is 18 years or older. If the individual is discovered to be younger than 18 then the alternative safeguards either of the Children Act or MHA should be followed. This process of age assessment is very straight-forward usually but in some circumstances it is not easy to establish age. The assessor should try to find the age from a source, such as the birth certificate, or any reliable evidence and the assessment must be made to the best of their knowledge and belief if they cannot fully establish the age by document. This assessment can be carried out by anyone whom the supervisory body consider eligible to be a best interest assessor.

No refusals

The purpose of the no refusals assessment is to establish whether the DOLS authorisation would conflict with a previous authority which exists to make decisions for the person. These previous refusals include:

- A valid and applicable advanced decision to refuse treatment;
- An objection by a donee of a registered personal welfare lasting Power of Attorney;
- An incompatible decision by the Court of Protection or an objection by a Court appointed personal welfare deputy.

This no refusal assessment can be carried out by anybody who the supervisory body is satisfied is eligible to be a Best Interest Assessor. If there is such a valid authority, the DOLS assessment cannot proceed.

Mental Capacity

This assessment needs to confirm that the person lacks capacity to decide whether to be admitted to or remain in the hospital or care home. The standard capacity test applies, i.e. the person cannot do one or more of the following things:

- understanding information given to them;
- retain the information long enough to be able to make a decision;
- weigh up the information available in order to make that decision;
- communicate that decision by speech, sign language or other means.

In relation to DOLS this decision is specifically related to deciding whether the person should be accommodated as stated above in a hospital or care home to be given care or treatment.

Sometimes, it may be best for the Mental Capacity assessment to be conducted by a professional who has previous acquaintance with the person being assessed. This is not always possible but any professional qualified to undertake either a Mental Health Assessment or a Best Interest Assessment may assess mental capacity.

Mental Health

A mental health assessment is required to determine if the person concerned is suffering from a mental disorder within the meaning of the MHA. A mental disorder is defined in the MHA as 'any disorder or disability of mind' but for the purposes of DOLS this MHA definition is extended to include people with a learning disability whether or not their disability is associated with abnormally aggressive or seriously irresponsible conduct.

The DOLS mental health assessor does not decide whether the individual requires mental health treatment, but simply confirms that the person has a mental disorder. The assessor also needs to consider what impact there would be on their mental health if they were to be deprived of their liberty. The mental health assessment must be undertaken by a registered medical practitioner who is either s12 approved and has undertaken MCA 2005 DOLS core mental health assessor training, or three years post registration and has completed the full DOLS mental health assessor training.

The mental health assessor can have previous knowledge of the patient but must not have a financial interest in or be related to the individual. The assessor is appointed by the supervisory body and should have relevant experience. It is good practice to consider a doctor who is both eligible and who already knows the relevant person if that would be of benefit. Assessors act as individual professionals and must be indemnified against any liability that might arise in connection with the assessment. Mental Health assessors must report their conclusions to the Best Interest assessor, in particular in relation to the potential effect on the person's mental health.

Eligibility

This assessment considers the person's status or potential status under the MHA. A person is not eligible for DOLS authorisation if they are detained under the MHA or subject to a requirement under the MHA which conflicts with a DOLS authorisation being sought. An example of this might be a s7 guardianship Order imposing conditions of residence. A DOLS authorisation cannot be granted in order to enable a treatment to which the patient objects being provided if he or she meets the criteria to be treated under s2 or s3 of the MHA. The eligibility assessment must be completed by a Mental Health Assessor who is also an s12 approved doctor or by a Best Interest Assessor who is also an Approved Mental Health Professional (AMHP).This is to ensure that the eligibility assessment is carried out by someone who is qualified to make MHA assessments.

The person undertaking the eligibility assessment must be able to decide whether detention under the MHA is more appropriate than a DOLS authorisation. The question of whether to use the MHA or DOLS is a current source of confusion and controversy which is discussed here. . It is recommended that people read Chapter 13 of the MHA Code which deals in depth with the issue. The following material summaries the issue and is based on Chapter 13 of the MHA Code.

Please note it only applies to decisions about admission to an in-patient facility.

Mental Health Act or DOLs- which to use?

Once a patient is identified as being deprived of their liberty, it can be difficult to determine which legal framework should be used to authorise this. This is a very complex area that still requires legal and clinical clarity and is being struggled with on a national level. There are concerns about a new legal gap, where for the same patient, a DOLS Best Interests Assessor recommends detention under the Mental Health Act and the Approved Mental health Professional (MHA assessor) advises use of a DOLS authorisation.

Clinicians have a duty to consider both the MCA/ DOLs and the MHA when a patient is being deprived of their liberty and should never conclude one is better or less restrictive than the other. **Both** should both be considered equally and a decision made, based on the patient and his or her particular situation.

The new Code of Practice does give some guidance regarding this issue part of which is a table as below:

Figure 5: Options grid summarising the availability of the Act and of DoLS

	Individual objects to the proposed accommodation in a hospital for care and/ or treatment; or to any of the treatment they will receive there for mental disorder	Individual does not object to the proposed accommodation in a hospital for care and/or treatment; or to any of the treatment they will receive there for mental disorder
Individual has the capacity to consent to being accommodated in a hospital for care and/or treatment	Only the Act is available	The Act is available. Informal admission might also be appropriate. Neither DoLS authorisation nor Court of Protection order available
Individual lacks the capacity to consent to being accommodated in a hospital for care and/or treatment	Only the Act is available	The Act is available. DoLS authorisation is available, or potentially a Court of Protection order **Note - in practice it is this group where there is most debate about whether to use DoLS or MHA**

© MHA Code of Practice 2015

Remember, as a general rule, the use of the MHA is to ensure a patient **with a psychiatric illness** receives appropriate **assessment and/or treatment.**

MCA/DOLS is more appropriate if the patient/person requires **physical or social care or treatment for a physical disorder.** There are of course, many grey areas, which is why it is important to make decisions on this after multidisciplinary discussion, involving family, carers and advocates, and document clearly the rationale for any decisions made.

Here is a summary of factors to consider when thinking about the most appropriate legal framework:

Factors making MHA more likely to be appropriate

- Patient actively objecting to assessment or treatment of mental disorder
- Patient currently undergoing active treatment plan for mental illness.
- Patient fulfilling criteria for Mental Health Act in terms of risk to health, safety and protection of others
- This particularly applies if client is a risk to others, as the Mental Capacity Act/DOLS is only appropriately used if there are risks to the client and is **NOT** to be used for protection of others.
- Patient has mental capacity to consent to treatment but is objecting. Only the Mental Health Act can be used for clients with mental capacity to consent to hospital admission and treatment.
- Mental Health Act is considered to be least restrictive alternative

Factors making MCA/DOLS more likely

- Client's primary needs are physical healthcare and/or social care needs
- Client is not actively objecting to staying in hospital for psychiatric treatment or assessment.
- Client's active treatment phase is over and they are either awaiting discharge arrangements (e.g. placement) or being cared for in a care home
- Client does not fulfil the criteria for nature and degree in terms of risk to health safety and others, and, in particular, risk to others, as this cannot be covered by Mental Capacity Act.
- Mental Capacity Act is considered to be the least restrictive alternative.

Figure 6: Deciding whether the Act and/or MCA will be available to be used

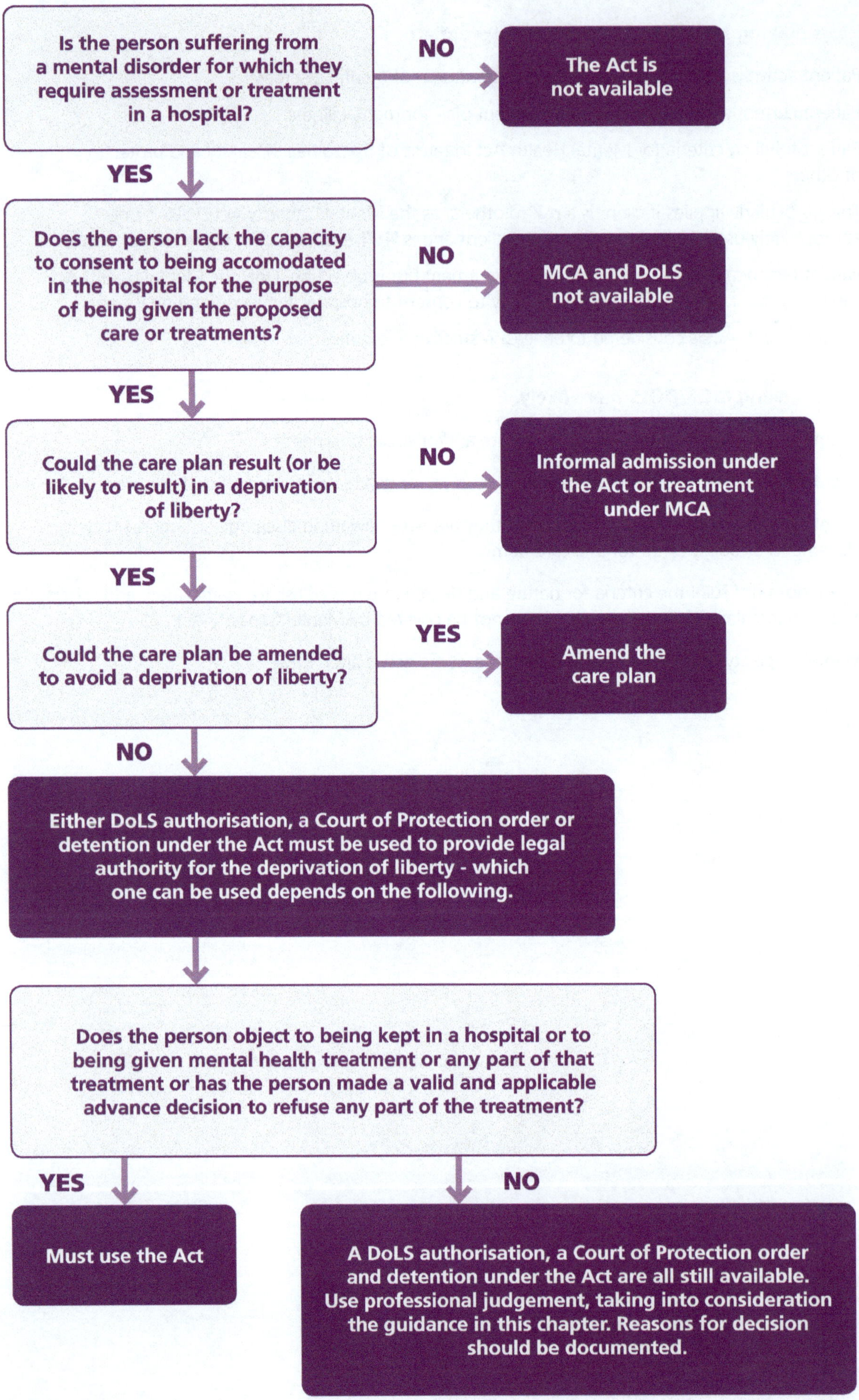

It is important to note that in some cases it may be legally justifiable to use either the Mental Health Act or the Mental Capacity Act/DOLS. It is this, that has led to some patients falling into a "gap" where DOLS assessors recommend MHA detention and Approved Mental Health Professionals favour DOLs authorisation; the result being that the patient is left apparently deprived of their liberty but with no legal framework in place. In these circumstances, it is prudent to bear in mind the central principle of the Mental Capacity Act and decide which Act would be in the patient's best interests. In dealing with any disagreements it is important to stress that the care plan of the patient should continue to be regularly reviewed with the attempt always to reduce the level of restriction.

Best Interests

The MCA uses the principle of best interests in order to facilitate decision making. All decisions made for or on behalf of an individual who lacks capacity must be made in their best interests.

The MCA s4 has a statutory checklist that must be considered in order to make decisions that are in the best interests of the individual which can be paraphrased in the following way:

- decisions about the person's best interests should not be determined by unjustified assumptions about them, such as for example their age, appearance or condition. Relevant circumstances should be taken into account if the decision maker is aware of them
- a decision maker must also consider whether the individual's capacity is likely to be regained and if necessary put off the decision until that point
- it is necessary to encourage the person to participate as fully as possible in any decision affecting him
- those making the decision should not be motivated to bring about the person's death. Decisions about withdrawal of life-saving interventions should be referred to the Court of Protection unless there is a valid written advance decision to refuse treatment
- those deciding must consider as far as possible the person's past and present wishes and feelings in any relevant written statements and the beliefs and values that would influence their decision if they had capacity
- the decision maker must take into account the views of anyone named by the person as someone to be consulted on the matter or someone engaged in caring for the person and must seek the consent of the donee of a valid lasting Power of Attorney granted by the person or any deputy appointed for the person by the Court.

The Best Interest Assessment must be undertaken by someone with the necessary skills, qualifications and experience specified in the regulations who has successfully completed an approved course of training. They must come from the following professions:-social worker, nurse (mental health or learning difficulty), occupational therapist, chartered psychologist or an AHMP. Doctors cannot carry out a DOLS best interest assessment.

The DOLS best interest assessment must establish whether Deprivation of Liberty is occurring or likely to occur and must also consider whether the Deprivation of Liberty is in the best interests of the relevant person and is necessary or proportionate to the likelihood of the person suffering harm (and the seriousness of that harm). Is it likely that harm could occur to the person if the deprivation did not take place? How likely would this be if other care options were available? Could these options be put in place in the future?

The best interest's assessor should seek the views of a range of people connected to the relevant person in order to determine whether the deprivation of liberty would be in the person's best interest. This would include the views of anyone the person has previously identified as someone they want to be consulted, anyone caring for the person or interested in the person's welfare and any donee or deputy who represents the person. The assessor needs to explain all the aspects of the care plan and what it aims to achieve.

They also need to consider the conclusions of the mental health assessor about how the person is likely to be affected in terms of their mental state by being deprived of their liberty. They will then need to offer an independent opinion to the supervisory body about whether there is justification for a Deprivation of Liberty. In addition they should recommend someone to be appointed as the relevant person's representative after the DOLS authorisation is given.

Granting of the authorisation

The supervisory body must consider the views of the best interest assessor and the conditions that they have laid down for the Deprivation of Liberty authorisation. This would include the length of time of the authorisation (up to 1 year).They must then give copies of the authorisation in writing to the managing authority, the relevant person, their representative, an IMCA and every person consulted or named by the best interest assessor and they must appoint a relevant person's representative. The supervisory body does not have to accept the recommendations of the best interest assessor, but if they do not they need to make it clear in communication with service users and carers.

The DOLS assessment process is potentially extremely stressful to service users and carers and it is important that assessors have excellent communication skills as well as their skills of assessment. They will also need to apply medical and legal knowledge in order to complete the assessments and must be familiar with the multi-disciplinary approach in order to be able to engage with the service user and carer and consider their abilities/interests; in addition the staff of the hospital or care home will need to give support to them. Some service users may be anxious or even decline to be assessed. It is important to be able to understand and remove barriers to communication with service users and carers.

The medical assessor must also take into account how the person's mental health will be affected by the Deprivation of Liberty authorisation and to inform the best interest assessor of their conclusions. In order to do this the mental health assessor must have a view about how the service user understands the current situation and how they view the prospect of having their liberty taken from them. They need to consider the specific home or hospital and how the interests of the family and friends will be met because, like the MHA process, a DOLS process could lead to damage and failure in family relationships.

Confidentiality should be respected but at times must be balanced by the need to avoid harm to the relevant person.

Role of the Relevant Persons Representative (RPR)

Following the granting of the authorisation the BIA will select a RPR. This will usually be a family member, friend or carer who is most involved in the care and treatment of the relevant person. The RPR must be willing and able to take on this role.

The Supervisory Body and Managing authority have a responsibility to give support to the relevant person's representative. The relevant person's representative must have good access and sufficient contact with the relevant person. Both managing authority and supervisory body have a duty to inform the representative about sources of support and information including that of an IMCA, but the managing authority need to make it easy for the representative to visit. They must, in addition, keep a record of contact to ensure that there is sufficient contact and inform the supervisory body if this is not the case.

Role of the IMCA

An IMCA needs to be appointed if it becomes apparent during the DOLS assessment that there is no one appropriate to consult other than staff or carers providing care and treatment for the relevant person in a professional capacity or for remuneration. An IMCA must also be involved when a DOLS authorization is in force if the person or their representative asks for access to an IMCA. Therefore, a person who is subjected to a standard DOLS authorisation and their representative must be informed about the IMCA Service because they have the statutory right of access to an IMCA.

IMCA's have the right to make submissions to the supervisory body and also to give information to any DOLS assessor carrying out a review. They can represent the person in any reviews or challenges that they might make about to the authorisation. They must also assist the person and their representative in understanding the DOLS process and must receive copies of authorisations. They are among the group of people who can apply to the Court of Protection if necessary.

Court of Protection

A new Court of Protection was established under the 2005 MCA. The Court offers an impartial point of referral for all cases under dispute. A Court of Protection can decide whether a person has capacity to make a particular decision for themselves. They can also make declarations, decisions or orders on financial and welfare matters affecting people who lack capacity to make such a decision. They appoint deputies, decide whether an Enduring Power of Attorney or Lasting Power of Attorney is valid and can remove deputies or attorneys who fail in their duties.

There is usually a fee for applications to the Court. A relevant person, or someone acting on their behalf, can apply to the Court of Protection before a decision has been made about a DOLS authorisation. This application can be related to whether the person has capacity or whether an act is lawful. A Court of Protection will decide whether to consider such an application.

An application to the Court of Protection can also be made after a standard authorisation is granted. This can be made by the person or anyone acting on their behalf, for example a donee or a deputy. This application would be related to the qualifications of a DOLS, the period of the authorisation, purpose or condition. It is however important to try and resolve things informally before referring to the expensive Court. The Court can vary or terminate the order or direct the supervisory body in the case of a standard authorisation or a managing authority in the case of an urgent authorisation to do so. Only the Court of Protection can authorise deprivation of liberty in other than a hospital or care home setting, for example in the person's own home.

Court Appointed Deputy

The powers of the deputy to make certain decisions for which a person lacks capacity will be set out in the relevant court order. Usually this is in relation to property and finance rather than a personal welfare order and any appointment of a personal welfare deputy by the Court is likely to be time-limited and with circumscribed powers. Deputies have to be 18 or over and of good character with appropriate skills and competence. They cannot make decisions if the person concerned has the capacity to make the relevant decision. They must always act in the person's best interest and cannot prevent contact with specified individuals.

DOLS Authorisations - Responsibilities of the Managing Authority Once In Place

The managing authority has a duty to monitor all cases to see if any circumstances have changed relating to the individual. A clear and precise care plan including responsibilities for monitoring must be set out. This must also make clear the circumstances in which a review is to be carried out. The managers must explain the process and must facilitate contact between the person and their representative. They must always ensure that all conditions are met. The managing authority should undertake a review at any time if the individual's circumstances change - for example if the person regains capacity.

DOLS Authorisations - Responsibilities of the Supervisory Body Once In Place

The supervisory body is responsible for undertaking reviews requested by the managing authority, by the relevant person or their representative, for example if the person no longer meets the requirements for the DOLS authorisation. The supervisory body must inform all relevant people and make sure the individual's best interests are being monitored by a representative. It is important to note an authorisation only permits; it does not indicate a person must be deprived of their liberty.

Review of an Authorisation

The supervisory body, on receiving a request for review from an involved party, must decide if any of the qualifying requirements needs to be reviewed. (A review application from a Managing Authority will always lead to a full review) If none need to be reviewed no further action is required.

A separate review assessment must be considered for each requirement needing a review. This must be recorded, along with the reasons for the decision. The supervisory body can simply vary the conditions if it is the best interest assessment alone that has been changed or if there is anyone contesting the condition. However, if there is a significant change in any other requirement or to the best interest assessment new assessments must be obtained.

Re-Application of an Authorisation

If the Managing Authority feels that a person still needs to be deprived of their liberty when an authorisation is due to end, they will need to request a further standard authorisation that will begin immediately after the current authorisation expires. The managing authority must apply in advance to the supervisory body as part of good care planning. The Code of Practice for DOLS suggests that this application should not be applied too far in advance.

Once underway, the process for re-application is the same as the process for that of obtaining an original authorisation and the same assessment process must take place.

Presumption of capacity

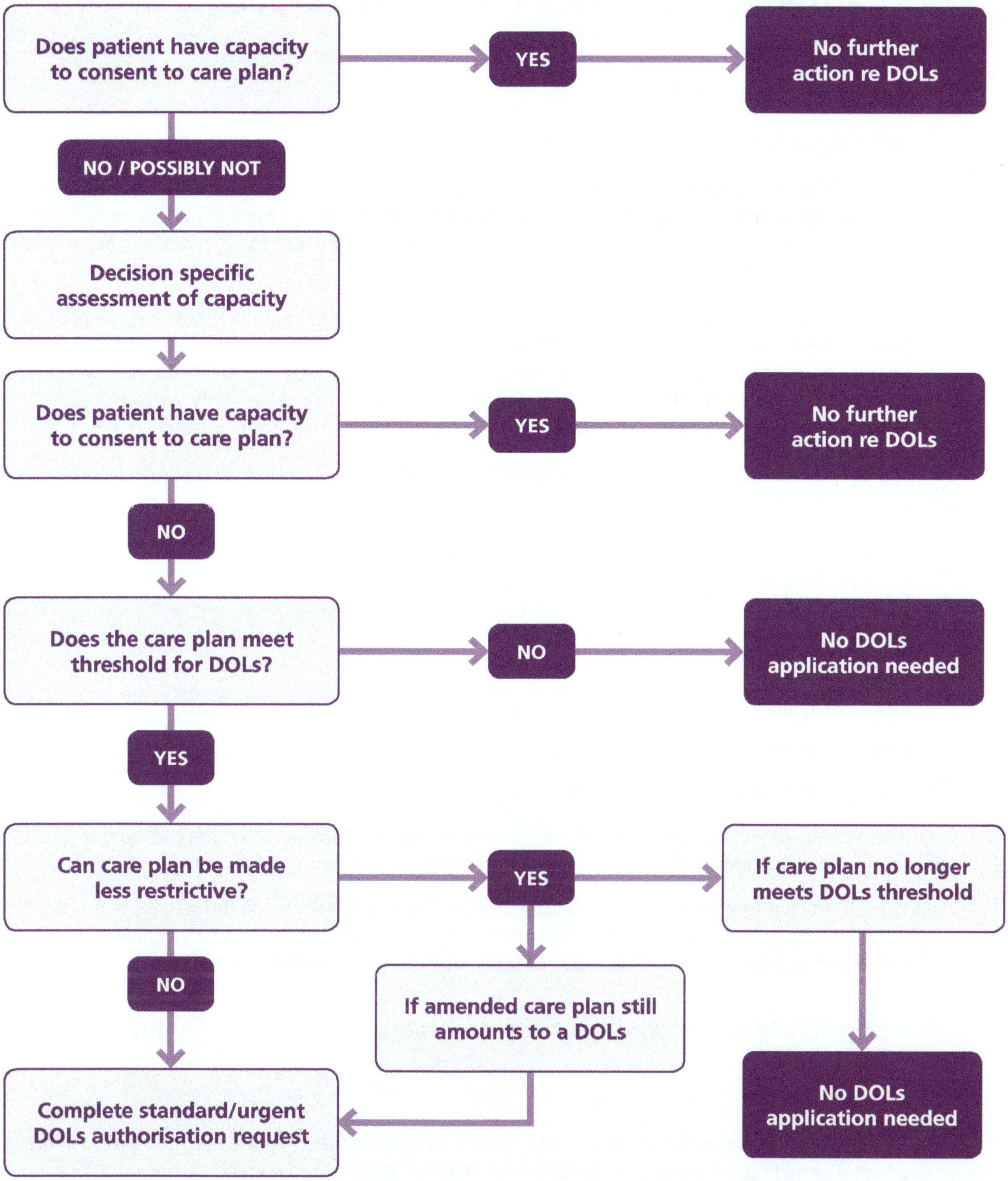

Part Six Specialist Areas

Chapter 25 MHA Part 3 - Forensic Sections

Overview

This chapter concludes with a flow chart summarising the main part 3 section

Part 3 of the Mental Health Act runs from s35 to s55 and provides options for the assessment and treatment of people who are being dealt with at varying stages within the criminal justice system. The sections enable people who are believed to be mentally disordered to be transferred from either prison or court to hospitals.

Forensic sections operate in a very different way to Part 2 civil sections both in terms of the origins of the detention and the procedures, which follow the patient's arrival in hospital. The creation of the Ministry of Justice (MOJ) in 2007 means that body now deals with aspects of MHA Part 3 previously dealt with by the Home Office. At the same time the role of the Home Secretary was replaced by the role of Secretary of State for Justice who is referred to in this chapter as the Secretary.

This chapter deals with the main Part 3 sections which are:

- s35
- s36
- s37 or s37/41
- s38
- s45A
- s47 or s47/49
- s48 or s48/49
- s41 (conditionally discharged patients).

It also covers the role of the Mental Health Casework Section (MHCS) within the MOJ and the key forms and documents staff who work with restricted patients need to be aware of.

The PPMHG has been formed by the merged former Mental Health Unit and the Public Protection Unit. The final part of the chapter deals with the Domestic Violence (Crime and Victims) Act 2004 including the extension of victims' rights introduced in the 2007 MHA amendments.

Section 35 Remand to hospital for assessment

Purpose of s35

This section is an alternative to remanding a person in custody for a medical report in circumstances where it would not be practicable to obtain the report if they were remanded on bail.
Home Office Circular No.71 from 1984 says s35 *'provides an alternative to remanding the accused person in custody for a medical report in circumstances where it would not be practicable to obtain the report if he were remanded on bail (for instance, if he decided to break a condition of bail that he should reside at a hospital, the hospital would be unable to prevent him from discharging himself)'.*

It is not necessary to establish a link between the person's mental disorder and the alleged offence.

Legal Criteria for s35

The court is satisfied on the written or oral evidence of an Approved Clinician (who must be s12 approved) that there is reason to suspect that the accused person is suffering from mental disorder. The court must also be satisfied that the patient will be admitted to hospital within seven days of the date of remand.

If the patient has learning disabilities their disability must be a mental disorder *'associated with abnormally aggressive or seriously irresponsible conduct'* (see Chapter One of this guide).

Implementation of s35

Section 35 is instigated either by a Crown Court or Magistrates' Court.

If implemented by a Crown Court it could be applied to someone awaiting trial for an offence which is punishable by imprisonment. This could include the situation where the trial process has begun but not yet been completed.

If implemented by a Magistrates' Court it could be applied in one of two sets of circumstances.

- Where the person had been convicted of an offence punishable on summary conviction with imprisonment.
- Where the person had been charged (but not convicted) of an offence punishable by imprisonment and the Court was satisfied that the person 'did the act'.

Section 35 paperwork and rights leaflets

The requirement is the remand order issued by the Court (which follows the recommendation made by one s12 doctor).

The rights leaflet for this section is **S35**.

Length of s35

The power to detain lasts initially for up to 28 days. If more time is needed to complete the assessment the Court can authorise further periods of 28 days detention but the maximum period of detention can never exceed 12 weeks in all. Further periods of remand (after the first 28 days) may only take place if it appears to the Court on the oral or written evidence of the patient's RC that more time is needed to complete the assessment. The power of further remanding the person may be exercised by the court in the patient's absence providing they are legally represented and the representative is given the opportunity to be heard.

Treatment under s35

Patients detained under s35 are not subject to Part 4 of the Act. If treatment is to be given for the patient's mental disorder it can only be given with the patient's consent or via one of the following methods:

- for someone with capacity under 'common law'
- for someone lacking capacity possibly using s5 or s6 of the MCA
- by 'dual detention' where the patient is concurrently detained under either s2 or s3.

Appeal Rights against s35

There are no rights of appeal to either the Tribunal or Hospital Managers against s35. However a patient detained under s35 can commission an independent psychiatric report at their own expense and apply to the Court for their remand to be terminated.

Leave of Absence for s35

It is not possible for either the Court or the patient's RC to grant leave of absence.

Absence without Leave for s35

If the person absconds they may be arrested without a warrant by any police officer and then brought before the Court that remanded them.

Outcome of s35

There are two possible outcomes to the use of s35.

- The conclusion reached by the patient's RC is that the person is not suffering from a mental disorder within the meaning of the Act, in which case the person will resume being dealt with using the normal powers of the Court. Note this conclusion could also be reached as a result of an independent medical report submitted by the patient.
- The conclusion reached is that the person is suffering from a mental disorder within the meaning of the Act, in which case detention under s36 or s37 could follow. These sections are dealt with below.

Section 36 Remand to hospital for treatment

Purpose of s36

Instead of transferring an un-sentenced prisoner to hospital under s48 s36 gives the option for a Crown Court to remand a patient to hospital for the purpose of treating the patient's mental disorder. Paragraph 36 of Home Office Circular No.71/1984 says that - *'where the need for treatment is urgent and an appearance before the court is not due in the immediate future'* - s36 is a preferable option to using s48.

A Magistrates Court cannot instigate s36.

Legal Criteria for s36

The Court must be satisfied on the written or oral evidence of two Approved Clinicians (one of whom must be s12 approved) that the person is suffering from mental disorder of a nature or degree which makes it appropriate for him to be detained in hospital for medical treatment, and that appropriate medical treatment is available for him/her.

If the patient has learning disabilities their disability must be a mental disorder *'associated with abnormally aggressive or seriously irresponsible conduct'* (See Chapter One of this guide).

Implementation of s36

There are two ways in which this section can be implemented.

- Where the patient is in custody awaiting trial by a Crown Court. The offence concerned must be punishable with imprisonment.
- Where the patient's trial has begun and they are in custody during that period.

It is not necessary to establish a link between the person's assessed mental disorder and the alleged offence. The Court must be satisfied that the patient will be admitted to hospital within seven days of the remand.

Section 36 paperwork and rights leaflets

The requirement is the remand order issued by the Crown Court which follows the recommendation of two doctors (one of whom must be s12 approved).

The rights leaflet for this section is **S36**.

Length of s36

The power to detain lasts initially for 28 days. Further periods of 28 days are possible with no more than 12 weeks in all. These further periods of detention depend on the written or oral evidence from the patient's RC to the Court that such a further remand is warranted.

The power of further remanding the patient may be exercised by the Court in their absence if they are legally represented and their representative is given the opportunity to be heard.

Treatment under section 36

Patients detained under s36 are subject to Part 4 of the Act.

Appeal Rights against s36

There are no rights of appeal to either the Tribunal or Hospital Managers against s36. However a patient detained under s36 can commission an independent psychiatric report at their own expense and apply to the Court for their remand to be terminated.

Leave of absence for s36

It is not possible for either the Court or the patient's RC to grant leave of absence.

Absence without Leave for s36

If the person absconds they may be arrested without a warrant by any police officer and then brought before the Court that remanded him or her.

Outcome of s36

There are two possible outcomes to the use of s36:

- If the conclusion is reached by the patient's RC that the person is not suffering from a mental disorder within the meaning of the Act, in which case the person will resume being dealt with using the normal powers of the court. Note this conclusion could also be reached as a result of the independent medical report submitted by the patient.
- If the conclusion is reached that the person is suffering from a mental disorder within the meaning of the Act, in which case detention under s37 could follow. This section is dealt with below.

Section 37 Hospital Order

Purpose of s37

This section enables an offender to be admitted to a hospital which has consented to admit them. This section can be instigated either by a Crown Court of a Magistrates' Court. This section directs the offender to a named hospital which has agreed to take them.

It is an alternative to a penal disposal for offenders who are found to be suffering from mental disorder at the time of sentencing. No causal relationship has to be established between the offender's mental disorder and their criminal activities.

Once in hospital s37 runs like s3 in all ways except for appeal rights which are dealt with below.

Legal Criteria for s37

The criteria are that the offender is suffering from mental disorder which is of a nature or degree which makes it appropriate for them to be detained in hospital for treatment and that appropriate medical treatment is available for him/her.

The court also needs to believe that in all the circumstances of the case that the most suitable disposal of the case is to use s37. The meaning of circumstances includes the nature of the offence and the character and antecedents of the offender.

If the patient has learning disabilities their disability must be a mental disorder *'associated with abnormally aggressive or seriously irresponsible conduct'* (See Chapter One of this guide).

Implementation of s37

Either a Magistrates' or Crown Court can implement s37. Written medical recommendations must be provided to the Court by two doctors one of whom must be s12 approved. The patient must be admitted to the named hospital within 28 days of the Order being made, or the order will expire.

Section 37 paperwork and rights leaflets

The requirement is the Court Order (which follows the recommendation of two doctors one of whom must be s12 approved).

The rights leaflet for this section is **S37**.

Length of s37

The length of s37 is for up to six months and it can be renewed for a period of up to six months by the patient's RC. Subsequent renewals would be for up to a year at a time. The renewal processes are the same as for s3 and are dealt with in Chapter 12 of this Guide.

Treatment under section 37

The treatment rules are the same as for s3. Note that the calculation of the three month period (see page 26) is from when the patient is admitted to hospital rather than from when the court order began. This is because a patient in prison is not covered by Part 4 of the MHA.

Appeal Rights against s37

The patient can appeal against the Order to a Court within 21 days of the order being made. The appeal would be to a Crown Court if a Magistrates' Court made the original order and the Court of Appeal if the Crown Court made the order. Patients admitted under s37 should be given both the leaflet **Appeals** and the S37 leaflet.

A patient under s37 can appeal to the Hospital Managers. The patient cannot appeal to the Tribunal during the first six months but can appeal during the second six months of the section if it has been renewed by their RC.

During subsequent periods of yearly renewals the patient has one right of appeal to the Tribunal during each year.

Leave of absence for s37

The RC may grant leave as for s3. The Court does not have to be informed.

Absence without Leave for s37

As for Section 3.

Outcome of Section 37

The patient may be discharged from detention by the RC, the Hospital Managers or the MHT. The Court which ordered the s37 does not need to be informed that the patient has been discharged. The patient's RC also has the option of making the patient subject to CTO.

The patient is entitled to s117 aftercare.

The patient's nearest relative has no powers of discharge. The nearest relative's right to make application to the Tribunal is dealt with in Chapter 13 of this Guide.

Section 37(4)

This section enables either a Crown Court or Magistrates' Court to place a person under s7 guardianship. If this is done the Court has no further involvement in the case. guardianship is dealt with in Chapter 22 of this Guide.

Section 38 Interim Hospital Order

Purpose of s38

When a person is convicted by a Court, but not yet sentenced, the Court may make this order to assess the patient for mental disorder; this is to see whether the person should be sentenced to hospital.

It is used to evaluate the person's response to hospital treatment without any irrevocable commitment on either side to this method of dealing with the person if it should prove unsuitable.

Legal Criteria for s38

The person is suffering from mental disorder and there is reason to suppose that the mental disorder is such that it may be appropriate for an s37 to be made.

Implementation of s38

The Court has to be satisfied by the AC who would have overall responsibility for the case that they will be admitted to hospital within 28 days of the order. Either a Crown Court or the Magistrates' Court can implement s38.

The Court has to be satisfied on the written or oral evidence of two AC's (one of whom must be s12 approved, and one who must be on the staff of the hospital specified in the order). Both doctors can be from the same hospital or one could be both s12 approved and on the hospital staff with a second recommendation from an external doctor.

Section 38 paperwork and rights leaflets

The paperwork for this section is the order issued by the Crown Court or the Magistrates' Court.

The rights leaflet for this section is **s38**.

Length of s38

This allows for the detention of the patient for an initial period of 12 weeks maximum with further periods of 28 days at a time but no more than twelve months in all.

Treatment under section 38

Patients detained under s38 are subject to Part 4 of the Act.

Appeal Rights against s38

There are no appeal rights either to the Hospital Managers or the Tribunal. As s38 is a form of sentence the patient can appeal against it to either the Crown Court or Court of Appeal.

Leave of Absence for s38

Leave of Absence cannot be granted by the patient's RC without prior permission from the court.

Absence Without Leave for s38

If the person is AWOL they may be arrested without a warrant by any police officer and then brought before the Court that made the order. The police should be contacted immediately the patient is AWOL.

Outcome of s38

The patient's RC has no power to discharge. The Court which made the order can end it at any time. One reason for ending the section could be on the basis of written or verbal evidence from the patient's RC which might lead to the Court deciding to deal with the patient in some other way.

The Court has the power to renew this section or to convert it to s37. This can happen in the absence of the offender if they are legally represented and that representative is given the opportunity to be heard.

Section 37/41 Hospital Order with restriction

Purpose of s37/41

When an s37 hospital order (see above) is made the Judge has the option of also imposing an s41 Restriction Order. This would be referred to as an s37/41. The Restriction Order means that the MOJ are responsible for granting leave and allowing discharge (apart from a Tribunal discharge). Only a Crown Court can make a Restriction Order. A Magistrates' Court cannot make a Restriction Order but s43 (1) does give a Magistrates' Court the power to commit an offender to the Crown Court with a view to that Court making the order.

Legal Criteria for s37/41

S41 (1) states that a Restriction Order is 'for the protection of the public from serious harm.'

In reaching their decision the Court should have 'regard to the nature of the offence, the antecedents of the offender and the risk of him committing further offences if set at large.'

Implementation of s37/41

Section 37/41 directs the admission of a patient to a named hospital which has agreed to the admission. The Court that makes the order is responsible for ensuring that hospital has the level of security needed in the case of the particular offender. Admission to the named hospital must be within 28 days of the Restriction Order being made.

Two medical recommendations must be provided, one of which must be from a s12 doctor. At least one of the two doctors must give evidence to the Court.

Section 37/41 paperwork and rights leaflet

This consists of the Court Order itself and a letter from the Secretary of State to the hospital which explains the restrictions imposed by the Court.

The rights leaflet is **S37/41**.

Length of s37/41

Prior to an amendment introduced to the MHA in 2007, s41 orders could be either time-restricted or without limit of time. Since that amendment all new orders are without limit of time. With the exception of the small number of time-limited restriction orders made before this amendment came in, the authority for detention does not end at a particular point in time. Therefore no processes are needed for renewing detention under s37/41.

Treatment under s37/41

As with a Section 3, the three month treatment period begins when the patient is admitted to hospital.

Appeal Rights against s37/41

A patient can apply to the MHT after the first six months of their detention. There is no bar to a Managers' hearing being arranged for a s37/41 patient but the Managers can only exercise their s23 powers of discharge with the authority of the Secretary of State for Justice (see Chapter 16).

Leave of Absence for s37/41

The restrictions do not permit the RC to grant leave or transfer the patient without the consent of the Ministry of Justice (MOJ). Requests for leave of absence transfer or discharge should be sent to the MOJ by the RC.

The RC will decide on the degree of supervision the person needs within the hospital and its grounds. The RC is permitted to grant 'ground leave' only within the grounds of the ward where the patient is detained. Any leave outside that ward or its grounds requires MOJ approval. Organisations need to clarify the definition of hospital grounds for their sites. This should be included in local policies which should be developed in conjunction with the MOJ.

Absence without Leave for s37/41

If a restricted patient is AWOL the MOJ and the local police should be informed as soon as possible. When the patient returns both the MOJ and the police should be informed of their return.

Outcome of s37/41

A Restriction Order can be ended at any time by the Secretary. If this happens from that point onwards the patient is detained under s37 only.

The patient's RC does not have the power to discharge a patient from s37/41 unless the Secretary expressly authorises it. For Hospital Managers powers in relation to s37/41, see Chapter 16.

The patient's nearest relative has no powers to discharge a patient from this section. The MHT has the power to grant either an absolute or conditional discharge. Information about conditionally discharged patients can be seen later in this chapter.

The RC has a duty to keep under review the suitability of discharge for a restricted patient.

The RC must report at least annually to the Secretary on each case for which they are responsible (the annual statutory report) and ideally address a checklist of points prepared by the MOJ.

Note also that the patient is entitled to s117 aftercare.

Section 45A Hospital Direction

Purpose of s45A

This section enables the Crown Court to sentence an offender to spend time both in prison and in hospital which is why the section is often referred to as a 'hybrid order'. The direction always begins with the convicted offender being directed to go to a hospital.

While in hospital the patient's RC has the option of seeking to transfer the patient to prison if he or she believes the patient no longer needs treatment or treatment is no longer beneficial. The decision at any point to transfer the patient to prison is made by the Secretary of State for Justice and may also happen following the recommendation of the Tribunal.

It is possible for the patient to spend the whole period of their sentence in hospital rather than in prison.

This sentencing option is only available where the offence is one which does not have a sentence fixed in law. The option to return the patient to prison is only available until the sentence runs out.

This section is always accompanied by an s45B limitation direction which operates in the same way as s41 (see above).

Guidance on possible uses of this power is contained in Home Office Circular No.52/1997.

Criteria for s45A

The criteria are that the offender is suffering from mental disorder which is of a nature or degree which makes it appropriate for them to be detained in hospital for treatment and that appropriate medical treatment is available for them.

If the patient has learning disabilities their disability must be a mental disorder *'associated with abnormally aggressive or seriously irresponsible conduct'* (See Chapter One of this guide).

Implementation of s45A

The law requires the Judge always to have first considered the use of s37. Evidence needs to be presented (either verbally or in writing) from two doctors (one of whom must be s12 approved) that the offender meets the legal criteria described above. The offender must be admitted to hospital within 28 days of them being sentenced.

Length of s45A

The length of this section is determined by the Court.

Treatment under s45A

The treatment rules are the same as for s3. Note that the calculation of the three month period (see page 26) is from when the patient is admitted to hospital.

Appeal rights against s45A

The patient has one right of appeal to the MHT during the second six months of the order and one appeal during each subsequent twelve month period.

Leave of Absence for s45A

The restrictions do not permit the RC to grant leave or transfer the patient, without the consent of the Ministry of Justice (MOJ). Requests for leave of absence transfer or discharge should be sent to the MOJ by the RC.

Absence without Leave for s45A

If a restricted patient is AWOL the MOJ and the local police should be informed as soon as possible. When the patient returns both the MOJ and the police should be informed.

Outcome of s45A

If the patient is in prison when the sentence ends both the hospital direction (s45A) and the limitation direction (s45B) ends. If however the patient is in hospital when this happens he or she becomes subject to s37 (without restrictions).

Note that the patient is entitled to s117 aftercare and CTO is an option available to the RC when considering discharge.

Section 47 Transfer of sentenced prisoners to hospital

Purpose of s47

This section is when the Secretary directs the transfer of a prisoner suffering from mental disorder to a hospital which has agreed to admit the patient. The Secretary may apply special restrictions (s49) to the direction which happens in the vast majority of cases. The Secretary can at any time order the person back to prison.

Legal Criteria for s47

The Secretary of State must be satisfied the prisoner is suffering from a mental disorder and that the nature or degree of that disorder makes it appropriate for them to be detained in hospital for treatment and that appropriate treatment is available.

If the patient has learning disabilities their disability must be a mental disorder *'associated with abnormally aggressive or seriously irresponsible conduct'* (See Chapter One of this guide).

Most patients admitted to hospital under s47 also have an s49 Restriction Order attached. The criteria for making an s49 Order are to be found in s41 (see above).

Implementing s47

Two medical recommendations are required, one of which must be by a s12 approved doctor. The medical officer of the prison, in consultation with the prison governor, makes the application to the Secretary for the transfer to take place. It is the responsibility of the medical officer in the prison to arrange for the necessary medical assessments by the two doctors.

Admission to the named hospital must be within 14 days of the transfer direction. The order ceases after this period if admission to hospital has not happened and a new s47 direction would be necessary.

Length of s47

The length of s47/49 is as long as the Restriction Order is in place. The date that the Restriction Order ends is the same date on which the sentence ends.

Treatment under s47

Patients detained under s47 are subject to Part 4 of the MHA.

Appeal Rights against s47

The patient can apply to the MHT immediately after arrival at hospital and then yearly.

Section 47 paperwork and rights leaflet

This consists of the order (following the recommendations of two doctors one of whom must be s12 approved). If accompanied by s49 the paperwork includes the transfer direction with the restrictions issued by the MOJ.

The patient rights leaflet is **S47** (if no restrictions are attached) or **S47/49** (if restrictions are attached).

Leave of absence for s47

Leave of absence can only be granted by the MOJ.

Absence without Leave for s47

The MOJ and local police should be informed immediately if a patient is AWOL. When the patient returns both the MOJ and local police should be informed.

Outcome of s47

Detention under s47 without restrictions has the same effect as a Hospital Order.

Most patients admitted to hospital under s47 also have an s49 Restriction Order attached to the s47. The effect of the s49 Restriction Order means neither the patient's RC nor the Hospital Managers (following a hearing) can discharge the patient without the consent of the Secretary. See Chapter 16 regarding discharge by Hospital Managers. The patient's nearest relative has no powers to discharge from this section.

Where the RC (or MHT) believes the offender no longer needs treatment in hospital, or that no effective treatment can be given, the Secretary of State for Justice can choose to release the patient on parole or require them to return to prison or take no action.

If the patient is in hospital on the date on which they could be released from prison the patient does not become an informal patient who would be able to decline treatment and/or leave hospital. From this point they become a 'notional s37 patient.' Though this term is not to be found within the MHA it is commonly used and is helpful as any patient in this category is treated from that point onwards as if they were on an s37 (without restrictions).

If the patient becomes a 'notional s37' the rights leaflet is **EndRes**.

If the patient is under either an s47 without restriction or becomes a notional s37 patient he or she is entitled to s117 aftercare and CTO would be a discharge option for the patient's RC.

Section 48 Transfer of un-sentenced prisoners to hospital

Purpose of s48

This section enables an un-sentenced prisoner to be transferred to hospital to receive treatment.

Legal Criteria for s48

These are the same as for s47 (see above) with the additional requirement that 'he is in urgent need of such treatment.'

If the patient has learning disabilities their disability must be a mental disorder 'associated with abnormally aggressive or seriously irresponsible conduct' (See Chapter One of this guide).

Implementation of s48

The medical officer at the prison in consultation with the prison governor should arrange for the necessary medical assessments and inform the Secretary. Admission must be within 14 days of the warrant.

On return to court for final sentencing the order will cease to have effect and would be followed by sentencing to prison or possibly detention under s37 or s37/41. If, prior to the patient's next Court appearance, the RC decides the patient does not require treatment for mental disorder the Secretary should be informed and arrangements will be made for their removal from hospital.

Section 48 paperwork and rights leaflet

This consists of the order (following the recommendations of two doctors one of whom must be s12 approved). If accompanied by **s49** the paperwork includes the transfer direction with the restrictions issued by the MOJ.

The patient rights leaflet is **S48** (if no restrictions are attached) or **S48/49** (if restrictions are attached).

Appeal Rights against s48

The patient has a right of appeal to the MHT once in the first six months. Subsequently the patient has one right of appeal during the second six months and subsequent appeals yearly.

Leave of Absence for s48

Leave of absence can only be granted by the MOJ.

Absence without Leave for s48

The MOJ and local police should be informed immediately if a patient is AWOL.
When the patient returns both the local police and MOJ should be informed.

Outcome of s48

There are a number of ways in which this section can end;

- when Court proceedings are completed in the case concerned
- where the patient had been remanded into custody by a Magistrates' Court and that period of remand ended. Note this would not apply if following a period of remand the patient was then committed into the custody of the Crown Court
- if the patient is discharged by the MHT. If this happens the patient resumes being under the criminal justice system and it would be for the Court to decide what happens next
- if the patient's RC reports to the MOJ that the patient no longer requires treatment or that effective treatment can no longer be given. This means that the patient resumes being under the criminal justice system and it would be for the Court to decide what happens next

Note the entitlement to s117 aftercare applies irrespective of whether the s48 is accompanied by a transfer direction.

If the patient is under either an s47 or s48 without restriction they are entitled to s117 aftercare and CTO would in time be a discharge option for the patient's RC.

Conditionally discharged patients - s41

A conditionally discharged patient is someone who was detained under s37/41 where either the MOJ or the MHT have 'conditionally discharged' them.

This means that the s37 is ended but the s41 remains in place. Such patients normally have conditions set by the MOJ (such as seeing their Consultant and Social Supervisor regularly). If these conditions are broken the s41 means that the person can be recalled by the MOJ to hospital where they revert to being under s37/41.

The conditions imposed upon a patient may vary but can include the following:

- requiring the person to live at a particular place
- requiring the person to receive particular treatment (though the person's consent is always required for that)
- requiring the person to keep appointments with their RC and/or their Social Supervisor and to grant access to them.

Conditionally discharged restricted patients (s41 only) may apply to an MHT twelve months after their conditional discharge and every two years thereafter, for an absolute discharge.

MHA PT 3 SUMMARY OF FORENSIC SECTIONS

ARREST (AWAITING TRIAL)

SECTION 35

Remand to hospital for report on mental condition

Initially up to 28 days renewable up to 12 weeks maximum

OR

SECTION 36

Remand to hospital for treatment

Initially up to 28 days renewable up to 12 weeks maximum

COURT (AWAITING TRIAL)

SECTION 38

Interim hospital order to evaluate response to hospital treatment

Intially up to 12 weeks with further periods of 12 weeks maximum but no more than 12 months in all

OR

SECTION 48/49

Unsentenced prisoner M of J manages the s49 Restriction Order)

SENTENCE

SECTION 37

Hospital Order (broadly the same as s3 following hospital admission)

OR

SECTION 37/41

Hospital Order with restriction direction for more serious offences. M of J manages the s41 Restriction Order

PRISON

SECTION 47/49

Transfer direction for sentenced prisoner. M of J manages the s49 Restriction Order

OR

SECTION 36

If patient is in hospital at point that EDR happens becomes a **notional s37**

Recall of conditionally discharged patients

Section 42 deals with the processes by which a conditionally discharged patient is recalled to hospital. A Recall Order by the MOJ entitles the police to retake the patient and bring them to the hospital.

If a patient is recalled to hospital the MOJ must refer his/her case to a MHT within one month of their being readmitted to hospital. When such a patient is recalled to hospital the original s37/41 comes back into force on the original date. The patient is liable to the three month treatment rule from the date of re-admittance.

Reasons for recall

The reasons for recall are not defined within the Act. Paragraph 71 of Supervisions and After-Care of Conditionally Discharged Patients - Notes for the Guidance of Social Supervisors' says *'it is not possible to specify all the circumstances in which the Home Secretary may decide to exercise his power (under this provision) to recall to hospital a conditionally discharged patient, but in considering the recall of a patient he will always have regard to the safety of the public.'*

This Guidance makes clear that the patient's Supervisor must always make an immediate report to the MOJ where:

- there appears to be an actual or potential risk to the public
- contact with the patient is lost, or the patient is unwilling to co-operate with supervision
- the patient's behaviour or condition suggests a need for further inpatient treatment in hospital
- the patient is charged with or convicted of an offence.

The Ministry of Justice - Mental Health Unit

The creation of the Ministry of Justice in 2007 means that body now deals with aspects of MHA Part 3 previously dealt with by the Home Office. At the same time the role of the Home Secretary is replaced by that of the Secretary of State for Justice.

The main operational functions for Part 3 patients are dealt with by the Mental Health Casework Section (MHCS) which functions within the Ministry of Justice Public Protection and Mental Health Group. The MHCS is based on the Ground Floor, Grenadier House, 99-105 Horseferry Road, London SW1P 2DD

The Ministry of Justice Public Protection and Mental Health Group (PPMHG) only deals with psychiatric patients detained under the following Mental Health legislation:

- sections 37/41 of the MHA
- sections 47/49 of the MHA
- sections 48/49 of the MHA
- Criminal Procedure Insanity (Unfitness to Plead Act 1964 (CPI); **and**
- section 45a of the MHA (Hospital Directions).

The Unit issues at regular intervals a very useful Bulletin. It also issues Guidance and a number of forms some of which are summarised below. The forms and copies of the guidance can be downloaded from the PPMHG website.

Guidance

- Guidance for clinical supervisors and social supervisors
- Recall of conditionally discharged restricted patients
- Leave guidance for responsible clinicians
- Guidance for the courts on remand and sentencing powers for mentally disorder offenders
- Guidance on repatriation of foreign national restricted patients
- Guidance for clinicians on duties under the Domestic Violence Crime and Victims Act 2004
- Guidance on applications for trial leave or full transfer to another hospital.

Forms

- Report on conditionally discharged restricted patient
- Remission to prison of s47 and s48 patients
- Leave applications for restricted patients

New guidance on s17 leave has been issued with effect from March 2015.This guidance includes the request forms for general leave and for medical leave. Note this guidance refers to Annex C as containing the form which records completed leave. There is no Annex C and the form in question can be found in the April 2014 guidance on leave.

- Report on completed leave (reissued August 2009)
- Application for trial leave or full transfer to another hospital (reissued June 2009)
- Assessment of patient by Medical Officer at proposed accepting hospital (reissued June 2009).

Domestic Violence (Crime and Victims) Act 2004

The Domestic Violence (Crime and Victims) Act 2004 (DVCVA) became law in 2004 as a way of ensuring that the victims of particular crimes were able to express their views about both the sentencing and release of the offender concerned. These crimes (of a violent or sexual nature) are defined within that Act. The Act gave the local probation board the responsibility for finding out whether the victim of the crime in question wanted to give their view about what conditions should be attached to the offender if made the subject of either a Transfer Direction or Restriction Direction (see above).

The 2007 MHA extended the rights of victims to being able to give their views about conditions which might be attached to offenders either being conditionally discharged or being considered for discharge under CTO. The local probation board retains the responsibility for liaising with the victim concerned. The DVCVA places particular responsibilities on Tribunals and the Secretary of State in connection with the implementation of this Act.

Responsibilities for clinical staff (working in either the NHS or independent sector) who work with this group of patients are dealt with in 'Mental Health Act 2007: guidance on the extension of victims' rights under the Domestic Violence (Crime and Victims) Act 2004' which was published in October 2008.

This can be downloaded at the following link.

http:/webarchive.nationalarchives.gov.uk/2013107105354/http:/www.dh.gov.uk/prod consum dh/groups/dh digitalassets/@dh/en/documents/digitalasset/dh 089407.pdf

Chapter 40 of the Code deals with information for victims.

Chapter 26 Issues for Children and Young People

The Guidance on the use of the Mental Health Act with respect to Children and Young People is largely contained within Chapter 19 of the Code of Practice.

When considering the use of the Mental Health Act with anyone under the age of 18 there are a number of issues that must be considered. The Act does not have a lower age limit so theoretically any child could be subject to detention. In reality this is unlikely in very young children for whom treatment will largely be provided with the consent of those with parental responsibility. This chapter will consider when the Act is appropriate to use and the distinctions between those aged 16 and 17 years and younger children. It will look at the differences in the consent rules for young people aged 16 and 17 and younger children and the role of those with parental responsibility and how and when this differs from the role of the nearest relative

The Mental Health Act applies to children in exactly the same way as to adults and they are entitled to the same safeguards as adult patients. However there are a number of other legal frameworks which guide the care and treatment of children. These include the Children Acts 1989 and 2004, the Mental Capacity Act 2005, the Human Rights Act 1998 and the Family Law Reform Act 1969. Because this is a complex area of law, decisions regarding the care and treatment of children must be very carefully considered with access to expert CAMHS advice and, if necessary, further legal advice.

A child as defined by the Children Act 1989 is anyone under the age of 18 years.

The Code of Practice 19.5 states that, when making decisions under the Act:

- the best interests of the child or young person must always be a significant consideration
- everyone who works with children has a responsibility for keeping them safe and to take prompt action if welfare needs or safeguarding concerns are identified
- all practitioners and agencies are expected to contribute to whatever actions are needed to safeguard and promote a child or young person's welfare
- the developmental process from childhood to adulthood, particularly during adolescence, involves significant changes in a wide range of areas, such as physical, emotional and cognitive development – these factors need to be taken into account, in addition to the child and young person's personal circumstances
- the child or young person's views, wishes and feelings should always be sought, their views taken seriously and professionals should work with them collaboratively in deciding on how to support that child or young person's needs
- any intervention in the life of a child or young person that is considered necessary by reason of their mental disorder should be the least restrictive option and the least likely to expose them to the risk of any stigmatisation, consistent with effective care and treatment, and it should also result in the least possible separation from family, carers, friends and community or interruption of their education
- where hospital admission is necessary, the child or young person should be placed as near to their home as reasonably practicable, recognising that placement further away from home increases the separation between the child or young person and their family, carers, friends, community and school

- all children and young people should receive the same access to educational provision as their peers
- children and young people have as much right to expect their dignity to be respected as anyone else
- children and young people have as much right to privacy and confidentiality as anyone else unless they may suffer significant harm if information is not shared.

Summary of Issues regarding children and changes in the MHA 1983 as revised 2007

- s.131 governs the informal admission of young people aged 16 and 17 to hospital and their right to consent to their own admission
- Requirements of CAMHS professionals to assess
- Requirements on hospitals managers to consult those with expertise in the care of children
- Age appropriate environments
- Role of those with parental responsibility
- Role of the local authority if children are looked after
- Use of alternative legislation
- 'Scope of Parental Responsibility'.

Informal Admission to hospital

Under s131 (3) and s.131 () a young person aged 16 or 17 who 'has capacity to make such arrangements' may consent to their own admission

- If the patient consents to the making of the arrangements, they may be made, carried out and determined on the basis of that consent even though there are one or more persons who have parental responsibility for him.
- If the patient does not consent to the making of the arrangements, they may not be made, carried out or determined on the basis of the consent of a person who has parental responsibility for him.

This means that it is not possible to admit a non-consenting 16 or 17 year old on the wishes of someone with parental responsibility unless that young person does not have capacity as defined by the MCA 2005 and admission is in their best interests and does not amount to a deprivation of liberty.

It is also possible to admit a competent young child whose competence has been determined (so called 'Gillick' competence) without the consent of someone with parental responsibility. Whilst a parent can still overrule a child's refusal to consent if they are considered to be competent, it is suggested in the code of practice that it would be inadvisable (Code19.59) to use parental responsibility to overrule a child's refusal. In this case if possible the MHA should be used.

For children and young people who lack capacity and young children who are not competent admission can be agreed by someone with parental responsibility. Their agreement can overrule a child's refusal to consent so long as the admission does not amount to a deprivation of liberty.

Requirements of CAMHS professionals to assess

The Code of Practice (14.39) suggests that 'at least one' of the professionals assessing a child for detention under the MHA should be a CAMHS specialist and if this is not possible to arrange then a CAMHS specialist should be consulted by those carrying out the assessment.

Age appropriate Environments

S131 makes specific the requirements on hospitals to provide care and treatment in an 'age appropriate' environment which is suitable for their age and subject to their needs. This refers to the treatment of children in CAMHS specialist units all Trusts must provide the following specialist environments for children.

- Appropriate physical facilities
- Staff specifically trained to work with children (including a requirement for all staff to have enhanced DBS clearance)
- A routine which allows access to education and to promote social and personal development
- Equal access to educational opportunities as their peers
- Access to leisure facilities and support for visiting

In exceptional cases if a child cannot be accommodated on a specialist CAMHS ward then discrete facilities within an adult ward with appropriate staffing might be a 'satisfactory solution'. This will require care by child specialists and single sex accommodation for young women.

There may be occasions when according to a young person's needs it is actually more appropriate to care for them in an adult facility, particularly when this is very close to a young person's 18th birthday and they themselves consider that they may be best cared for on an adult ward. This might be appropriate if care is very likely to extend beyond the age of 18 and therapeutic relationships are likely to be disrupted.

In any event if a young person is cared for on an adult ward those caring for the child should be given access to CAMHS specialists for advice and consultation and there is a requirement on hospitals managers to consult those with expertise in the care of children and young people.

Role of those with parental responsibility

The role of those with parental responsibility is extremely important in the care and treatment of children and they hold a vital legal role in being responsible for consenting to their child's care, if that child is unable to consent for themselves. It can be a complex role which combines rights and responsibilities as defined by the Children Act 1989 with those enshrined in the MHA 1983.

Anyone involved in the assessment and care of children must establish who has parental responsibility for that child. Parental responsibility is defined by the Children Act s.3 as:

'all the rights, duties, powers, responsibilities and authority which by law a parent of a child has in relation to the child and his property.'

Determining who has parental responsibility is important and this role can be held by more than one person.

Who holds Parental responsibility for a child? (from s.2 Children Act 1989)

- Where a child's father and mother were married to each other at the time of his birth, they shall each have parental responsibility for the child.
- Where a child's father and mother were not married to each other at the time of his birth—
  - the mother shall have parental responsibility for the child;
  - the father shall not have parental responsibility for the child, unless he acquires it in accordance with the provisions of this Act.
- Unmarried fathers can acquire parental responsibility either by formal agreement with the mother or by being granted this by a court
- Other people MAY hold PR for a child (e.g. those who have a Child Arrangements Order) but foster carers will NOT have PR unless they have a residence or special guardianship order in relation to the child.
- More than one person may have parental responsibility for the same child at the same time.

Parental Responsibility			
Who holds it?		**Who does not hold it?**	
Married Parents	Both	**Unmarried fathers**	Unless they are named on the birth certificate for a child born after 1.12.2003 Unless he has applied for a court order, has a parental responsibility agreement with the mother or has another order conferring parental responsibility
Unmarried Parents	Mother alone	**Step Parents**	Unless they have a Child Arrangement Order, Special Guardianship Order or have adopted the child.
Divorced Parents	Both, even if the child lives with one parent		
Anyone with a Child Arrangements Order, Special Guardianship Order or who has adopted a child			

If a local authority has a Care Order for a child under s31 Children Act they will share parental responsibility with the parent/s. In this case it is for the local authority to determine the extent to which a parent may exercise their responsibilities. In relation to mental health treatment it will normally be the local authority who decides the extent to which they wish to make decisions on a child's behalf and MUST be consulted in all cases.

Parental Responsibility and Nearest Relative

It is important to note that the person with parental responsibility will not always be the person identified as being the nearest relative within the meaning of the MHA. In the case of the father who does not have parental responsibility he will not be the nearest relative in terms of the MHA unless this status is transferred to him by some other means (e.g. if the nearest relative is displaced by a court or a child has lived with him for five years thus qualifying him as NR under the 'five year rule').

If a parent or other person has a child arrangements order or a special guardianship order then that person will the nearest relative.

Role of the local authority if children are looked after

If a child or young person is 'looked after' by the local authority ('in care') they may either be cared for on a voluntary basis with agreement with the parent (s20 Children Act 19089) or compulsorily under a Care Order or Interim Care Order (s31 or s38 Children Act 1989). If the local authority has either of these orders then treatment decisions and consent for a child's admission (if they are unable to consent for themselves) must come from the local authority. This will normally be taken at a senior management level and the local authority will advise who they consider to be the appropriate person to make such decisions. If the young person is assessed under the MHA 1983 the local authority will be the Nearest Relative.

Use of alternative legislation

It is not always appropriate to use MHA legislation in the care of children if the primary purpose for their admission is a behavioural one, i.e. the young person is primarily in need of care and control rather than treatment for a mental disorder. If the young person needs to be detained but this is **NOT** for the purpose of treatment of a mental disorder then it may be appropriate to consider **other legislation**. In these cases it will always be necessary to seek further legal advice .

'Scope of Parental responsibility and Consent to Treatment

This concept covers the rights of parents to consent to treatment on behalf of their children if the child is unable to do so. It covers the areas of treatment which can be consented to by a parent and which it is or is not reasonable to expect a parent to consent to on behalf of a child. The key to the ability of parents to consent to their child's treatment lies in the ability or otherwise of the child to consent to their own treatment and the reasons why a child might not be able to do so (i.e. are they unable to consent because they are temporarily overwhelmed by the decision they are making or because they lack capacity by reason of their mental disorder or because developmentally they have not yet reached the stage where they are able to understand the nature of what they are consenting to).

The extent to which parents can consent to treatment is outlined in the grid below making reference to the different ages and competencies of children *(adapted from NIMHE Legal Aspects of the Care and Treatment of Children and Young People with Mental Disorder 2009)*

Admission and Treatment of Children

Age/Capacity of child	Consent to treatment
16-17 year old with capacity	■ Patient may consent or refuse, parents may not overrule but should be involved subject to confidentiality ■ If patient refuses and meets criteria for detention, MHA may be used ■ If MHA criteria not met, patient's wishes should be respected or Court declaration may be needed ■ In life-threatening emergency, refusal can be overridden.
16-17 year old lacking capacity	■ Permissible if in best interests under the MCA ■ Parental views should usually be taken into account but are not decisive ■ If patient refuses a person with parental responsibility may also be able to consent on behalf of the young person who lacks capacity to make decisions about their treatment so long as the treatment decision is within the scope of parental responsibility. ■ If patient refuses and proposal is not in the scope of parental responsibility but patient meets criteria for detention, MHA may be used ■ Where parents object Court declaration may be needed ■ In life-threatening emergency, refusal can be overridden
'Gillick' competent < 16 year old	■ Patient may consent ■ If patient refuses, views of person with parental responsibility must be sought but 'inadvisable' to overrule the objecting competent child ■ If patient refuses and meets criteria for detention, MHA may be used or seek Court declaration ■ Where parents object and/or MHA does not apply Court declaration may be needed ■ In life-threatening emergency, refusal can be overridden
Incompetent < 16 year old	■ If within scope of parental responsibility, rely on parental consent ■ Seek agreement for each component of care as it arises ■ If not, detain under MHA if criteria met ■ If criteria not met, seek Court declaration ■ If life-threatening emergency, treat to save life.

If a parent is making a decision on behalf of an 'incompetent child' then the decision must be within their scope of parental responsibility.

The Code of Practice gives guidance (19.41):

Whether the particular intervention can be undertaken on the basis of parental consent will need to be assessed in the light of the particular circumstances of the case. Practitioners will need to consider a range of factors. These are set out below, under the two key questions that must be addressed (the term 'parent' is used to cover all people with parental responsibility):

First, is this a decision that a parent should reasonably be expected to make? If the decision goes beyond the kind of decisions parents routinely make in relation to the medical care of their child, clear reasons as to why it is acceptable to rely on parental consent to authorise this particular decision will be required. When considering this question, any relevant human rights decisions made by the courts should be taken into account. Significant factors in determining this question are likely to include:

- the type and invasiveness of the proposed intervention – the more extreme the intervention, the greater the justification that will be required. Relying on parental consent to authorise an intrusive form of treatment might be justified because it is necessary to prevent a serious deterioration of the child or young person's health, but this would need to be balanced against other factors such as whether the child or young person is resisting the treatment; whether the specific form of treatment is particularly invasive and/or controversial (e.g. careful consideration should be given to the appropriateness of relying on parental consent to authorise electro-convulsive therapy (ECT)
- the age, maturity and understanding of the child or young person: the role of parents in decision-making should diminish as their child develops greater independence, with accordingly greater weight given to the views of the child or young person
- the extent to which the decision accords with the wishes of the child or young person, and whether the child or young person is resisting the decision, and whether the child or young person had expressed any views about the proposed intervention when they had the competence or capacity to make such decisions; for example, if they had expressed a willingness to receive one form of treatment but not another, it might not be appropriate to rely on parental consent to give the treatment that they had previously refused.

Secondly, are there any factors that might undermine the validity of parental consent? Irrespective of the nature of the decision being proposed, there may be reasons why relying on the consent of a person with parental responsibility maybe inappropriate; for example:

- where the parent is not able to make the relevant decision; for example, this may arise, if the parent lacks capacity as defined in the MCA, because of their own mental health problems or learning disabilities. In cases of doubt, the parent's capacity will need to be assessed in accordance with the MCA
- where the parent is not able to focus on what course of action is in the best interests of their child; for example, where the parents have gone through a particularly acrimonious divorce, they may find it difficult to separate the decision whether to consent to their child's admission to hospital from their own hostilities
- where the poor mental health of the child or young person has led to significant distress and/or conflict between the parents, so that they feel unable to decide on what is best for their child and/ or cannot agree on what action should be taken, and
- where one parent agrees with the proposed decision but the other is opposed to it. Although parental consent is usually needed from only one person with parental responsibility, it may not be appropriate to rely on parental consent if another person with parental responsibility disagrees strongly with the decision to admit and/or treat their child, and is likely to take action to prevent the intervention, such as removing the child from hospital or challenging the decision in court.

Consent and Capacity assessments

Given the complexities of decision making regarding children and young people it is vital that ALL decisions with regard to their care are carefully assessed for the child's ability to make decisions for themselves and the extent to which they are able to consent to their own treatment. This should be carefully recorded or each decision that consent is sought. If the consent of the parent is sought this must be fully recorded on each occasion. In making capacity assessments on a young person over the age of 16 the provisions of the MCA 2005 should be used to determine whether or not a young person has capacity. For younger children the concept of 'Gillick' competence is used. This refers to the child being able to *'have sufficient understanding and intelligence to enable them to fully understand what is involved in a proposed intervention.'* The concept of 'Gillick' competence reflects the increasing level of developmental maturity in a child. It is important to recognize that the level of understanding may vary according to what is required for specific interventions. 'Gillick' competence may therefore vary according to the decision a child is being asked to make.

Duties on Local Authorities

The Mental Health Act and Children Acts' place certain duties on Trusts and local authorities to inform each other of the care and treatment of young people in hospital.

s85 Children Act (1989) requires NHS Hospital Trusts to inform local authorities of any child who is looked after by them for a period of more than three months. Once the local authority have been notified that a child has been placed in accommodation, including a hospital, local education authority, independent hospital or residential accommodation, and the placement is likely to last for three months or more, then the local authority must 'take such steps as are reasonably practicable to enable them to determine whether the child's welfare is adequately safeguarded and promoted while he is accommodated by the accommodating authority' and 'consider the extent to which (if at all) they should exercise any of their functions under this Act with respect to the child.'

s116 of the Mental Health Act places a duty on the local authority to provide for visits to be made to a child patient on their behalf, whether or not they are subject to a care order:

The Children Act 1989 requires that local authorities:

- Promote contact between children and young people and their families, if they live away from home; and
- Arrange for independent visitors to visit and befriend children and young people, if they have not been visited by their parents.

s116 of the Mental Health Act places a duty on the local authority to provide for visits to be made to a child patient on their behalf, whether or not they are subject to a care order:

The Children Act 1989 requires that local authorities:

- Promote contact between children and young people and their families, if they live away from home; and
- Arrange for independent visitors to visit and befriend children and young people, if they have not been visited by their parents.

The Code requires that local authorities are alerted if the whereabouts of the person with parental responsibility is not known or if that person has not visited the child or young person for a significant period. The local authority should then consider the arrangement of visits by an independent person.

Part Seven MHA Resources

Chapter 27 Mental Health Law Resources

This list is not exhaustive.

Primary sources for the Mental Health Act

- Mental Health Act 1983:
- Code of Practice 2015 by Department of Health
- Reference Guide to the Mental Health Act 1983 by Department of Health.

Mental Health Act Textbooks / Guides

These include the following:

- Blackstone's Guide to the Mental Health Act 2007 by Paul Bowen
- Mental Health Act Manual by Richard Jones
- Mental Health:Law and Practice by Phil Fennell
- A Clinician's Brief Guide to the Mental Health Act by Tony Zigmund
- The Approved Mental Health Professional's Guide to Mental Health Law by Robert Brown

Mental Capacity Act & DOLS Textbooks / Guides

These include the following:

- Mental Capacity Act 2005 Code of Practice
- Deprivation of Liberty Safeguards Code of Practice
- Mental Capacity Act by Robert Brown
- Mental Capacity Act Manual by Richard Jones

Valuable Websites

- Department of Health - Mental Health
- Mental Health Tribunal
- Care Quality Commission
- Mental Health Law Online
- The Masked AMHP
- Institute of Mental Health Law (members only website).

Both the Rethink and Royal College of Psychiatrists' Websites contain clear and informative material about the MHA and MCA/DOLS

Briefings

- 39 Essex Street Barrister's Chambers (mainly MCA and DOLS)
- RadcliffeLeBrasseur Mental Health Law Brief

Appendix A - Summary of all the MHA sections

Section	Summary
1	Application of Act and 'mental disorder'
2	Admission for assessment
3	Admission for treatment
4	Admission for assessment in emergency cases
5	Application in respect of patients already in hospital
6	Effect of application for admission
7	Application for guardianship
8	Effect of guardianship application etc
9	Regulations as to guardianship
10	Transfer of guardianship in case of death, incapacity etc. of guardian
11	General provisions as to applications
12	General provisions as medical recommendations
12A	Conflicts of interest
13	Duty of mental health professionals to make applications for admission or guardianship
14	Social Reports
15	Rectification of applications and recommendations
16	There is no longer a s16
17	Leave of absence from hospital
17A	Community treatment orders
17B	Conditions
17C	Duration of community treatment order 17D Effect of community treatment order
17E	Power of recall to hospital
17F	Powers in respect of recalled patients
17G	Effect of revoking community treatment order
18	Return and readmission of patients absent without leave
19	Regulations as to transfer of patients
19A	Regulations as to assignment of responsibility for community patients
20	Duration of authority
20A	Community treatment period
20B	Effect of expiry of community treatment order
21	Special provisions as to patients absent without leave
21A	Patients who are taken into custody or return within 28 days
21B	Patients who are taken into custody or return after more than 28 days
22	Special provisions as to patients sentenced to imprisonment etc.
23	Discharge of patients
24	Visiting and examination of patients
25	Restrictions on discharge by nearest relative
26	Definition of 'relative' and 'nearest relative'
27	Children and young people in care
28	Nearest relative of minor under guardianship etc
29	Appointment by court of acting nearest relative
30	Discharge and variations of orders under s29

Section	Summary
31	Procedure on application to county court
32	Regulation for purpose of Part 2
33	Special provision as to wards of court
34	Interpretation of Part 2
35	Remand to hospital for report on accused's mental condition
36	Remand to hospital for treatment of accused person
37	Powers of court to order hospital admission or guardianship
38	Interim hospital orders
39	Information as to hospital
39A	Information to facilitate guardianship orders
40	Effect of hospital orders, guardianship orders and interim hospital orders
41	Power of higher courts to restrict discharge from hospital
42	Powers of Secretary of State in respect of patients subject to restriction orders
43	Power of magistrates' courts to commit for restriction order
44	Committal to hospital under s43
45A	Power of higher court to direct hospital admission
45B	Effect of hospital and limitation directions
46	There is no longer a s46
47	Removal to hospital of persons serving sentences of imprisonment etc.
48	Removal to hospital of other prisoners
49	Restriction on discharge of prisoners removed to hospital
50	Further provisions as to patients under sentence
51	Further provisions as to detained patients
52	Further provisions as to persons remanded by magistrates' courts
53	Further provisions as to civil prisoners and persons detained under they Immigration Acts
54	Requirements as to medical evidence
54A	Reduction of period for making hospital orders
55	Interpretation of Part 3
56	Patients to whom Part 4 apply
57	Treatments requiring consent and a second opinion
58	Treatment requiring consent or a second opinion
58A	Electro-convulsive therapy etc.
59	Treatment Plans
60	Withdrawal of consent
61	Review of treatment
62	Urgent treatment
62A	Treatment on recall of community patients or revocation of order
63	Treatment not requiring consent
64	Supplementary Part 4 provisions
64A	Meaning of 'relevant treatment'
64B	Adult community patients
64C	Supplement to s64B
64D	Adult community patients lacking capacity
64E	Child community patients
64F	Child community patients lacking capacity

Section	Summary
64G	Emergency treatment for patients lacking capacity or competence
64H	Supplementary provisions regarding certificates
64I	Liability for negligence
65	Mental Health Review Tribunals
66	Applications to tribunals
67	Referrals to tribunals by Secretary of State concerning Part 2 patients
68	Duty of hospital managers to refer cases to tribunals
68A	Power to reduce s68 periods
69	Applications to tribunals concerning patients subject to guardianship and hospital orders
70	Applications to tribunals concerning restricted patients
71	References by Secretary of State concerning restricted patients
72	Powers of tribunals
73	Power to discharge certain restricted patients
74	Restricted patients subject to restriction directions
75	Applications and references concerning conditionally discharged restricted patients
76	Visiting and examination of patients
77	General provisions concerning tribunal applications
78	Tribunal procedures
79	Interpretation of Part 5
80	Removal of patients to Scotland
80ZA	Transfer of responsibility for community patients to Scotland
80A	Transfer of responsibility for conditionally discharged patients to Scotland
80B	Removal of detained patients to Scotland
80C	Removal of patients subject to compulsion in the community from Scotland
80D	Transfer of conditionally discharged patients from Scotland
81	Removal of patients to Northern Ireland
81ZA	Removal of community patients to Northern Ireland
81A	Transfer of responsibility for patients to Northern Ireland
82	Removal to England and Wales of patients from Northern Ireland
83	Removal of patients to Channel Islands or Isle of Man
83ZA	Removal or transfer of community patients to Channel Islands or Isle of Man
83A	Transfer of responsibility for conditionally discharged patients to Channel Islands or Isle of Man
84	Removal to England and Wales of offenders found insane in Channel Islands or Isle of Man
85	Removal of patients from Channel Islands or Isle of Man
85ZA	Responsibility for community patients transferred from Channel Islands or Isle of Man
85A	Responsibility for conditionally discharged patients transferred from Channel Islands or Isle of Man
86	Removal of alien patients
87	Patients absent from hospitals in Northern Ireland
88	Patients absent from hospitals in England and Wales
89	Patients absent from hospitals in the Channel Islands or Isle of Man
90	Regulations for the purposes of Part 6
91	General provisions as to patients removed from England and Wales
92	Interpretation of Part 6

Section	Summary
93-113	There are no longer these section.
114	Approval by local social services authority
114A	Approval of courses etc. for approved mental health professionals
115	Power of entry and inspection
116	Welfare of certain hospital patients
117	After-care
118	Code of Practice
119	Practitioners approved for Part 4 and s118
120	General protection of detained patients
121	Care Quality Commission
122	Provision of pocket money for in-patients in hospital
123	Transfers to and from special hospitals
124-5	There are no longer these sections
126	Forgery, false statements etc.
127	Ill treatment of patients
128	Assisting patients to absent themselves without leave etc.
129	Obstruction
130	Prosecution by local authorities
130A	Independent mental health advocates
130B	Arrangements under 130A
130C	Supplement to 130A
130D	Duty to give information about independent mental health advocates
131	Informal admission of patients
131A	Accommodation etc. for children
132	Duty of hospital managers to give information to detained patients
132A	Duty of hospital managers to give information to community patients
133	Duty of hospital managers to inform nearest relatives of discharge
134	Correspondence of patients
135	Warrant to search for and remove patients
136	Mentally disordered persons found in public places
137	Provisions as to custody, conveyance and detention
138	Retaking of patients escaping from custody
139	Protection for acts done in pursuance of this Act
140	Notification of hospitals having arrangements for special cases
141	Members of Parliament suffering from mental illness
142A	Regulations as to approvals in relation to England and Wales
142B	Delegation of powers of managers of NHS foundation trusts
143	General provisions as to regulations, orders and rules
144	Power to amend local Acts
145	Interpretation
146	Application to Scotland
147	Application to Northern Ireland
148	Consequential and transitional provisions and repeals
149	Short title, commencement and application to Scilly Isles

Appendix B - MHA Forms

Form	Description of the Form
A1	S2 Nearest Relative Application
A2	S2 Approved Mental Health Professional Application
A3	S2 Joint Medical Recommendation
A4	S2 Medical Recommendation
A5	S3 Nearest Relative Application
A6	S3 Approved Mental Health Professional Application
A7	S3 Joint Medical Recommendation
A8	S3 Medical Recommendation
A9	S4 Nearest Relative Application
A10	S4 Approved Mental Health Professional Application
A11	S4 Medical Recommendation
H1	S5(2) report
H2	S5(4) Nurse's Holding power
H3	Record of Detention
H4	Transfer form
H5	Renewal form
H6	S21B Authority to detain after AWOL for 28 days
G1	Nearest Relative Guardianship Application
G2	Guardianship Approved Mental Health Professional Application
G3	Guardianship Joint Medical Recommendation.
G4	Guardianship Medical Recommendation
G5	Guardianship Record of Acceptance
G6	Guardianship Transfer
G7	Guardianship Transfer to another Guardian
G8	Guardianship Transfer to Hospital
G9	Renewal of Guardianship
G10	Guardianship S21B Authority to detain after AWOL for 28 days
M1	Reception of a patient in England
M2	S25 Report Barring Discharge by Nearest Relative
T1	S57 Certificate of Consent to treatment and second opinion
T2	S58(3)(a) Consent to Treatment
T3	S58(3)(b) Second opinion
T4	S58A(3) Consent to Treatment (patients at least 18 years old)
T5	S58A(4) Certificate of consent to treatment and Second opinion (patient under 18)
T6	S58A(5) Certificate of Second opinion

Form	Description of the Form
CTO1	Community Treatment Order (CTO)
CTO2	Variation of conditions of a CTO
CTO3	Notice of Recall to Hospital
CTO4	Record of patients detention in hospital after Recall
CTO5	Revocation of Community Treatment order
CTO6	Transfer a recalled patient to a hospital under different managers
CT07	Report extending the Community Treatment period
CTO8	Extend CTO after AWOL for more than 28 days
CTO9	Community Patients transferred to England
CTO10	Authority for assignment of responsibility of community patients to hospital under different managers
CTO11	S64C(4) Certificate of appropriateness of treatment to be given to community patient (part 4A certificate)
CTO12	S64C(4A) Consent to Treatment form completed by RC

Appendix C - Patient Information Leaflets

A number of patient information leaflets revised in June 2009 to incorporate information about the role of Independent Mental Health Advocates. These leaflets are published by the Department of Health and are only available in English and Welsh. The Northamptonshire Healthcare NHS Foundation Trust have, in collaboration with a number of other organisations, translated the leaflets into 25 of the most commonly used languages. The available languages are listed below.

Leaflet	Section
S2	Admission to Hospital For Assessment
S3	Admission to Hospital For Treatment
S5(4)	Nurse's Holding Power
S4	Emergency admission for assessment
S5(2)	Detention of in-patient
S136	Admission of mentally disordered ordered person found in public place
S135	Admission of patients removed by police under a court warrant
S37/41	Admission to hospital by a hospital order with restrictions
S37	Admission to hospital by a hospital order without restrictions
S45A	Admission to hospital by hospital and limitation direction
S38	Interim hospital order
S35	Remand to hospital for assessment
S36	Remand to hospital for treatment
APPEALS	Right to appeal for patients admitted from courts
S48	Transfer to hospital of un-sentenced prison (with or without restrictions)
S47/49	Transfer to hospital with restrictions of person serving a prison sentence
S47	Transfer to hospital without restrictions of person serving a prison sentence
EndRes	Patient whose restrictions have come to an end
G7	Guardianship
G37	Guardianship Order
CTO-Pt2	Community Treatment Order - Part 2 patients
CTO-Pt3	Community Treatment Order - Part 3 patients
CTO-Recall	Recall to hospital of Community Treatment Order patients
CTO-RevPt 2	Revocation of - s3 patients
CTO-RevPt 3	Revocation of Community Treatment Order - Part 3 patients

Leaflets have been translated into the languages listed below. There is a set of DVDs also available with visual and verbal information in the same languages. In addition there is a visual/verbal version in British Sign Language and Patois.

Albanian
Arabic
Bengali
French
Gujarati
Hebrew
Hindi
Italian
Korean
Lithuanian
Mandarin
Pashto
Persian
Polish
Portuguese
Punjabi
Russian
Somali
Spanish
Swahili
Sylheti
Tamil
Turkish
Urdu
Vietnamese

Notes

Notes

Notes

Notes

Notes

Notes

Notes

Notes

Notes

Notes

Notes

Notes

Notes

Notes

Notes